Understanding Mathematics
for Young Children

4th Edition

Education at SAGE

SAGE is a leading international publisher of journals, books, and electronic media for academic, educational, and professional markets.

Our education publishing includes:

- accessible and comprehensive texts for aspiring education professionals and practitioners looking to further their careers through continuing professional development

- inspirational advice and guidance for the classroom

- authoritative state of the art reference from the leading authors in the field

Find out more at: **www.sagepub.co.uk/education**

4th Edition

Understanding Mathematics for Young Children

A guide for teachers of children 3–8

Derek Haylock and Anne Cockburn

Los Angeles | London | New Delhi
Singapore | Washington DC

Los Angeles | London | New Delhi
Singapore | Washington DC

SAGE Publications Ltd
1 Oliver's Yard
55 City Road
London EC1Y 1SP

SAGE Publications Inc.
2455 Teller Road
Thousand Oaks, California 91320

SAGE Publications India Pvt Ltd
B 1/I 1 Mohan Cooperative Industrial Area
Mathura Road
New Delhi 110 044

SAGE Publications Asia-Pacific Pte Ltd
3 Church Street
#10-04 Samsung Hub
Singapore 049483

Editor: Marianne Lagrange
Development editor: Robin Lupton
Editorial assistant: Kathryn Bromwich
Project manager: Jeanette Graham
Assistant production editor: Thea Watson
Copyeditor: Rosemary Campbell
Proofreader: Sharon Cawood
Indexer: Derek Haylock
Marketing manager: Catherine Slinn
Cover designer: Wendy Scott
Typeset by: C&M Digitals (P) Ltd, Chennai, India
Printed and bound in Great Britain by Ashford
Colour Press Ltd

Library of Congress Control Number: 2012949195

British Library Cataloguing in Publication data

A catalogue record for this book is available from
the British Library

ISBN 978-1-4462-4865-2
ISBN 978-1-4462-4866-9 (pbk)

CONTENTS

ABOUT THE AUTHORS

Derek Haylock is an education consultant and writer in the field of mathematics education. He is a Senior Fellow in Education at the University of East Anglia, Norwich, where he worked for over 30 years in primary teacher training and in education research. He is a major author in education, with a large number of published books and chapters in books. His best-selling *Mathematics Explained for Primary Teachers* (SAGE) has been the leader in the field for many years, with a fourth edition published in 2010. Derek's work is characterized by a commitment to explain mathematics in simple and accessible ways and to enable the subject to be taught and learnt with understanding and confidence. He is married, with two grown-up daughters and three grandsons. Outside of mathematics, he is a Free Church elder, plays the trumpet, and is passionate about classical music, cricket, walking (quickly) and cycling (slowly).

Professor Anne Cockburn is Professor in Early Years Education at the University of East Anglia, Norwich. Her research interests focus on mathematics education in the primary school and teacher well-being, recruitment and retention. She has completed a range of research projects, including Understanding the Primary Mathematics Classroom Part 2 (Economic and Social Research Council Award) with Paola Iannone; and Mathematical Misconceptions in the Primary Years (British Academy) with international partners. She is currently disseminating the findings of her most recent project – Challenging Colleagues: Primary Head Teachers Managing Mediocre Practitioners – which was funded by the Nuffield Foundation. Professor Cockburn chaired the International Meeting of the Psychology of Mathematics Education Group in 2002 and was an Associate Editor of the *Journal of Mathematics Teacher Educators*.

ACKNOWLEDGEMENTS

We again express our appreciation to those teachers who attended our in-service course at the University of East Anglia prior to the writing of the first version of this book and those many teachers and trainees who have met with us since to share their experience of teaching and learning mathematics in the age range 3–8 years. Special thanks go to Catherine Bates, Emma Yerby-Smith, Sarah Johnston and Kate Oakley, who have allowed us to spend time in their classes gathering material for this book and who have shared with us their insights; to Joe Haydn for the drawings in Figure 1.5; and to Inge Schwank for the idea and photographs used in Chapter 11. We also wish to thank Alison Barnes, Lynne Greenwood and Sheena Smart of the University of Brighton for their helpful comments on this new edition.

INTRODUCTION

This book is about teaching and learning mathematics in the age range 3–8 years. The first book that we wrote together, way back in 1989, was called *Understanding Early Years Mathematics*. It covered the age range 4–8 years. After its publication, however, the phrase 'early years' began to be used solely for the age range up to 5 years. So the next two incarnations in 1997 and 2003, more substantial and comprehensive, were called *Understanding Mathematics in the Lower Primary Years*. We then found that in the educational set-up in England the phrase 'lower primary' no longer sent out the right signals for a book that has as much focus on the Early Years Foundation Stage (3–5 years) as Years 1 to 3 (5–8 years). So, in producing the previous version to the current edition we yet again changed the title, to *Understanding Mathematics for Young Children*. We are relieved that we have been able to retain that title for this new edition, and happy to have the opportunity to ensure that the book remains up-to-date and relevant to those teaching or being trained to teach children in this age range.

The aims of the book

The book is written for those who teach or who are preparing to teach mathematics to children in the age range 3–8 years and who wish to have a clearer understanding of the mathematical ideas behind the material they deal with in the classroom. Although it draws mainly on the curriculum and classroom context of schools in England, we are confident that, as has proved to be the case with earlier versions, the book will be useful and relevant to colleagues involved in elementary or primary education in other countries in the United Kingdom and, indeed, around the world.

Our interest in writing this book arose from our concern about the long-term effects on children's confidence in mathematics resulting from their teachers' own mathematical misconceptions and limited understanding of the subject. This is no doubt often because they and their teachers before them were taught mathematics by drill, as a set of rules and recipes. Understanding as a goal may have played little part in their mathematics education. Our aims are therefore that this book will help prospective and experienced teachers who work in this age range to understand:

- the mathematical ideas that underpin what they teach
- what understanding of that mathematics entails
- how children can be helped to construct that understanding for themselves.

We hope that we can demonstrate that understanding mathematics and mathematical pedagogy need not be the sole prerogative of those who call themselves mathematicians.

This is not a book of superficial tips for teachers and we guarantee that you will not be able to canter through it. It is a book that should make you think and reassess your own understanding of basic mathematical ideas. We hope, of course, that it will make you a better teacher of mathematics to young children, by increasing your confidence and dispelling some of the fears and anxieties that you might have accumulated over the years (see Chapter 1 of Haylock, 2010). It is essential that teachers themselves should have a thorough understanding of the basic mathematical concepts and principles that underpin the mathematics that is taught and learnt as a young child embarks on their educational journey. The reader should note that, to help early years practitioners develop this understanding, we find that it is necessary here and there to discuss some material that goes a little beyond the 3–8 age range.

Input from teachers

To explore the nature of the mathematical understanding of Early Years Foundation Stage and lower primary teachers, we have met at the University of East Anglia in Norwich with various groups who work with this age range. They have shared with us honestly their experience of teaching the subject to young children and the aspects of mathematics where their own understanding needed boosting. We have also been privileged to visit a number of nurseries and classes to observe children learning mathematics. We quote generously and gratefully from these conversations and observations throughout the book.

Input from research

In this new edition we have included a Research Focus in each chapter, to indicate how a range of research studies in the field of mathematics education relate to the content of the chapter. We begin some of these with reference to seminal or classic studies, which are often the foundation on which more recent work is built. We have also been able in these research sections to draw on Anne's extensive contacts with the international mathematics education community. These research sections are not intended to be a comprehensive survey of the field. Rather, we have chosen a few particularly interesting studies on which to focus, in order to whet the reader's appetite for exploring the field further. All the details of the publications referred to in these Research Focuses (and in our Suggestions for Further Reading) are given in the References at the end of the book.

Pauses to reflect

For this new edition we have also included in each chapter one or two Pauses to Reflect. These, we hope, may intrigue you, amuse you, or help you to relate the content of the chapter to your own experience or that of young children. We have in mind that these might best be discussed with a colleague, so that you can share each other's perspectives and observations.

Classroom activities

Although the book focuses mainly on the understanding of mathematical ideas rather than on how to teach mathematics, pedagogical implications are considered throughout. At the end of each chapter we include examples of activities that might be used with children in the nursery or lower primary years. The activities are all aimed at developing what we might recognize as understanding. They are not intended to cover comprehensively the material in the chapter, but we hope that they may provide you with some indication of ways in which the ideas we have outlined in the preceding pages might influence your practice. Many of these activities can be used with a variety of ages of children, adapting them as appropriate. For each activity we have given an indication of the ages (3–4, 4–5, 5–6, 6–7 or 7–8 years) for which we expect it to be most suitable, but this is certainly not intended to be prescriptive.

Derek Haylock and Anne Cockburn

A NOTE ON TERMINOLOGY

In this book the following terminology is used as it relates to education in England.

Nursery   The year group of children who have their fourth birthday within the school year.

Reception class   The year group of children who have their fifth birthday within the school year; normally the year in which children enter primary education.

Early Years Foundation Stage   The two years of schooling comprising nursery and reception.

Year 1, Year 2, Year 3   The year groups of children who within the school year have their sixth, seventh and eighth birthdays respectively.

Key Stage 1 (KS 1)   The period of schooling comprising Years 1 and 2.

Key Stage 2 (KS 2)   The period of schooling comprising Years 3–6.

Primary school   Usually a school with children in the age range 4–11 years. Many primary schools have a nursery attached.

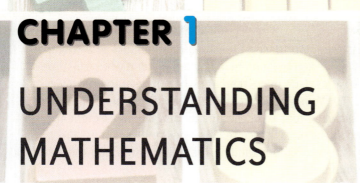

CHAPTER 1

UNDERSTANDING MATHEMATICS

A REVEALING CONVERSATION

Gemma, aged 6 years, had no problems with questions like 2 + 3 = □ and even 8 + □ = 9. Her teacher said that she thought Gemma had a good understanding of the equals sign. But then the teacher asked Gemma how she did 2 + □ = 6. Gemma replied, 'I said to myself, two (then counting on her fingers), three, four, five, six, and so the answer is four. Sometimes I do them the other way round, but it doesn't make any difference.' She pointed to 1 + □ = 10. 'For this one I did ten and one, and that's eleven.'

This conversation prompts us to ask the following questions:

- How does Gemma show here that she has some understanding of the concept of addition?
- What about her understanding of the concept represented by the equals sign?
- How would you analyse the misunderstanding shown at the end of this conversation?

In this chapter

In this chapter we discuss the importance of teaching mathematics in a way that promotes understanding. So we aim to help the reader understand what constitutes understanding in mathematics. Our main theme is that understanding involves establishing connections. For young children learning about number, connections often have to be made between four key components of children's experience of doing mathematics: symbols, pictures, concrete situations and language. We also introduce two other key aspects of understanding that will run through this book: equivalence and transformation.

Learning and teaching mathematics with understanding

This book is about *understanding* mathematics. The example given above of Gemma doing some written mathematics was provided by a Key Stage 1 teacher in one of our groups. It illustrates some key ideas about understanding. First, we can recognize that Gemma does show some degree of understanding of addition, because she makes connections between the symbol for addition and the process of counting on, using her fingers. We discuss later the particular difficulties of understanding the equals sign that are illustrated by Gemma's response towards the end of this conversation. But we note here that, as seems to be the case for many children, she appears at this point to perceive the numerical task as a matter of moving symbols around, apparently at random and using an arbitrary collection of rules.

Learning with understanding

Of course, mathematics does involve the manipulation of symbols. But the learning of recipes for manipulating symbols in order to answer various types of questions is not the basis of understanding in mathematics. All our experience and what we learn from research indicate that learning based on understanding is more enduring, more psychologically satisfying and more useful in practice than learning based mainly on the rehearsal of recipes and routines low in meaningfulness.

For a teacher committed to promoting understanding in their children's learning of mathematics, the challenge is to identify the most significant ways of thinking mathematically that are characteristic of understanding in this subject. These are the key cognitive processes by means of which learners organize and internalize the information they receive from the external world and construct meaning. We shall see that this involves exploring the relationship between mathematical symbols and the other components of children's experience of mathematics, such as formal mathematical and everyday language, concrete or real-life situations, and various kinds of pictures. To help in this we will offer a framework for discussing children's understanding of number and number operations. This framework is based on the principle that the development of understanding involves building up *connections* in the mind of the learner.

Two other key processes that contribute to children learning mathematics with understanding are *equivalence* and *transformation*. These processes also enable children to organize and make sense of their observations and their practical engagement with mathematical objects and symbols. These two fundamental processes are what children engage in when they recognize what is the same about a number of mathematical objects (equivalence) and what is different or what has changed (transformation).

Teaching with understanding

This book has arisen from an attempt to help teachers to understand some of the mathematical ideas that children handle in the early years of schooling. It is based on our experience that many teachers and trainees in nursery and primary schools are helped significantly in their teaching of mathematics by a shift in their perception of the subject away from the learning of a collection of recipes and rules towards the development of understanding of mathematical concepts, principles and processes. So our emphasis on understanding applies not just to children learning, but also to teachers teaching: in two senses. First, it is important that teachers of young children teach mathematics in a way that promotes understanding, that helps children to make key connections, and that recognizes opportunities to develop key processes such as forming equivalences and identifying transformations. Second, in order to be able to do this the teachers must themselves understand clearly the mathematical concepts, principles and processes they are teaching. Our experience with teachers suggests that engaging seriously with the structure of mathematical ideas in terms of how children come to understand them is often the way in which teachers' own understanding of the mathematics they teach is enhanced and strengthened.

Concrete materials, symbols, language and pictures

When children are engaged in mathematical activity, as in the example above, they are involved in manipulating one or more of these four key components of mathematical experience: concrete materials, symbols, language and pictures.

First, they manipulate *concrete materials*. We use this term to refer to any kind of real, physical materials, structured or unstructured, that children might use to help them perform mathematical operations or to enable them to construct mathematical concepts. Examples of concrete materials would be blocks, various sets of objects and toys, rods, counters, fingers and coins.

Second, they manipulate *symbols*: selecting and arranging cards with numerals written on them; making marks representing numbers on pieces of paper and arranging them in various ways; copying exercises from a work card or a textbook; numbering the questions; breaking up numbers into tens and units; writing numerals in boxes; underlining the answer; pressing buttons on their calculator; and so on.

Third, they manipulate *language*: reading instructions from work cards or textbooks; making sentences incorporating specific mathematical words; processing the teacher's instructions; interpreting word problems; saying out loud the words that go with their recording; discussing their choices with the teacher and with other children; and so on. This language will include both formal mathematical words, such as 'subtract two, equals', and less formal language that describes particular actions or observations, such as 'take two away, how many are left?'

Finally, they manipulate *pictures*: drawing various kinds of number strips and number lines, set diagrams, arrow pictures and graphs.

An example in a nursery class

In a nursery class some children aged 3 to 4 years are propelling themselves around the playground on tricycles. The tricycles are numbered from 1 to 9 (see photograph). At the end of the time for free play they put the tricycles away in a parking bay, where the numerals from 1 to 9 are written on the paving stones, matching their tricycle to the appropriate numbered position in the bay. There are conversations prompted by the teacher about why a particular tricycle is in the wrong place and which one should go next to which other ones. When all the tricycles are in place the children check them by counting from 1 to 9, pointing at each tricycle in turn.

We begin to see here how understanding of elementary mathematical ideas develops, as children begin to make connections between real objects, symbols, language and pictures. The children are making connections between the ordering of the numerical symbols and the ordering of the actual tricycles. The numerals on the paving stones form an elementary picture of part of a number line, providing a visual image to connect with the language of counting. Already the children are beginning to understand what we will call (in Chapter 2) the ordinal aspect of number, by making these simple connections between real objects lined up in order, the picture of the number line, the symbols for numbers and the associated language of counting.

Understanding as making connections

A simple model that enables us to talk about understanding in mathematics is to view the growth of understanding as the building up of cognitive connections. More specifically, when we encounter some new experience there is a sense in which we understand it if we can connect it to previous experiences or, better, to a network of previously connected experiences. In this model we propose that the more strongly connected the experience is, the greater and more secure is our understanding of it. Using this model, the teacher's role in developing understanding is, then, to help the child to build up connections between new experiences and previous learning. Learning without making connections is what we would call learning by rote.

Connections between the four key components

We find it very helpful to think of understanding the concepts of number and number operations (that is, number, place value, addition, subtraction, multiplication, division, equals, number patterns and relationships, and so on) as including the building up of a network of cognitive connections between the four types of experience of mathematics that we have identified above: concrete experiences, symbols, language and pictures. Any one of the arrows in Figure 1.1 represents a possible connection between experiences that might form part of the understanding of a mathematical concept.

So, for example, when a 3-year-old counts out loud as they climb the steps on the playground slide or when they stamp along a line of paving stones, they are connecting the language of number with a concrete and physical experience. Later they will be able to connect this experience and language with the picture of a number strip. When 4-year-olds play a simple board game they are connecting a number symbol on a die with the name of the numeral and the concrete experience of moving their counter forward that number of places along the board. And so, through these connections, understanding of number is being developed.

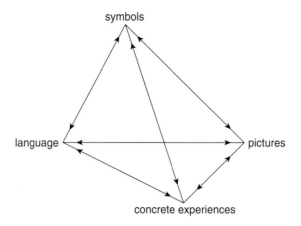

Figure 1.1   *Significant connections in understanding number and number operations*

Consider a child just starting to use Numicon plates to explore early ideas of number. These are coloured plates carefully structured to represent numbers in sequence (see www.numicon.com). The shape for 5, as shown in Figure 1.2, is a picture that through playing with the materials is connected with the language 'five' and, eventually, the symbol 5. The shape is seen as having a position in a pattern of shapes, which places 'five' between 'four and 'six'. The child learns to connect this shape with the physical process of filling the holes in the plate with pegs, while counting one, two, three, four, five. The materials are effective for promoting understanding of number because they enable the child to make such key connections between language, pictures and patterns, physical action and symbols.

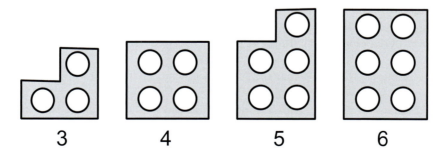

Figure 1.2   *Some Numicon shapes for promoting understanding of number*

We should make clear that the diagram in Figure 1.1 does not represent all the possible connections that might contribute to understanding mathematical concepts or processes. Particularly for young children, in their learning about number and counting, we could include physical movements, gestures and music – such as the rhythmic patterns in both the words and the music of counting songs and the actions that go with them. Then, of course, there are connections within one of the four categories of experience suggested in Figure 1.1. For example, the learner will make connections between one kind of visual image and another, such as connecting four steps of two on a number line with four rows of two dots; or between formal mathematical language, such as 'not vertical', and everyday language, such as 'tilted'. Our point is simply this: the more connections, the more secure and the more useful the understanding.

PAUSE TO REFLECT   'By George, she's got it!'

These are the words of Professor Higgins in *My Fair Lady* when Eliza shows significant progress in her learning! Think about all the different expressions you might use – or hear other people use – to indicate that you (or they) understand something or do not understand something. For example, you might say things like:

- Oh, I see!
- Now it's clicked.
- Everything is falling into place.
- Sorry, I don't get it.
- I'm still in the dark.
- I can't see the sense in that!

Reflect on what insights these forms of words might give you about the nature of understanding. Do any of the expressions you identify resonate with the connections model of understanding for mathematics that we have introduced in this chapter?

An illustration: 7-year-olds and the concept of division

Below is one teacher's description of some children in her class engaged in a mathematical activity designed to develop their understanding of the concept of division. The emphasis on making connections is clearly what we would recognize as developing understanding, as opposed to just the processes of handling division calculations. The children's recording is shown in Figure 1.3. This illustrates how the activity involves

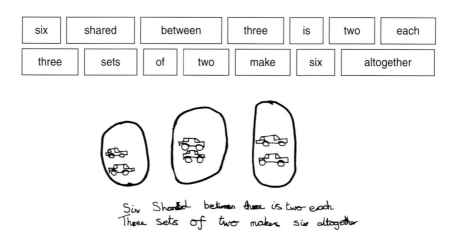

Figure 1.3   *Language patterns and a picture for a sharing experience*

children in handling the four key components of mathematical experience – real objects, pictures, mathematical symbols and mathematical language – and in making connections between them.

Three 7-year-olds in my class were exploring the early ideas of division. On their table they had a box of toy cars, paper and pencil, a collection of cards with various words written on them (*shared, between, is, each, sets, of, make, altogether, two, three, six, nine, twelve*) and a calculator. Their first task was to share six cars between the three of them. They discussed the result. Then they selected various cards to make up sentences to describe what they had discovered. The children then drew pictures of their sharing and copied their two sentences underneath. One of the children then picked up the calculator and interpreted the first sentence by pressing these keys: 6 ÷ 3 =. She seemed delighted to see appear in the display a symbol representing the two cars that they each had. She then interpreted their second sentence by pressing these keys: × 3 =. As she expected, she got back to the 6 she started with. She demonstrated this to the other children who then insisted on doing it themselves. When they next recorded their calculations as 6 ÷ 3 = 2 and 2 × 3 = 6, the symbols were a record of the keys pressed on the calculator and the resulting display. Later on I will get them to include with their drawings, their sentences, their recording in symbols, and a number line showing how you can count back from 6 to 0 in jumps of 2 (see Figure 1.4).

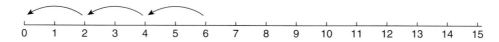

Figure 1.4   *Division connected with a number line*

We can identify some of the connections being made by these children in this activity. They make connections between concrete experience and language when they relate their manipulation of the toy cars to the language patterns of '... shared between ... is ... each', and '... sets of ... make ... altogether'. They connect their concrete experience with a picture of three sets of two things. The language of their sentences is connected with the symbols on the keys and display of the calculator. And then, later, they will be learning to connect these symbols with a picture of three steps of two on a number line. It is because of these opportunities to make so many connections between language, concrete experience, pictures and symbols that we would recognize this as an activity promoting mathematical understanding.

We should comment here on the role of calculators in this example, since they are not normally used with children in this age range. However, here they helped children to connect the mathematical symbols on the keys with the concrete experiences and the language of division, showing how calculator experiences even with young children can be used selectively to promote understanding. A more detailed analysis of understanding of multiplication and division is provided in Chapter 4.

We can see, therefore, that much of what is involved in understanding can be identified as the building up of a complex network of connections between language, symbols, concrete materials and pictures. We find it helpful to regard many mathematical concepts as networks of such connections.

The function of a mathematical symbol

Other than just marks we learn to write on paper and manipulate according to certain rules, what are mathematical symbols? What is the function of a symbol in mathematics? What is the relationship of a mathematical symbol to our experiences of doing mathematics and handling mathematical ideas? These are some comments from some of our Foundation Stage and Key Stage 1 teachers, in response to these questions:

- I think of mathematical symbols as abbreviations. They're a sort of shorthand.
- They have very ambiguous meanings for me. They have different meanings depending on the situation you're using them in.
- They sometimes mean you have to do something. Perform an operation. Move some blocks around.

Mathematical symbols are not just abbreviations

Are mathematical symbols just abbreviations? Of course, there is a sense in which mathematical symbols (such as 4, 28, ×, =) are abbreviations for mathematical ideas or concepts. But it is important to note that this does not mean that a symbol in mathematics is just an abbreviation for a specific word or phrase. It is tempting to think of, say, the division sign as being essentially an abbreviation for the words 'shared between'. Children often appear to view mathematical symbols in this way. One 9-year-old was using a calculator to do '28 ÷ 4', saying to himself as he pressed the keys, 'Twenty-eight shared …'. At this point he turned to the teacher and asked, 'Which button's *between*?' It was as though each word had to have a button or a symbol to represent it. When we see children writing 41 for fourteen it is clear that they often say 'four' and write 4, then say 'teen' and write 1, again using the symbols as abbreviations for the sounds they are uttering. And so the same child will happily write 41 for forty-one a few lines later! It is a similar error when children record a number like three hundred and seventy-five as 30075 or 3075. The zeros are written down as abbreviations for the word 'hundred'.

But once we think of understanding, particularly understanding of number and number operations, as the building up of connections between concrete experiences, symbols, words and pictures, we begin to see that a mathematical symbol is not simply an abbreviation for just one category of concrete experiences, or just one word or phrase, or just one picture. The child has to learn to connect one symbol with what, at times, can seem to be a confusing variety of concrete situations, pictures and language.

A symbol represents a network of connections

Hence we suggest that a symbol in mathematics is a way of representing a concept, by which we mean a network of connections. The symbol then becomes a means whereby we can manipulate that concept according to various rules. Without the symbols it would be virtually impossible for us to manipulate the concepts. The symbols of mathematics allow us to both discover and express relationships between various concepts. For example, when we write down a statement in symbols like $4 + 2 = 6$ we are expressing a relationship between the concepts of four, two and six, addition and equality, each of which, as we shall see, is itself a complex network of connections represented by a specific symbol.

The teacher's suggestion above that mathematical symbols have different meanings depending on the situation in which they are being used is a very perceptive observation. One symbol can indeed represent a complex network of connections. It can therefore be applied to a variety of situations and pictures. And it can be associated with a variety of language. This is one of the major themes in our discussion of understanding number and number operations in this and subsequent chapters. We explore in considerable detail how a statement in symbols, such as $4 + 2 = 6$, can be connected to an extensive range of different pictures, language and concrete situations.

For example, these symbols could be connected with such different experiences as: throwing a 4 on one die and a 2 on another and combining these to get a score of 6; starting on square 4 and moving on 2 squares to get to square 6 in a board game; or the price of an item costing £4 being increased by £2 to give a new price of £6. So, the symbols for the numbers, the symbol for the operation of addition and the equals sign itself each has a variety of meanings depending on the situation and the manner in which they are being used. And there is wide variety of language required in these differing contexts: altogether, counting on, increasing, and so on. Put all this together and the simple-looking statement 4 + 2 = 6, represents a surprisingly complex network of connections. This is at one and the same time the reason why mathematics is so powerful and the reason why it is for many such a difficult subject to understand.

The symbol for zero

Consider, for example, understanding the concept of zero. The formal mathematical language is the word 'zero' and the symbol is 0. Sometimes we use the symbol 0 to represent 'nothing' or 'none'. If a child playing a game has six counters and then loses six, the child has no counters left: 0 counters, nothing. If children in a class are sorted into sets according to their ages and there are no 7-year-olds, then the set of 7-year-olds is an 'empty set'. There is nothing in it. The number in the set is zero. Similarly, if Derek's bank balance is zero, then he has nothing; the zero indicates a complete absence of money in his account. In discussing zero as a place holder in Chapter 7 we shall see that in a number like 206 the zero represents an absence of tens. So when we say the number 'two hundred and six' the zero does not even get a mention!

But we shall also see in Chapter 2 and elsewhere in this book that there are other situations where the same symbol (0) and the word 'zero' are connected with something that is not 'nothing'. For example, the point on a number line connected with 0 is not nothing; it is a very important point on the line. The point labelled 0 degrees on a thermometer does not indicate 'no temperature'. It is not surprising then that understanding the concept of zero is such a challenge for young learners. It involves building up a varied and complex network of pictures, language and real-life situations all to be connected with the symbol. And it is the symbol 0 that represents for us this network of connections.

> **PAUSE TO REFLECT   An absence of something**
>
> In this chapter we have introduced the idea that although zero sometimes represents 'nothing' there are also situations in which it represents something (for example, a temperature or a point on a number line). We should also make the point that in real-life contexts, even when it represents *nothing*, a zero usually indicates
>
> *(Continued)*

(Continued)

nothing of something – in other words an absence of something. The 'something' that is absent is a significant component of the meaning of the zero.

Having spent years thinking of zero as 'nothing' rather than 'an absence of something', we may find it quite hard to think of real-life examples to make this point. Thoughts of zero teeth or zero money might be pretty shocking for us, while the thought of zero tasks to be done may be highly appealing! (See Figure 1.5.)

Children may be less likely to be taken by these particular examples. So how might you portray for them this idea of zero being 'an absence of something'? Reflect on the day-to-day experiences that young children might have of a total absence of something. Come up with some examples where zero of something is desirable for the children as well as some examples where it is undesirable.

Figure 1.5   *Zero teeth, zero money, zero tasks*

Transformation and equivalence

The concept of 'equals' is another example of a complex network of connections, which we represent by the equals sign. To analyse this concept we first discuss two fundamental ideas that run right through mathematics. These are the notions of *transformation* and *equivalence*.

What is different? What is the same?

We introduce these principles with an example from everyday experience, namely, paper sizes. Figure 1.6 represents two pieces of paper, one A4 size and the other A5 size. We should explain that you get A1 paper by folding A0 paper in half, A2 by folding A1 in half, and so on, and that the dimensions of the paper are cunningly chosen so that each rectangle has exactly the same proportions as the original. So the A5 rectangle is the shape produced by folding in half the A4 rectangle. Now when we begin to make mathematical statements about the relationships between the two rectangles in Figure 1.6, we find they fall into two categories. On the one hand, we may look at the rectangles and make observations about the ways in which they differ from each other:

- One rectangle is on the left and the other is on the right.
- One is half the area of the other.
- The length of one is about 1.4 times the length of the other.

Statements like these are essentially using the notion of transformation. We are concerned with the changes that are observed when we move our attention from one

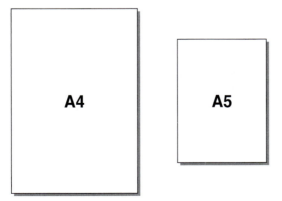

Figure 1.6   *The same but different*

rectangle to the other. We are hinting at what would have to be done to one rectangle to transform it into the other. But, on the other hand, we may look at these rectangles and make statements about the ways in which they are the same. Statements like these are essentially using the notion of equivalence. We are concerned with what stays the same when we move our attention from one rectangle to the other:

- They are both rectangles.
- They are the same shape.
- Their sides are in the same proportion.

More generally, then, when we make statements about what has changed in a situation, what is different about two things, what something has become, and so on, we are using the idea of transformation. When we concern ourselves with what is the same, with similarities rather than differences, what remains unchanged in spite of the transformation, then we are talking about equivalence. The key questions in everyday language for teachers to prompt children to recognize transformations and equivalences are simply 'What is different?' and 'What is the same?'

> So when my 4-year-olds sort the shapes in the shape box into sets and put all the squares together, for example, they are seeing an equivalence. And when they look at two of the squares and say something like 'this one is bigger than that one' they are seeing a transformation.

What stays the same when things change?

Much of mathematics, not just geometrical experiences like the example above, is concerned with recognizing and applying equivalences and transformations. Often a crucial mathematical principle involves the recognition of which equivalences are preserved under which transformations. An example of this, which illustrates the point nicely, is that of equivalent fractions. The reader may recall that you can transform the fraction $\frac{4}{6}$ by dividing top and bottom by 2 to produce the equivalent fraction $\frac{2}{3}$ (and record this as $\frac{4}{6} = \frac{2}{3}$). This is a transformation that preserves the equivalence. But it is apparently not in order to transform $\frac{4}{6}$ by, say, adding one to top and bottom, because $\frac{4}{6}$ does not equal $\frac{5}{7}$. This transformation does not preserve the equivalence.

But there are other situations where adding 1 to each of two numbers does preserve an equivalence, such as when calculating the difference between two numbers. For example, 77 − 49 can be correctly and usefully transformed into 78 − 50. At times one feels sorry for the poor child trying to make sense of this subject, particularly if the processes are taught as recipes and routines without understanding.

If the appropriate connections are not made, it must seem entirely arbitrary as to whether a particular transformation is acceptable and warrants a tick or is unacceptable and generates a cross.

The equals sign

Finally, to bring together the major ideas about understanding introduced in this chapter, we return to the equals sign (=) and the difficulties illustrated by Gemma at the start. We can now see that the essence of the problem with this symbol is that the concept of equals is such a complex network of ideas and experiences. We find that there is not just one form of words that goes with the symbol (=) but that there is a range of language and situations to which the symbol may become attached, including both the ideas of transformation and equivalence. Some of the teachers with whom we worked articulated their anxieties about the meaning of this symbol.

- My 6-year-olds had problems with some questions in their maths books where they had to put in the missing numbers, like this: $6 = 2 + \square$. Most of them put in 8, of course. When I tried to explain to them how to do these sums I realized I didn't actually know what the equals sign meant myself. We would say 'two add something makes six' if it were written the other way round, but 'six makes two add something' doesn't make sense.
- Is it wrong to say 'four add two makes six'? Should I insist that the children say 'equals six'?
- The word 'equals' doesn't mean anything to them. It's just a symbol, just some marks on paper that you make when you're doing sums.
- Doesn't it confuse children to say 'makes' when you're adding and then to say 'leaves' when you're taking away?
- And sometimes we just read it as 'is', like 'three add four is seven'.

The equals sign representing an equivalence

Strictly speaking, the equals sign represents the idea of equivalence. When we write down $2 + 4 = 6$ we are expressing an equivalence between $2 + 4$ and 6. We are making a statement that there is something the same about 'two added to four' and 'six'. Probably the most straightforward language to go with this statement is 'two add four is the same as six'. To emphasize the underlying equivalence in statements in arithmetic that use the equals sign, this phrase 'is the same as' is particularly significant. It connects very clearly with the concrete experience of doing addition and subtraction with some structured materials, as shown in Figure 1.7.

Figure 1.7   *Two add four is the same as six*

When the child makes a train with a 2-rod and a 4-rod the problem is to find another rod to match this train. Recording this experience as 2 + 4 = 6 is an expression of the equivalence: the 2-rod added to the 4-rod is in one sense the same as the 6-rod. Of course, they are only the same in that they are the same length. A train made up of a blue rod and a brown rod is very different from a red rod. But lying there side by side they represent an equivalence, and this is expressed by the symbols 2 + 4 = 6. It is worth noting that this interpretation of the equals sign makes sense of the problem that Gemma started with: '6 = 2 + □' can be read as 'six is the same as two add something'.

The equals sign representing a transformation

However, when the child puts out sets of two counters and four counters, forms their union and counts the new set to discover that there is now a set of six counters, it is a bit obscure to suggest that this is an experience of 'two add four is the same as six'. The child has actually *transformed* the two sets of two and four counters into a set of six (see Figure 1.8). The child's attention therefore is focused on the transformation that has taken place. This being so, it seems perfectly natural, and surely appropriate, to use the language 'two and four makes six' to describe the transformation the child has effected. One of the teachers quoted above said that she regarded the symbols as instructions to do something. In other words, the equals sign tells you to apply some sort of transformation. There is evidence that this is how children most frequently interpret the equals sign.

So, in practice, the equals sign represents both the equivalence and the transformation aspects of the relationship between 2 + 4 and 6. Thus we would not want to suggest that it is wrong or in some way mathematically incorrect to associate 'makes', 'leaves', 'is', and so on, with the equals sign, and insist on using only one particular form of words, such as 'is the same as' or even 'equals'. Rather, we would advocate a combination of experiences emphasizing the notions of both equivalence and transformation. As we have already argued, mathematical symbols are not just abbreviations for particular words or phrases. We have to recognize that the statement 2 + 4 = 6 is actually at one and the same time a representation in symbols of the transformation that has been applied to 2 and 4, and the equivalence that has emerged between 2 + 4 and 6.

Figure 1.8   *Two add four makes six*

One symbol, two meanings

It could be, therefore, that the child's attention might on some occasions be directed to the transformation of two and four into six, particularly when using counters, fingers, sets of toys, pencils, sweets, and so on. And on other occasions, particularly when using some structural apparatus or when making steps on a number line, the attention might be directed to the equivalence of 'two added to four' and 'six'. On both occasions the child might record their activity as 2 + 4 = 6. But this might be accompanied in the first case by the language pattern 'two add four makes six', and in the second case by the language pattern 'two add four is the same as six'. The use of different language appropriate to the situation is inevitable and perfectly acceptable, demonstrating that the child is gaining experience of both the transformation and the equivalence built into the relationship between 2 + 4 and 6. However, we should note that, as in the case of Gemma, it is often the dominant association of the equals sign with the idea of 'makes' that is the root cause of difficulties with missing number questions. Activity 1.4 at the end of this chapter provides an opportunity to explore the use of the phrase 'is the same as' in such questions.

These two ideas of transformation and equivalence are almost always present whenever we make statements of equality. In the fractions example above, when we write down $^4/_6 = {}^2/_3$ we are both recording a transformation that has been applied to the $^4/_6$ and recognizing an equivalence that has emerged. There is a sense in which $^4/_6$ is not the same as $^2/_3$. Using one meaning of the fraction notation, four slices of a cake cut into six equal parts is actually different from two slices of a cake cut into three equal parts. But there is something very significantly the same about these two situations – they produce the same amount of cake – which prompts us to recognize an equivalence and to record it with the equals sign. This is just the same with 2 + 4 = 6. Two piles of cubes, one containing two and the other containing four, look quite different from a pile of six cubes, yet there is an aspect of sameness about the two situations that warrants the use of the equals sign.

So, what does the equals sign mean? Strictly we should concede that it means 'is equivalent to', or 'is the same as', in whatever sense is determined by the context. And we should say that perhaps this is an aspect of the meaning of the symbol that is underplayed by teachers. It would be no bad thing for children's mathematical development for the phrase 'is the same as' to occur more frequently in their talk and in the talk of their teachers. But as with all mathematical symbols we have to learn to connect the equals sign with a complex variety of situations, operations and language, sometimes focusing on the transformation and sometimes on the equivalence.

Understanding mathematics right from the earliest years involves us in learning to attach the same symbol to a potentially bewildering variety of situations and language. We saw this earlier in this chapter with the symbol for zero. But it is actually true about all the symbols we use for numbers, the first mathematical symbols the learner encounters. That will be the subject of Chapter 2.

RESEARCH FOCUS   The equals sign

Full details of the publications mentioned here and in Research Focuses in subsequent chapters are given in the References section at the end of the book.

Off and on over the years there have been bursts of interest among researchers in young children's understanding of the equals sign. Some have focused on younger children (e.g. Behr et al., 1980; Falkner et al., 1999; Freiman and Lee, 2004), while others such as Kieran (1981) and Marchini and his colleagues (Marchini et al., 2009) have gone across the age range, extending into high schools and beyond. What is interesting is that they have all reached similar conclusions, as may be summarized thus:

> … the concept of equivalence is an elusive one not only for elementary school students but for high schoolers as well. That the equals sign is a 'do something signal' is a thread which seems to run through the interpretation of equality sentences throughout elementary school, and even college. (Kieran, 1981, p. 324)

Notice the date and language of Carolyn Kieran's remarks: they are over 30 years old and written from a North American perspective, and yet, despite teachers' best efforts, Marchini et al.'s work suggests that the same still applies within a modern European context.

Carlo Marchini has spent many years working in advanced mathematics with graduate and undergraduate students at the ancient University of Parma in Italy. He became fascinated by the concept of equality when working with Paul Parslow-Williams and the second author (Anne) on a study of mathematical misconceptions in primary schools in the UK, the Czech Republic, Italy and Israel. He was so intrigued by these findings that he decided to try out some of the tasks used there with young children on his students. The following problem appeared to create particular difficulty:

$$48 - \square = 47 - \square = 46 - \square = \square$$

What are your responses? Why do you think some might have found the task tricky? Some of the possible answers are given at the end of this chapter.

More recently Carlo has been working with a Greek colleague – Ioannis Papadopoulos – exploring ways to help young children in the early stages of their written work (Marchini and Papadopoulos, 2011). They have been investigating whether using brackets is a useful technique to enhance children's understanding of equality. Thus, for example, they have been comparing data collected from Year 2 and 3 classes where some children are given tasks in a conventional format such as '7 + 2 = $\square$' and '1 + $\square$ = 6 + 2', while others have been presented with the same problems but with brackets added, resulting in '(7 + 2) = $\square$' and '(1 + $\square$) = (6 + 2)'. They concluded that the presence of brackets enabled children (1) to perform slightly better and (2) to be more aware of the symmetrical property of equality. Interestingly, however, their research led to a lively debate among delegates at the Psychology of Mathematics Education Annual Conference. Why do you think people might feel strongly about such an issue? What do you think about their ideas?

Some activities to use with children

The activities below are chosen to illustrate ways in which teachers might focus particularly on the development of understanding through making connections, in the ways discussed in this chapter.

		3–4	4–5	5–6	6–7	7–8
ACTIVITY 1.1 Number of the Week		$\square$	$\square$			

Objective

To develop connections between the name for each number from zero to ten and the symbol, pictures and concrete embodiments of the number.

Materials

A card with instructions for the activity to be shared each week with the child's family. Here is an example, using the number five.

The number of the week is 5.
Please try to do some or all of these activities with your child this week and let us know how he or she gets on. Thank you!
Look around for examples of sets of *five* things at home and outside in the street and ask your child to count them.

(Continued)

(Continued)

When you are out and about ask the child to look out for the number 5 and to point it out to you.

Write down 3 2 5 1 6 8 and ask the child to point to *five*.

Ask the child to find page *five* in a book.

Then ask the child to find a word with *five* letters.

If you have stairs, get the child to go up *five* stairs, counting up to *five*, and then down again, finishing with zero. Do the same thing with a row of paving stones or tiles.

Ask the child to count out *five* buttons or counters and then arrange them in lots of different ways.

Ask the child to draw a monster with *five* heads, *five* legs and *five* tails.

Method

Each week a particular number is chosen to be the focus. The parent/guardian is encouraged to do the activities at home with their children and to share what happens at home with the teacher.

 ACTIVITY 1.2   Tidying the Books

3–4	4–5	5–6	6–7	7–8
☐	☐			

Objective

To develop connections between number symbols, the language of ordering numbers and putting objects in order.

Materials

A set of ten (or more) reading or picture books in a nursery class and bookshelves.

Method

Compare the example of cars in the nursery playground earlier in this chapter. Number the books 1 to 10, and number the spaces on the bookshelves 1 to 10 – or further, as for example, in the photograph where the books and spaces are numbered up to 15. When the time for tidying up comes, children take it in turns to put the books back in their right places. The teacher or classroom assistant takes the opportunity to talk with the child about the ordering process. Why does this book not go here? Which number goes after number two? Does this book match that space? Which number book is missing? What number book is that one over there? When all the books are in place, ask the child to point at the books and say the numbers from left to right; when they are efficient at this, ask them to do the same from right to left.

This activity can be done equally well with numbered bowls for snacks, lunch boxes, wellington boots, and so on.

		3–4	4–5	5–6	6–7	7–8
	ACTIVITY 1.3 Connections (Add, Subtract)				□	□	

Objective

To develop the concepts of addition and subtraction by making connections between symbols, concrete experiences, language and pictures.

Materials

A box of counters (or toys, or pennies); paper and pencil; strips of card with words associated with addition and subtraction written on them (such as: take away, add, leaves, make); cards with numbers from 1 to 20 written on them; cards with +, −, = symbols on them; a duplicated sheet of number lines marked from 0 to 20.

(Continued)

(Continued)

Method

Develop an activity, for a small group of children, using subtraction, similar to that using division outlined in this chapter (see Figure 1.3). Do not provide everything outlined here at the start, but gradually introduce a wider range of experiences to be connected with subtraction. The children can be provided with a prompt sheet with these words written on it: *counters, sentences, picture, numbers, number line*. The children should start with two of the numbered cards, such as 12 and 5. It is explained to them that this means they put out twelve counters, move five to one side, and count how many are left. They then have to connect this with the appropriate language. For example, they use the cards provided to make up two sentences: 'twelve take away five leaves seven' and 'seven add five make twelve'. They then have to draw a picture on their paper to show what they have done and assemble or write the sentences underneath, as shown in Figure 1.9.

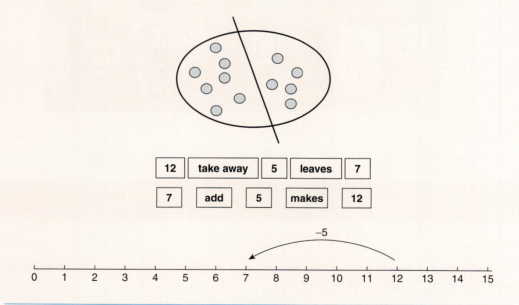

Figure 1.9   *Making subtraction connections*

When the children are at the stage when they can begin to make connections with symbols they then replace the words in the number sentences with the +, − or = cards, to produce 12 − 5 = 7 and 7 + 5 = 12. Finally they must represent the relationship on a number line, as shown in Figure 1.9. The teacher should discuss with the children how their number-line diagram shows both 12 − 5, and 7 + 5.

	3–4	4–5	5–6	6–7	7–8
ACTIVITY 1.4 Missing Numbers			□	□	

Objective

To help children understand statements with missing numbers and the meaning of the equals sign.

Materials

Some structured materials representing the numbers from 1 to 10, such as coloured rods, sticks of coloured cubes joined together, or Numicon plates.

Method

First investigate how the children handle a collection of missing number additions, where the box for the missing number might be in any one of six positions. For example, using the number statement $5 + 3 = 8$, they could look at: $5 + 3 = \square$, $5 + \square = 8$, $\square + 3 = 8$, $\square = 5 + 3$, $8 = \square + 3$ and $8 = 5 + \square$. Which type of questions do they find easier? More difficult? Talk with the children about how they interpret the questions, and discover what language they use for the equals sign. Explore the suggestions that children might be helped to make more sense of these questions by using the phrase 'is the same as' to go with the equals sign, and by connecting the symbols in these questions with corresponding manipulations of the materials.

Summary of key ideas

1 A simple model for talking about understanding is that to understand something is to connect it with previous learning or other experiences.
2 Mathematical activity involves the manipulation of concrete materials, symbols, language and pictures.
3 Connections between these four types of experience constitute important components of mathematical understanding.
4 A mathematical concept can be thought of as a network of connections between symbols, language, concrete experiences and pictures.
5 A mathematical symbol is a way of representing a mathematical concept that enables us to manipulate it and to discover and express relationships with other concepts.
6 Equivalence and transformation refer respectively to statements of sameness and statements of difference or change.

(Continued)

(Continued)

7   The equals sign strictly means 'is the same as' or 'is equivalent to'. But often in practice it represents both an instruction to apply a transformation – in which case language such as 'makes' and 'leaves' is appropriate – and the equivalence that emerges.

8   One mathematical symbol, such as the equals sign, can be connected with a wide variety of different concrete situations, language and pictures.

 ## Suggestions for further reading

Full details of the publications mentioned here and in Suggestions for Further Reading in subsequent chapters are given in the References section at the end of the book.

The entries on *Making Connections, Concept Learning, Rote Learning* and *Meaningful Learning* in Haylock with Thangata (2007) are relevant to the discussion of understanding mathematics in this chapter.

Chapter 3 of Anghileri (2006) provides a useful account of young children's growing understanding of the use of mathematical symbols.

Turner and McCullough (2004) emphasize teaching strategies that seek to establish relationships between language, symbolic notation and pictorial representation.

Section 1 in Gifford (2005) shows how the development of mathematical understanding in children aged 3–5 years involves consideration of cognitive, emotional and social processes.

Using practical examples and research evidence, Montague-Smith and Price (2012) demonstrate how, through the provision of a range of experiences, discussion and sensitive and skilled adult intervention, young children can develop their mathematical understanding within an early years environment.

Tucker (2005), basing her advice on research literature, provides a wide range of stimulating and practical suggestions to help young children develop mathematical connections through play.

In an engaging book, full of practical suggestions and interesting insights, McGrath (2010) shows how a play-based curriculum shaped by clear principles can promote mathematical understanding in young children.

Rowland et al. (2009) is a book that will help primary teachers to develop their own understanding of mathematics and thus to promote understanding in the children they teach. Chapter 5 is about making connections in teaching mathematics.

Note: *Responses to Carlo's task (see Research Focus)*

Quite a few of the university students responded with: $48 - 1 = 47 - 1 = 46 - 1 = 45$. Why do you think they did this? Of the 112 students, 2% wrote: $48 - 48 = 47 - 47 = 46 - 46 = 0$. More commonly (i.e. 6% of) students answered: $48 - 2 = 47 - 1 = 46 - 0 = 46$. The commonest correct response, which was presented by 61%, was $48 - 3 = 47 - 2 = 46 - 1 = 45$. How did you get on?

CHAPTER 2

UNDERSTANDING NUMBER AND COUNTING

A CHARMING STORY

A 7-year-old child was asked to write a story to go with the subtraction 5 − 3. This is what the child wrote (child's spelling retained!):

Once upon a time there lived a nubere and he was called 5 and he was very lonly. Won day he saw a nubere 3 and he was lonly to saw he went up to him and sad well you be my frinde. Yes he sad becase I have no frinde to play with. Saw five and three were good frinds and they were happy and the nexed day they went four a pikenik and had a good time. They had cakes and drink and sandwich and biskites and they came home and got into bed with a hot water botel.

This child chooses here to interpret numbers as characters in a story with lives of their own. This is hardly surprising, given children's experience of writing stories in literacy lessons. But, nevertheless, this child's response may prompt the reader to reflect on these questions:

- To what kinds of concrete situations and pictures might a child connect the symbols and names of numbers if they are to show an understanding of number?
- What exactly is a number?

In this chapter

In this chapter we focus first on this question: what exactly is a number? We do this by analysing the network of connections that are involved in understanding number. The middle section of the chapter explores the idea of counting. In the final section we provide the reader with an analysis of how the concept of number is developed from a mathematical perspective.

What is three?

We begin our exploration of what is a number by asking this question. What is three? We asked teachers in one of our groups to close their eyes and to bring to the forefront of their consciousness an image of the number three. They described the image in their minds:

- I can see three dots arranged in a triangle.
- A set of three fruits: an apple, an orange and a banana.
- Three dots in a line.
- A triangle, a shape with three sides.
- The symbol 3.
- Someone holding up three fingers.

This question has been asked of hundreds of teachers and trainees and almost invariably the responses are similar to those above. They usually fall into two categories. Either the image described is a set of three things: dots, sides of a triangle, fingers, sweets, vague unspecified objects or splodges, and so on; or, less frequently, the picture imagined is just the symbol 3.

Numbers, numerals and digits

Clearly the symbol that we use for three (3) is not the number three. As discussed in Chapter 1, the symbol allows us to represent the concept of 'three', to manipulate it and to relate it to other numbers. But the actual symbol that we use to represent three is fairly arbitrary. Other scripts and languages use other symbols and other words, but the same network of connections constituting the concept of three lies behind them. The Roman numeral for three (III), for example, represents the same number as does the numeral 3. If we want to distinguish the symbol from the number it represents then we can refer to the *numeral* 3. So, numerals are the marks we make on paper, such as 3, 26, 819, when we record and manipulate *numbers*. In practice we do not often need to make this distinction, because the symbol (that is, the numeral) plays such an important role in representing the number. Another important word that we might mention here is *digit*. There are just ten digits in our number system: 0, 1, 2, 3, 4, 5, 6, 7, 8, 9. We use the word *digit* to refer, for example, to the 8, the 1 and the 9 in the numeral 819.

Sets of three and one-to-one matching

The image of three that clearly dominates the thinking of most adults is the idea that three is a *set* of three things. When a teacher needs to explain to a child a problem involving the number 3 the most likely thing to appear on the table will be a set of three things: three counters, three toys or three fingers, for example. Not surprisingly, therefore, children's own stories about number usually interpret numbers in this way – as sets of things: three children, three teddies, three sweets, three bears, and so on. It could be suggested then that 'three' is what all these sets of three things have in common. In this way, three is seen as a concept abstracted from many examples of sets of three things. One-to-one matching of objects in one set of three with objects in another set of three, as illustrated in Figure 2.1, is an important part of the learning here. It is a visual or practical experience that is designed to focus the child's perception on what is the same about the two sets.

In one-to-one matching, we see the concepts of equivalence and transformation in operation. For example, when a child matches a set of three cups, one to one, onto a set of three saucers, the operation of matching shifts the focus from what is different about the cups and the saucers to what is the same, namely, that there are three of them.

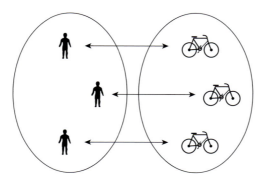

Figure 2.1   *One-to-one matching*

Adjective or noun?

The following conversation with some of our Key Stage 1 teachers highlights another important point about understanding number:

> D. *Is three an adjective or a noun?*
> C. *It must be an adjective, because you talk about three things. Three apples, three bananas, and so on. It describes the set.*
> E. *I think it can be both.*
> D. *To convince me that it can be a noun you need to give me a sentence beginning with the words 'Three is ...'*
> C. *Three is a number.*
> E. *Three is less than five.*
> A. *Three is a factor of twelve.*
> D. *Three is a prime number.*

When three changes from an adjective to a noun like this, it is no longer attached to the sets of three things; it has a life of its own. We can talk about three as though it exists independently of the sets to which we might connect it. We would suggest, therefore, that a key step in the development of the concept of number is this transition from number as an adjective to number as a noun.

Nominal, cardinal and ordinal

In fact, the view outlined above of the way in which number concepts develop is rather simplistic and does not recognize the complex network of connections between concrete experience, language, pictures and the symbol 3, which constitute the concept of three. So far we have only talked about connecting the symbol with concrete situations consisting of sets of three things. This is only one aspect of a number, referred to as the *cardinal* aspect. When we talk about three bears, three fingers, three children, or any other set of three things, we are using the cardinal aspect of number. But to what else, apart from sets of things, can we attach the symbol 3?

> • What about the 3 on a clock face – that's not denoting a set of three things, is it?
> • I live at number 3, but I don't live in a set of three houses!
> • Or page 3 in a newspaper?
> • It's like the number 3 bus. It's just a label that helps us identify one bus from another.

The 3 on a number 3 bus is indeed just a label, a number being used in what is called the *nominal* aspect. This is where a number is used just to label various items and to distinguish the items from one another. The 3 on the number 3 bus enables us to know that this is the bus we want to catch and distinguishes it from all the buses with other numbers. When used like this the symbol is hardly operating as a number at all. For a start, the 3 certainly does not mean that there are three of these buses (even though you may wait for ages and then three arrive at the same time!). And when we see a number 3 bus coming we do not expect the previous bus to have been a number 2 and the next one to be a number 4. Other examples that are essentially using just the nominal aspect of numbers would be telephone numbers and television channels. Numbers used simply as labels are all around us.

However, behind the other responses from the teachers above is another very important category of images of the number 3. This is called the *ordinal* aspect of number: numbers used not just to label things but also to *put them in order*. Room number 3, flat number 3, the 3 on the clock face, page 3 in a book – these are labelled 3 because there is some kind of ordering system involved in which they come between 2 and 4. The page before page 3 is invariably page 2 and the page following it is page 4. These are ordinal numbers because they are labelling the pages and telling us where they come in relation to other pages.

Notice that in this ordinal use of the number 3 there is no 'threeness' in the cardinal sense. Page 3 is not a set of three pages: it is, in fact, just one page. It does not have to contain a photograph of a set of three people or a set of three objects, nor does it contain just three words or three sentences. So why is it labelled page 3? The reason is simply that it is located between page 2 and page 4.

We want to emphasize that this ordinal aspect is not an obscure or in any sense a secondary aspect of the concept of number. In spite of the fact that so few people bring to mind an ordinal image when asked to think of three, this ordinal aspect of the number is as central and important as the cardinal aspect. It is one we use frequently in our everyday lives, whether it be locating a page in a book, finding a room in a strange building, looking up a date in a calendar, or deciding whether it's our turn to get padded up ready for the next wicket to fall. We shall see later that in mathematical terms the image of a number line is one that embodies most strongly the ordinal aspect of number.

Understanding number

So, in answer to the question, 'What is a number?', we see already that numbers like three are used as labels for identifying things (the nominal aspect), as labels for putting things in order (the ordinal aspect) and as indications of how many there are in a set of things (the cardinal aspect).

Connecting symbols with the number line

The importance of the ordinal aspect means therefore that a very significant part of understanding number is the connection between the symbols for numbers (the numerals) and the picture of number incorporated in a number strip or a number line. Examples of these are shown in Figure 2.2. In the number strip, as in many board or playground games, the squares or spaces are labelled with the numerals. In the more sophisticated number line, it is the points rather than the spaces that are labelled. For convenience, the number line in Figure 2.2 is shown as a horizontal line.

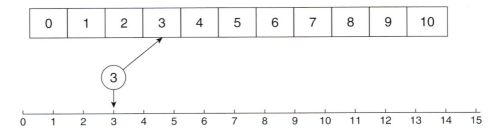

Figure 2.2   *The ordinal aspect of number in a number strip and a number line*

Possibly even more effective for developing number concepts is a similar line arranged vertically, so that the numbers get larger as you go up and smaller as you go down (see photograph). Either of these lines is a picture of number that emphasizes particularly the ordinal aspect. The number three is one point on the number line, or one square on the number strip, not a set of three points or a set of three squares. Its main property is that it lies between two and four.

A network of connections

It appears, therefore, that the answer to the question 'What is three?' is far from straightforward. The concept of a number like three appears to involve a network of connections between the symbol 3, the word 'three', concrete situations of sets of things, using the cardinal aspect, and pictures of number involving the ordinal aspect, such as number lines and number strips. Hence it seems that at a very early age the child encounters one enormous difficulty – a difficulty that runs right through mathematics – that one symbol can be used to represent vastly different situations. Not just different in the way in which a set of three sweets is different from a set of three plates, but as different as the questions, 'How many pages have you read today?' and 'What page are you on?' Both questions might elicit a response of 'three', but with two completely different meanings, one a cardinal number (the number of pages) and the other an ordinal number (the page number).

Of course, the different meanings of the symbol are not totally unrelated and arbitrary, as, for example, two different meanings of some words might be, such as 'well' (in good health) and 'well' (of water). As we shall see, the cardinal and ordinal aspects come together in counting. But the connections are by no means at a simple level of perception, and the teacher has a major task to help the child to make the connections and to build them into a coherent network.

Nor is it the case that the cardinal and ordinal aspects of number are the whole story. Consider the use of number in the following sentence, overheard when a teacher was talking to a group of children: 'There are three children in class four who are five.' This demonstrates the way in which we expect even young children to connect number symbols and words to very different situations. In the space of ten simple words the teacher has used numbers in three widely differing ways. The three children constitute a cardinal 3 and class four is an ordinal 4. The five (years old) is an example of number used in a measuring context. The different ways in which numbers are used in measurement will be discussed in Chapter 8 of this book.

Laying the foundations for later experiences of number

It is important, then, for teachers of young children to lay foundations of experience and networks of connections on to which future experiences of number can be built. In this respect the cardinal aspect of number is a very limited view of what numbers are. Later on, for example, children will meet negative numbers, a source of great mystery for many students of mathematics. But, in fact, it is not difficult to extend understanding of numbers to make connections with negative numbers if the ordinal aspect and the associated picture of the number line are a strong part of the concept of number. All that is required is to extend the number line the other side of zero and to use appropriate labels for the new points. In a local department store the buttons in the lift are labelled 3, 2, 1 and 0 for the 3rd, 2nd, 1st and ground floors. How mathematically pleasing to note that the button for the basement is labelled −1! This is a straightforward and obvious extension of ordinal number in a real-life context. In fact, some of the teachers we worked with assured us that by extending the ordinal aspect of number below zero, children as young as 5 can handle negative numbers confidently, using appropriate contexts such as number lines, temperatures, page numbers in a book and going up and down in lifts. One teacher reported her experience of using a number line with 5-year-olds, as follows:

> I put a vertical number line on the wall with zero and numbers written above it, up to about 10. We did some counting forwards and backwards. Start at 3 and count forward two; where do you get to? That sort of thing. I had marked some points below zero, but not labelled them. I then asked them to start at 1 and count back three. They did this quite happily and one of the girls amazed me by saying that the point we had arrived at was minus two! I don't know where she got this idea from, but the others picked it up immediately and handled the idea with no difficulty. One of the children pointed out that there was the same pattern of numbers above zero as below zero.

Overemphasis on the cardinal aspect

We propose that young children should do as much of their number work moving up and down number lines, or similar manifestations of the ordinal aspect, as they do manipulating counters and blocks and counting objects in sets. This is so that they learn to connect the symbol 3 and the word 'three' just as much with the idea of a label for a point or a position as with sets of things. We cannot stress too strongly that numbers are not just ways of representing sets of things.

We have talked about mathematical concepts as networks of connections between concrete situations, symbols, language and pictures, and highlighted the problem that understanding the concept involves one symbol being connected to a wide range of often very different situations. We have seen that even the basic and seemingly elementary concept of number has this problem built into it, with the same numeral being applied to very different experiences. The discussion about the possible overemphasis on the cardinal aspect at the expense of the ordinal aspect raises another point of general applicability and great significance to teachers in the Foundation Stage and Key Stage 1. There is a danger that we might continually reinforce just one particular connection in the network of connections constituting a mathematical concept at the expense of equally important or even ultimately more significant connections. If this one connection dominates the child's thinking about the concept, it may be difficult later to build on new experiences that do not readily connect with this part of the network. For example, if the idea that numbers are sets of things is continually reinforced in the early years and is the dominant connection, it is not surprising that negative numbers appear very mysterious when they are met later on. You cannot think of −3 as a set of things! And if you cannot make connections with previous learning then no real understanding but only rote learning can occur.

Assimilation, restructuring and accommodation

Learning with understanding progresses most smoothly by what Piaget and his associates called a process of *assimilation* of new ideas into existing networks of connections; however, when material does not connect readily to the existing network, understanding usually requires a *restructuring* of that network in order to *accommodate* the new experiences (Inhelder and Piaget, 1958). Skemp (1971, Chapters 2 and 3) showed how Piaget's ideas were particularly significant in the formation of mathematical concepts and 'schema' – what we call 'networks of connections'. Many children clearly fail to achieve the appropriate restructurings, particularly in mathematics, and continue with their limited and inadequate networks of connections, relying on memorization of rules and procedures that make little sense to them. It is because of this that we are emphasizing the importance of providing experiences of number early on – particularly activities with the number line – that will provide a basis for later learning with understanding when children encounter numbers other than those used for counting. It is very important that teachers are aware of the nature of the restructurings required as new mathematical experiences are encountered, so that by skilful, directed questioning, they can help children to reorganize their existing networks of connections in order to accommodate the new experiences. In this way children learn with understanding, rather than by rote.

Understanding zero

We asked the teachers in one of our groups to close their eyes and to think of zero. We asked them to describe the images that came into their minds:

- It's very hard to think of nothing!
- I can see a set with nothing in it, like a circle with nothing inside.
- I thought of putting out three chocolates then eating them!

Is zero a number? Many people feel that it isn't really a proper number; not like one, two or three. It's just nothing. A group of trainees was given a table showing the numbers of children in a class with birthdays in each month and asked which month had the smallest number of birthdays. Some of them had great difficulty in accepting that the month without any birthdays had the smallest number, because they did not think of zero as a number.

Part of the problem with zero is that it's not uncommon for the word 'nothing' to be used for the symbol 0. This fixation on the idea that zero is nothing is, of course, a consequence of the overemphasis on the cardinal aspect of number. If you have a set of zero objects in your hand then, of course, you do actually have nothing in your hand. But is zero nothing more than nothing? We have already seen that the cardinal view of a number is very limited. Once we consider the ordinal aspect, zero (as a label on the number line, for example) has at least the same status as any other number. In fact, it becomes a very significant and important number. It is the point before 1 on the number line, and sometimes the starting point; it is the point on the number line that separates positive numbers from negative numbers; it is the ground floor in the department store; it is midnight on my digital watch; it is freezing point on the thermometer.

A line of pegs in a classroom is labelled like a number line; there is a bag hanging on each peg, the bag on peg 1 containing one block, that on peg 2 containing two blocks, and so on. The photograph shows the peg labelled 0 and, hanging on this peg, there is an empty bag. This is a bag containing zero blocks. Here we see the two ideas of zero coming together: the position labelled zero (an ordinal zero) and the accompanying bag with nothing in it (a cardinal zero).

So understanding the concept of zero involves connecting the symbol and the language, not just with 'nothing', an 'absence of something' and empty sets but also with ordinal pictures of number where zero is very definitely something. Our teachers added some insightful comments on this special number:

- *The problem is that we sometimes call it zero, we sometimes call it nought, and sometimes nothing. Other numbers like 1 have only one name.*
- *When children do take away questions and get nothing left they tend to say 'nothing', but when they count backwards they always say 'zero' at the end, like a countdown for a spaceship.*
- *Counting down is very clearly an ordinal aspect of number, isn't it?*
- *Do books have a page numbered zero?*

Does this book have a page numbered zero? How could you label the pages that come before page 1, other than the way it is done in this book?

PAUSE TO REFLECT   Zero, zero everywhere

Make a list of situations in your everyday life in which you come across the symbol for zero (0). Compare your list with that of a colleague. In each example you come up with, discuss how or why the symbol is being used, what language goes with it, what it means in that context, and any other questions that might occur to you or puzzle you. Try to come up with some examples that are very different in the way the symbol is used.

Here are two examples we came up with:

1 All the area telephone codes in Britain begin with a zero (0); for example Norwich is 01603. Most people read this as 'O' (pronounced 'oh') apart from a few pedants (like Derek) who insist on saying 'zero'. Does this matter? What is this zero for? Does it mean 'nothing' or does it just mean nothing?
2 On the formatting palate for a Word document on a computer we spotted: *Indentation (cm) Left 0.* How do you read this symbol? What does it mean in this context? How is it connected with the picture of a number line on the ruler that can be displayed on the screen? How is it connected with the layout of the text you are typing? Note how you can change the setting in the indentation box up or down: what numbers are available either side of the zero?

Understanding counting

For young children their understanding of the concept of number is closely bound up with their experience of counting. Children's first experiences of counting both at home and in the nursery class will include preparing, matching and comparing. Many activities in the early years classroom provide opportunities for children to participate in the preparation of resources, and this often involves counting; for example, to prepare for playing shops the children may count out five pennies (or tokens of some kind) for each child to use to buy items from the play shop. Likewise, there are frequent opportunities for children to match numbers; for example, at snack time they may count ten children and count out ten pieces of banana and then match one piece of banana to each child. Similarly, children will often count to compare, motivated by their strong sense of what is fair; for example, counting to check that there are three children in each group, or to check that each child has three and no more than three pieces of fruit.

> My 3- and 4-year-olds know that only three children at a time are allowed to play on the slide in the playground. I see the others keeping an eye on the slide and as soon as the number drops to two they rush to get in as quick as they can. If two arrive at the same time they call me over to sort it out because they realize that there are four children now and that's not allowed!

From a mathematical perspective we may see numbers as describing sets or labelling points, but most significantly for young children numbers are words you use to count with. In fact, we shall see that it is in the process of counting that the ordinal and cardinal aspects of number come together. So, now we ask, what is counting? What is there to be understood? What connections must be made for a learner to be able to count with meaning? We shall identify a number of key components that are involved in learning to count, drawing substantially on the influential work of Gelman and Gallistel (1986).

Pre-counting experiences

It is important to recognize first that learning to count requires a considerable background of experience, much of which many children bring to the Foundation Stage classroom from their life at home. We mention here three kinds of prerequisite experience for counting.

Top of the list is the whole idea of sorting objects into sets and categorization. In order to engage with counting some objects you clearly need to have the notion of the objects being separated off from those you are not counting. This is an early experience of forming equivalences: identifying a set of objects on the basis of them being in some sense the same; the same colour, the same size, the same family, and so on. Young children's play provides many examples of sorting and categorizing. They will sort blocks, toy animals, model cars, dolls, and so on, into different sets and categories. They categorize when they make distinctions between those in their family and those who are not; between children and adults; between boys and girls. In fact, categorization lies at the heart of language development and is the basic process by which we make sense of our experiences. What we are pointing out here is that this process is the first stage of learning to count: to be able to identify and separate off the members of a set in order that you can then count just these objects and no others.

> It's like when you say, 'How many children are here today?' The children in my reception class know they don't count the adults. Or if you ask how many boys, they don't count the girls. When you think about it, that's quite a sophisticated thing for young children to learn to do. There are two steps: they have to separate the children into a category and then count them.

Second, we should not underestimate the importance of the child having a rich experience of talk using language such as 'one more' and 'another one', within the context of family life at home. A basic idea in counting is that numbers increase as you count; that six is more than five, for example. So, when a child learns at such a young age to ask for 'another one', they are getting essential prerequisite experience for learning to count. Parents are probably unaware of the significant experience being provided by the repetition of phrases such as 'one more, then no more'. Teachers, in their own conversations with children, should not be.

Third, there is some evidence to suggest that before they engage in actual counting children are able to distinguish between small numbers, such as one, two and three. Three-year-olds will look at picture books and be able to recognize which picture has one cow, two cows or three cows. So, they are beginning to learn that numbers are used to describe sets of objects and to distinguish between sets of various sizes. This is also experienced when small numbers are used in conversation. Children, before they can count, know that they have two feet, two hands and two eyes, but only one nose. They have stories about three little pigs and three bears. All this experience is invaluable preparation for counting.

Perceiving at a glance the number of items in a set without actually counting them is called *subitizing*. Recognizing a small number like two or three without recourse to any mathematical process or pattern is often called *perceptual* subitizing (Clements, 1999). Children move on from this to *conceptual* subitizing, where it is the pattern in the arrangement of a number of items that leads to its recognition. The arrangement of dots on dice and dominoes (see Figure 6.2 in Chapter 6) and the holes in Numicon plates (see Figure 1.2 in Chapter 1) are therefore important visual images for the development of young children's ability to subitize in a conceptual way.

> I find that many of the 3-year-olds arriving in my nursery class can already recognize three items at a glance – and four items if they are arranged in a square. I have one exceptional 3-year-old, who, when she is counting, will sometimes spot a group of three things in the set and start from there, counting on 3, 4, 5, 6, …

The order of numbers is invariant

When children start to learn to count they learn first a pattern of noises, memorized by repetition in all sorts of situations both in and out of school: 'One, two, three, four …' and so on. This set of sounds is probably just as meaningless as many traditional nursery rhymes, demonstrating the young child's amazing capacity for sequential learning. But what they learn from this repetition is the underlying principle of counting that the order of the numbers is fixed. It is invariant: when you are counting, three always comes after two, and so on. Gelman and Gallistel (1986) call this the stable order principle.

One-to-one matching of number names to objects

Then the child has to learn to co-ordinate the utterance of these noises with the physical movements of a finger and the eye along a line of objects, matching one noise to one object. So the child has to learn that one number name must be matched to one object, until all the objects have been used up. Gelman and Gallistel call this the one–one principle. This is a significant skill to learn. Teachers working with children learning to count will know that the two-syllable word 'seven' sometimes poses a difficult problem of co-ordination. Also, children sometimes over count. A way to see if they have a good understanding of the principle is to arrange the objects to be counted in various ways, such as in a straight line, in a circle and in a heap. This will show whether or not the child is aware that they have to keep track of what has been counted and what remains to be counted.

Connecting cardinal and ordinal aspects

An underlying principle of counting is that the last number that you get to when you are counting a set is the number in the set. Gelman and Gallistel call this the cardinal principle. This is where the ordinal and cardinal aspects come together. As each number is spoken it is being used essentially in an ordinal sense, to label the objects and to order them – number one, number two, number three, and so on. But then the child has somehow to discover that the ordinal number of the last object is the cardinal number of the set. What a stunning and powerful discovery this is! One teacher reported the following:

> A 4-year-old girl was counting objects in her head and suddenly announced with great excitement, 'Three is three, isn't it!' She did some more counting in her head and then announced, 'Four is four! And five is five!' It was as though she was counting to three and then realizing that when you got to three you actually had a set of three things. And then that when you got to four you actually had a set of four things, and so on.

Counting as an abstraction

A major challenge in learning to do mathematics is to learn to abstract the mathematical concepts from the context in which they are embedded. For example, when a child adds 3 to 4, what actual objects are used makes absolutely no difference to the mathematical process: three sweets and four sweets, three boys and four boys, three counters and four counters, these are all represented by the same abstraction, 3 + 4 = 7. This is a significant way in which mathematics is so different from so many of the other things children learn at school. In a poem, a story, a picture, a song, a game, a piece of drama, and so on, the context is the essence of the activity. But in mathematics it is often the case (but by no means always) that the context is of little significance. In counting, children first meet what Gelman and Gallistel call the abstraction principle. It makes no difference what you are counting; whether it be children, animals, counters or fingers, the process is exactly the same. You use the same number names, in the same order, with the same one-to-one matching procedure.

The order of the objects is irrelevant

Gelman and Gallistel also identify what they call the order-irrelevance principle. Children have to learn, for example, that whether they count a row of objects from left to right or from right to left makes no difference. In fact, you can count the objects in any order, provided you match them all one to one with a number name in the prescribed sequence. This is again a very sophisticated piece of learning and something that teachers should target specifically in the counting experiences of young children and in their assessment of their understanding.

The arrangement of the objects is irrelevant

An associated principle is that the arrangement of the objects in a set is irrelevant when you are counting them. If a line of seven objects is spread out, there are still seven objects. If they are arranged in a cluster, or a circle, or some other pattern, there are still seven objects. This and the previous principle together constitute what is called the principle of conservation of number. We can understand this in terms of the child learning that whatever transformation is applied to the arrangement of the objects in a set, there is an equivalence that is preserved: there is still the same number. See the Research Focus at the end of this chapter and also Chapter 8 where conservation is discussed more generally in the context of measurement.

Matching the names to the numerals

Clearly, at some stage, children have to learn to match the names of numbers to the numerals that represent the numbers. In the early stages of counting they just recite the number names: 'one, two, three, four, five, …' as they point to objects. At a later stage they will learn to recite these names as they point to the symbols: 1, 2, 3, 4, 5, and so on, doing this often, until eventually the connection between each name and the corresponding numeral is clearly established.

Connecting 'one more' and the 'next number'

There is a basic principle of counting that we should make explicit here, so that teachers reading this book are aware of it and ensure that the principle is targeted in their interactions with children. The principle is simply that the next number after any given number is always one more. So seven is one more than six, because it is the next number after six.

> That seems so obvious when you point it out, but it had never occurred to me that it's something children have to learn! I was asking a 4-year-old yesterday what number is one more than five and he couldn't do it. But he can count up to 20 with no trouble!

Again, we suggest this is a sophisticated piece of learning and it is helpful for teachers of young children to be aware of it and to ensure that they make the principle explicit. Even more sophisticated and challenging is the complementary principle: that the previous number is always one less.

> Young children find it really hard to think about the previous number. When I ask some of my Year 1 children, 'What comes after five?' they will say 'six', no problem. But if I then ask them what comes before six, they don't have a clue!

The pattern in counting

Figure 2.3 shows a hundred square. The hundred square is a spatial arrangement of numbers that makes transparent (a) the ordinal aspect of number, and (b) the relationships associated with place value (see Chapter 7). So, for example, the number 43 is defined by its *position* in the hundred square. What is significant about 43 is that it comes in a row between 42 and 44. This emphasizes the ordinal aspect of number, which, as we have argued above, is often emphasized insufficiently in the Foundation Stage and Key Stage 1, with a consequent overemphasis on the cardinal aspect. The number 43 here is not a set of things (it is not a cardinal number) – it is a label for one square in an ordered arrangement of squares. The number 43 also refers to the square that comes between 33 and 53 in the column of numbers all ending in the digit 3. This pattern is, of course, significant in terms of children's

1	2	3	4	5	6	7	8	9	10
11	12	13	14	15	16	17	18	19	20
21	22	23	24	25	26	27	28	29	30
31	32	33	34	35	36	37	38	39	40
41	42	43	44	45	46	47	48	49	50
51	52	53	54	55	56	57	58	59	60
61	62	63	64	65	66	67	68	69	70
71	72	73	74	75	76	77	78	79	80
81	82	83	84	85	86	87	88	89	90
91	92	93	94	95	96	97	98	99	100

Figure 2.3   *A hundred square*

developing understanding of our base ten place-value system – which is explained in Chapter 7 – and is related to the fact that there are ten squares in each row.

The hundred square makes clear the patterns in counting up to 100, which are crucial to children's learning to count. First there is the recurring sequence in the last digits. Each sequence of ten numbers ends in 1, 2, 3, 4, 5, 6, 7, 8, 9 and 0. When said out loud the pattern of sounds at the end of the numbers in each row of ten numbers (after 20) is always 'one, two, three, four, five, six, seven, eight, nine, something-ty'. Then there is the pattern in the tens position of the numbers: the way you get a whole row of twenty-somethings, then a whole row of thirty-somethings, then forty-somethings, and so on. Being aware of these patterns in counting and learning to use them are key principles in learning to count beyond twenty.

- One of my 4-year-olds who can count up to 100 emptied the treasure box onto the table, looked at the items and said, 'There's probably more than 100 there.' He uses this phrase 'more than 100' to mean too many for him to count!
- I heard about a kindergarten in Israel that has a clever idea for helping children get a sense of a hundred. They introduced the idea of a 'hundred day celebration'. On the hundredth day at the school the children – either individually or in pairs – are asked to bring in 100 items. They (and their parents!) often prepare for the event with rather grand ideas, but they quickly realize that they would need a very big bag to take in, for example, 100 tennis balls!

It is unfortunate that, in common with most European languages, English does not settle down to a systematic relationship between the language and the symbols until we get beyond the number 19. We would find it much easier to help children to connect the language and the symbols if we counted: '... seven, eight, nine, ten, onety-one, onety-two, onety-three ...' and so on. In this respect children learning about counting and place value in Japan would seem to have a distinct advantage. For example, the names of the numbers 12, 15 and 25 in Japanese (*ju-ni, ju-go, ni-ju-go*) are all built up from the words for 'ten' (*ju*), 'two' (*ni*) and 'five' (*go*) and could be translated into English as 'ten two', 'ten five' and 'two tens five'. All the number names up to a hundred are constructed in the same logical way, making the place-value principle transparent. By contrast, we might feel sorry for the poor French child who has to learn to connect the symbol for 92, for example, with a name (*quatre-vingt-douze*) that makes no reference to either the 9 tens or the 2 ones, but which could be translated as 'four twenties twelve'!

- The 3- and 4-year-olds in my nursery class always find counting from 11 to 20 the most difficult. Once they've got that sorted they seem to take off and most of them learn the pattern for counting up to 100 very quickly. They love it when they get to 100! It's as though that's the target to aim for and once you get there counting stops!
- Just recently I've noticed that several of the children in my nursery class miss out 15 when they are counting up to 20, which puzzled me. I wonder if it's because when they say the 'four' in 'fourteen' it's the first time they repeat a number they have learnt already; and the pattern of sounds 'four, five, six' that's already fixed in their brains leads them to say 'four-, teen, six ...' and so it comes out as 'fourteen, sixteen'.
- I find that children often get to twenty-nine and then want to say twenty-ten. To help them get over this I find myself changing the way I say 29, 39, 49 and so on, when we are counting, slowing down a bit and intoning the 'nine' in a way that suggests something different is coming!

Numbers go on for ever

Once the pattern in counting is clearly established beyond 20 and up to a hundred, children learn a further pattern that enables them to go on into the hundreds, and then the thousands. They begin to get hold of another key idea in counting: that it goes on for ever! There is always the possibility of one more.

Children are always fascinated by the question, what's the biggest number? Then they like it when someone says something like, a million, billion, zillion, or something, and they can say, 'what about a million, billion, zillion and one!'

Teachers should recognize that the child who learns this 'and one' trick has got hold of a key principle of counting.

Not all numbers are counting numbers

The final principle to learn about counting is that there is more to the concept of number than counting. Because counting is so strongly linked with our early ideas about numbers and our first experiences of number, we can easily develop a mind set that numbers are just the words and symbols that we use for counting, in other words, positive, whole numbers. This mistaken, naive notion persists into adult thinking, even though we may have met and used many other kinds of numbers in our lives. So, for example, when some trainee teachers were asked how many numbers there are between 1 and 20, the majority gave the answer 18. They ignored numbers such as 7.8 and $9^1/_2$, even though all of them had presumably used decimals and fractional numbers for years. Many of these trainees were unable to find two numbers that add up to 9 and differ by 4, simply because when they hear 'number' they automatically think of the numbers we use for counting. In the following section, therefore, we explore the concept of number from a more mathematical perspective. But we hope that we do this in a way that will make clear the challenging and intriguing pedagogical implications of this analysis.

A mathematical analysis of number

So, in this section we outline the development of number from a mathematical point of view. Although this introduces some fairly abstract mathematical material, the teachers we have worked with were unanimous that this analysis was both comprehensible and helpful to them in their own understanding of what they are doing in teaching number to young children. It is important for those laying the foundations of number to know what later ideas will have to be built on to those foundations, so that they do not limit children's experiences of number to only those that are appropriate to the numbers we use for counting. Figure 2.4 is a diagrammatic representation of the different kinds of numbers that children will encounter as their experience of mathematics grows.

Moving outwards from the centre of Figure 2.4, we will see that this development of number begins with the positive whole numbers, the numbers we use for counting, called the *natural numbers*. It then proceeds to expand the set of what we understand to be numbers to what are called *integers*. The set of numbers is then expanded further to *rational numbers*, and finally to *real numbers*. Notice that in this sequence each of these sets includes the previous sets.

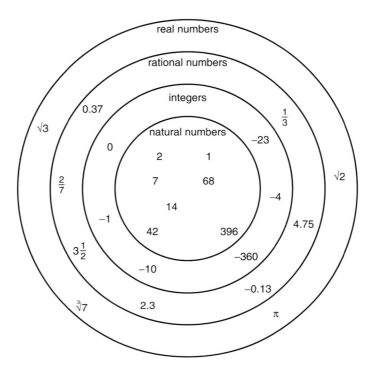

Figure 2.4   *A mathematical development of number*

Unstable truths, changing properties and new possibilities

In the course of the following analysis, we consider each set of numbers in turn. Although the material here is directed at developing the teacher's own under-standing of what numbers are, at each stage some pedagogical implications will become apparent. One important theme is that as we move from one set to the next larger set, certain mathematical properties change. Readers who think of mathematics as the subject that offers stability and certainty in its concepts and principles may be somewhat surprised to see it in this light. In fact, as the concept of number is enlarged, some things that were true become no longer true, some things that were false become true and some things that were not possible become possible.

It is important for teachers of young children to be aware of this phenomenon. For example, many children from their early experiences of multiplying with whole num-bers (such as 2 × 3 or 5 × 2) get the idea that multiplication makes things bigger. This would appear to be true in most cases they encounter – three sets of two objects make a set of six, 5 multiplied by 2 becomes 10, and so on. Perhaps their teachers even encourage them in this notion? But this is a false assertion when you come to multiply by other sorts of numbers. For example, if you multiply 5 by 0.4 the answer (2) is smaller than the 5 you started with. The problem for us – as teachers – is that these ideas, picked up through early experiences of number, are very persistent and resistant to change. One 15-year-old girl, tackling a complicated algebraic equation, had correctly simplified it to $10 \times x = 5$. Then, having demonstrated impressive mathematical skills in attaining this point, she turned to her teacher and announced that this was stupid because you could not multiply 10 by something and get an answer less than 10! The idea that multiplication makes things bigger – which presumably she had picked up when she was about 7 years of age – had persisted through all those years of subsequent mathematical experience.

A similar misconception is that subtraction makes things smaller. In Chapter 3 we will discuss why $6 - (-3)$ is equal to 9, a case where subtraction clearly makes something larger! Children also get told that you cannot subtract a larger number from a smaller number. If you think that this statement is true yourself, then get a calculator and see what happens when you enter $2 - 6 =$.

The natural numbers

The set of *natural numbers* consists of those numbers that we use for counting: 1, 2, 3, 4, 5, 6, 7, 8, 9, 10, 11, … going on for ever. We have discussed earlier in this chapter how these numbers have both cardinal and ordinal aspects. The basic properties of these numbers are (a) that there is a starting number (one), and (b) that for each number there is a *next* number, also called a *successor*. As one of our teachers noted above, this 'nextness' property is an important idea that children find fascinating, particularly with big numbers. They will often ask what is the biggest number in the whole world and will like the idea that no matter how big a number you write down there's always another one following it.

The basic operation that can be performed on this set of natural numbers is *addition*. Any two numbers can be combined using this operation of addition to produce a number, called the *sum* of the two natural numbers, which is still in the set of natural numbers. So, for example, the natural number 12 added to the natural number 14 produces the natural number 26. Mathematicians say that the set is *closed* under addition. In other words, the addition of two natural numbers always produces a natural number. The set of natural numbers together with the basic operation of addition is a closed set. It is because of this that addition with natural numbers does not present us with any challenges to our understanding of how numbers work. It is when we introduce other operations to combine our numbers that problems begin to arise.

Integers

The *inverse* of addition is the operation known as *subtraction*. The concept of inverse is a fundamental mathematical idea that we explain in more detail in Chapter 6. We call subtraction the inverse of addition because, for example, 6 – 2 is defined mathematically as meaning what must be added to 2 to give 6. Now, it is soon apparent that the set of natural numbers is not closed under this operation of subtraction. For example, we cannot find a natural number that is equivalent to 2 – 6. This, of course, is where we get the idea that you cannot subtract a larger number from a smaller one. This is a true statement if you are dealing with natural numbers. However, this does become possible if we extend the set of numbers to include negative numbers and zero. The new set produced by this extension is called the set of *integers*. This set consists of all whole numbers, positive, negative and zero, going on for ever in both directions: ..., –4, –3, –2, –1, 0, 1, 2, 3, 4, ... Note that the set of integers includes the set of natural numbers.

So, we now take 'number' to mean a member of this set of integers. We then find that subtraction – which was previously not always possible – is now always possible. We can now always subtract one number from another, even when the second number is larger than the first, for example, 2 – 6 = –4. But other things have changed as well. For a start we have lost the idea of a first number, since now our set of numbers goes on for ever to the left of zero as well as to the right. So we could no longer say, for example, that there's nothing less than 1, or even that there's nothing less than zero. We now have a number line extending for ever to the left as well as to the right, with points to the left of zero being labelled –1, –2, –3, and so on.

Significantly we should note that we have lost the cardinal aspect of number. We can no longer think of all our numbers as representing sets of things and all our operations on numbers as things that you do with sets of things. We could not demonstrate 2 – 6, for example, by putting out sets of counters and manipulating them in some way. We could, of course, demonstrate it very simply with a number line, by starting at 2 and counting back 6 – as one of our teachers showed with her 5-year-olds in the example quoted earlier in this chapter. This idea of a number being a set of things, which, as we have seen, so dominates our thinking about number, really does not survive for very long in this mathematical development of the concept of number.

The next operation that appears in this development is multiplication. The set of natural numbers is closed under multiplication. In other words, if you multiply one natural number by another, the result, called the *product* of the two numbers, is a natural number, every time. So, for example, the product of 6 and 2 is 12. This is also true of integers. The set of integers is closed under multiplication. We can always multiply any two integers together and find their product. For example, the product of the integers 6 and –2 (think of six steps of –2 on the number line) is the integer –12. The product of the integers –2 and –3 is the integer 6. (The explanation of why mathematicians choose to define the product of –2 and –3 to be the positive integer 6 is abstract and formal and beyond the scope of this book.) So the set of integers is closed under addition, subtraction and multiplication.

Rational numbers

The next step in the development is to think about the inverse of multiplication. This is the operation known as *division*. As with the relationship between subtraction and addition, we call this the inverse because, for example, 6 ÷ 2 is defined mathematically as meaning what must be multiplied by 2 to give 6. We find that the set of integers is not closed under this operation of division. For example, we cannot find an integer that is equivalent to 2 ÷ 6. Colloquially, we say '6 does not go into 2', meaning there is no integer by which we can multiply 6 to get 2. Similarly, we cannot find an integer equal to 13 ÷ 5. We say '5 does not go into 13', meaning there is no integer by which we can multiply 5 to get 13. The only way to deal with this in practical situations where we are restricted to whole numbers is to use the idea of a remainder.

So, from a mathematical perspective, the challenge presented by the fact that the set of integers is not closed under division is to extend the set of numbers to make division always possible. We do this by extending the set of numbers to include *fractions* – and decimals, of course, since decimals, like 0.37 and 4.3, are just fractions, such as $\frac{37}{100}$ and $\frac{43}{10}$, written in a different way. The new set produced by this extension is called the set of *rational numbers*. This set consists of all those numbers that are the *ratio* (hence the word *rational*) of two integers. For example, 2.3 is a rational number because it is the ratio of 23 to 10 (this is also written sometimes as 23:10). It is equivalent to $\frac{23}{10}$ or 23 ÷ 10. Similarly, $3\frac{1}{2}$ is a rational number because it is equivalent to $\frac{7}{2}$. And −0.13 is a rational number because it is equivalent to $\frac{-13}{100}$. Note that our set of rational numbers includes the set of integers, which itself included the set of natural numbers. So, for example, the integer −3 is also a rational number because it can be expressed as the ratio $\frac{-3}{1}$, and the natural number 6 is also a rational number because it can be expressed as the ratio $\frac{6}{1}$.

So, we will now take 'number' to mean a member of the set of rational numbers, which includes all whole numbers, positive, negative or zero, and fractions or decimals. One thing we are now able to do is to label points on the number line between the integers. And now we are always able to divide one number by another (with one exception: division by zero is not permissible – see Chapter 5). In other words, the set of rational numbers (excluding zero) is closed under division. We have moved on from the stage where the only ways we can deal with 13 ÷ 5 are by saying '5 doesn't go into 13', or by giving the result as '2 remainder 3'. We are now able to recognize an equivalence between 13 ÷ 5 and the rational number 2.6, and to record this as 13 ÷ 5 = 2.6.

So something that was not always possible is now possible. Other things have changed as well. Suddenly we have lost the nextness property. Numbers no longer have successors. What is the next number after 2.8? Is it 2.9? How about 2.81? or 2.801? Clearly, there is no next number. But an associated gain is that it is now always possible to insert a number between two given numbers. When 'number' meant integer we could not always do this. There was no number between 6 and 7, for example. But now that 'number' means rational number, this is always possible. And you can go on and on doing this for ever.

For example:

- Between 6 and 7 are the numbers 6.5 and 6.6.
- Between 6.5 and 6.6 are 6.63 and 6.64.
- Between 6.63 and 6.64 are 6.638 and 6.639.
- Between 6.638 and 6.639 are … and so on.

This phenomenon is quite mind-boggling and requires a complete reorganization of our thinking about what numbers are and how they relate to each other. Given any two numbers, it appears that you can go on and on for ever putting more and more numbers in between them.

Young children find some difficulty with the concept of *between* when applied to numbers, which is not surprising if the cardinal aspect is dominant in their thinking. 'Between' is a spatial concept. Young children handle it quite successfully in spatial contexts, such as following an instruction to sit between two individuals. This is another case where the number line, which is a spatial image of number, helps to develop an important mathematical concept. For example, using this spatial notion of the concept of between, children can play simple games that involve finding numbers between two given numbers on a number line.

Real numbers

There is yet another extension to the set of numbers, to what mathematicians call the set of *real numbers*. In the set of real numbers we have all the rational numbers that we have identified already, together with what are called *irrational numbers*. These are numbers that are not rational (that is, not exact fractions or decimals) but which nevertheless still represent real points on the number line, or real lengths. For example, the length of the diagonal of a square whose sides are 1 unit in length is actually equal to the square root of 2 (this is written in symbols as $\sqrt{2}$). This is a real number, representing a real length. It comes on the number line somewhere between 1.4 and 1.5. To be more precise, it comes somewhere between 1.41 and 1.42; or, to be even more precise, somewhere between 1.414213 and 1.414214. But we find that we cannot write down the value of this number exactly in our base ten place-value number system. This means we could not write down a decimal number which, when multiplied by itself, gives the exact answer 2. We could get as close as we like but we could not get exactly 2. There is no rational number that we could put in both of the boxes to make this equation true: □ × □ = 2. All we can say is that √2 lies *between* two particular rational numbers. Think of it like this: you can take the bit of the number line between 1 and 2 and divide it into ten equal parts – when you have done this √2 will lie between two of the subdivisions, as shown in Figure 2.5. You can then divide this section into ten equal parts and √2 will again lie between two of them. And you can go on and on doing this for ever and ever, dividing the line into ten equal parts, becoming smaller and smaller, and none of your subdivisions will ever land exactly on √2.

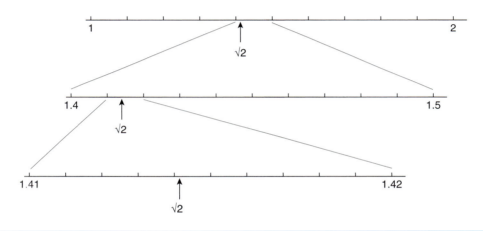

Figure 2.5   *Locating the square root of 2*

Now √2 is not a freak. There are millions of numbers like this – in fact an infinite number of them – the square root of 3, the cube root of 7, and so on – all real numbers in the sense that they represent real points on the number line and real lengths. And yet they are not rational numbers; they cannot be expressed exactly as a fraction or a decimal. So we cannot actually write them down exactly in our number system! This is quite a dramatic loss – and a major challenge to our understanding of what numbers are – but what we have gained in the set of real numbers (rational and irrational) is a continuum of numbers, a complete number line in which every point is associated with a number. In the end we get to the idea that the most comprehensive idea of what is a number is that it is a point on the number line. This notion allows us to embrace all the different kinds of real numbers that we have discussed: positive or negative, whole numbers or fractional numbers, rational or irrational.

The significance of this mathematical analysis

Some readers may have found some of the ideas in this last section difficult to under-stand. In other words, it may have been difficult to connect them with their existing network of ideas about what numbers are. We hope that this experience might enable us all to appreciate what it is like for children as their experiences of number are gradually broadened. Children learning mathematics have to come to terms with things that were true becoming false, the false becoming true, the impossible becom-ing possible and even, in our last step, the possible becoming impossible.

Finally, we emphasize that this analysis reinforces the view that, even when young children are only at the stage of handling natural numbers, it is important that their activities with number are not limited to those that are relevant only to natural num-bers. When other sorts of numbers are encountered later on, they will then have some framework of experience on which to build. In this chapter we have for this reason made much play, for example, of the importance of number-line experiences. In the next two chapters an analysis of number operations, particularly that of subtraction, provides further illustrations of this important principle.

PAUSE TO REFLECT   Your number's up!

Here's a way to do some personal research on how numbers are used in everyday experience. Choose a two-digit number that you might expect to hear or see quite often. For example, you might choose the number fifteen, represented by the numeral 15. Look out for every time your number turns up in your life for a week and record the context. Each time you meet it ask yourself, how is this number being used? What does it signify in this context? Is it some kind of a label? Is it being used to put things in order? Is it a number on a scale? In which case, between what other numbers does it sit? Is it telling you how many items there are in a set? Is it a measurement of some kind, attached to units of money, length, weight, time, or volume? For example, we have just spotted: page 15 in this book; there's an important conference coming up on 15 July; one of Derek's grandsons is about to have his 15th birthday; a particular breakfast cereal con-tains 15 grams of sugar per 100 grams; the weather forecast for today includes a temperature of 15 degrees Celsius …

Compare your record with that of a colleague who has used a different number. Between you discuss what meanings of your numbers seem to be most common in everyday experience. You may be surprised at how infrequently numbers are used to count the items in a set.

RESEARCH FOCUS   Talking and listening to children

By way of preparation for the research section in this chapter we read a wide range of material dating from the 1970s to the present day. The recurring theme was not so much about numbers and counting but more about exploring young children's understanding of the world. Of particular note was a re-appraisal of Piaget's classic experiments of the 1950s. Among the most famous of these were the tasks he used to explore young children's understanding of the conservation of number. So, for example, a child might be presented with two rows of six counters and asked whether there were the same in number in each row (see Figure 2.6(a)).

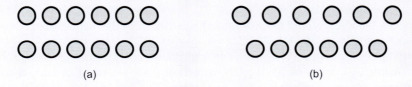

(a)   (b)

Figure 2.6   *Piaget and Szeminska's number conservation experiment*

Typically, young children replied that the number of counters in each row is the same. Piaget and Szeminska (1952) noted, however, that if one of the rows of counters was stretched out, as in Figure 2.6(b), and the question was repeated, many children under 8 years of age said that now there was not the same number of counters in each row. We discuss conservation further in Chapter 8 (see Figure 8.5). Piaget and Szeminska (1952) concluded that such young children were unable to conserve number because they were unable to appreciate that if you move a group of six objects around there will always be six items in the group.

Let us digress for a moment: if we asked you how many days there are in June you might immediately say, '30'. What would your reaction be, however, if we repeated the question immediately after your response? Most probably – we predict – you would wonder whether there really are 30 days in June and whether you might have made a mistake.

Reflecting on the possibility that young children might question their initial response if posed the same question a second time, McGarrigle and Donaldson (1974) devised a series of ingenious experiments involving a 'naughty' teddy. Thus, for example, children might be presented with two sets of counters as in Figure 2.6(a). A naughty teddy then intervened and 'accidentally' re-arranged one row of counters as the researcher exclaimed something along the lines of, 'Oh no, he is spoiling our game!' When the children were then asked whether the rows in the new arrangement (as in Figure 2(b), for example) each had the same number of counters they were far more likely to answer correctly. Indeed McGarrigle

(Continued)

(Continued)

and Donaldson (1974, p. 347) concluded: 'Most of these four- and five-year olds achieved the criterion for successful conservation of … number when the transformation was accidental, and yet most of the same children failed when the transformation was effected in the traditional manner.'

Even those who have considerable experience of working with young children sometimes find it hard to fathom what their responses really mean. In their seminal book, *The Child's Understanding of Number*, Gelman and Gallistel (1986, p. 226) reflected that: 'Those who attempt to question children of preschool age directly about their numerical knowledge generally find that the children are not very responsive, nor do their answers seem to indicate much numerical knowledge'. Almost 20 years later another Gelman concluded, 'Sometimes, though, it is hard to know what children mean by the number words they use' (Sarnecka and Gelman, 2004, p. 329).

Recently, the experiments of Nguyen, Kemp and Want (2011) with 84 children in grades 1 and 5 (ages 6–7 years and 10–11 years, respectively) revealed that '… making children's cognitive tasks funnier can enhance task performance' (p. 154). So what can we conclude? First, although we very much enjoy talking to young children, we can never be entirely confident as to the full extent of their understanding – and we may often underestimate this. Second, to enable an individual to perform at their best – be they young or old – it is a good idea to employ strategies that will engage them. Third, while our approach may seem logical and clear to us it may not to someone else, so it is wise to deploy a series of tasks to explore and evaluate another person's knowledge and understanding. And, finally, as a consequence of the above, we recommend that you read accounts and interpretations of children's work (including those of Haylock and Cockburn) with caution!

Some activities to use with children

Below are some examples of activities that might be used with children in the lower primary and nursery years to develop their understanding of both cardinal and ordinal number. The emphasis is on understanding. Clearly, activities like these should be complemented by others that focus more directly on counting skills.

	ACTIVITY 2.1 Snack Time	3–4	4–5	5–6	6–7	7–8
		☐	☐			

Objective

To develop children's understanding of one-to-one matching and counting sets.

Materials

Beakers, a jug of drink, a plate of pieces of fruit.

Method

Something along these lines can be made into a daily ritual at snack time. The children sit in a circle on the floor. The teacher asks how many children are here today and the class counts them together, with everyone pointing to each child in turn. The teacher gets the children to count the pieces of fruit to check that it is the same number. Then one child is asked to count out this number of beakers. One child then distributes the beakers, matching one beaker for each child. Another child distributes the fruit similarly. The children are encouraged to count out loud as the items are distributed.

 ACTIVITY 2.2   Number Displays

3–4	4–5	5–6	6–7	7–8
☐	☐			

Objective

To connect together the language, symbols, concrete experiences and pictures of natural numbers.

Materials

Anything appropriate that the children can find at school or at home!

(Continued)

(Continued)

Method

Make a class display of each natural number from 1 to 10, to which children can add examples from time to time as they come across them. Small groups of children can be given particular responsibility for one display and be encouraged always to be on the lookout for examples of their special number. For example, depending on the age of the children, the display for 4 might contain: pictures of four people cut from a magazine; pictures of other sets of four things, such as four legs on a table or four legs on an animal; some examples of the written word 'four' cut from newspapers; four plastic pennies, labelled 4p; non-English words for 'four'; a Roman numeral IV; a birthday card for a 4-year-old; a house number 4; a square; a photograph of a footballer with 4 on his shirt; a number line with 4 highlighted; page 4 from an old book; a clock showing 4 o'clock; a 4 o'clock programme cut from the television schedules; facts about 4 such as $4 = 3 + 1$, $4 = 7 - 3$.

Home-based element

Ask the families to be on the lookout with their children for examples of their special number to add to the display, and encourage them to help the children at home to find examples. This could include taking photographs to bring or send to school.

 ACTIVITY 2.3   **Between**

3–4	4–5	5–6	6–7	7–8
	☐	☐		

Objective

To develop the concept of 'between' in the context of ordinal numbers.

Materials

A blank number strip with spaces for the numerals 0 to 20; a set of cards labelled 0 to 20 to fit in these spaces.

Method

This is a very simple game for three or four children. One child, who is confident in using the number line, acts as umpire. The teacher first shows the children where all the cards from 0 to 20 would go on the number strip, ensuring they understand that it starts at 0 and finishes at 20. The cards are then shuffled and the pack placed face down on the table. The umpire turns over two cards and positions them in their places on the number strip. In the example shown in Figure 2.7 the cards 3 and 12 have been turned over and positioned. Children now take turns to pick up a card from the pack and show where it would go on the number strip. If the card goes *between* the two numbers the child retains the card. If not, it is discarded. The umpire checks that they do this correctly. For example, in Figure 2.7 a child who picks up 7 retains the card because 7 is between 3 and 12, but a child who picks up 14 has to discard it. The winner of the round is the child who has the most cards at the end. For younger children, use cards and a number strip from 0 to 10.

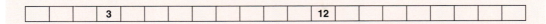

Figure 2.7 *The between game*

3–4	4–5	5–6	6–7	7–8
	☐	☐		

ACTIVITY 2.4   I Have, Who Has? (Cardinal Numbers)

Objective

To develop recognition of cardinal numbers.

Materials

Prepare a pack of ten cards, with sets of dots on one side and numerals on the other, as shown in Figure 2.8. Note that these are arranged so that the number of dots on one card corresponds to the numeral on the next, in a continuous cycle. For younger children, make a set of cards using numerals and arrangements of dots just from 0 to 5.

Method

This is a game that we use in a number of versions to help children to make various connections in mathematics. Three children play this version of the game. The cards are shuffled and dealt, the remaining card being placed dots upwards in the centre of the table. Each child spreads out their cards in front of them, numerals upwards. The child who has the card with the numeral corresponding to the number of dots displayed places it beside the card in the centre. When all players have agreed that this is correct the card is turned over to reveal the next number to be sought. The first player to dispose of all their cards is the winner. As they play the children should have a conversation along the lines of 'Who has three?' 'I have three ... Who has nine?' and so on.

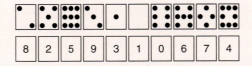

Figure 2.8 *Cards for Activity 2.4*

3–4	4–5	5–6	6–7	7–8
	☐			

ACTIVITY 2.5   Green Bottles

Objective

To develop connections between the cardinal and ordinal aspects of number.

Materials

Three number strips labelled from 0 to 10; a pack of 22 cards, two each depicting ten green bottles, nine green bottles, eight green bottles, ... one green bottle, blank.

Method

This is a game for three children, each of whom has a number strip to work on. The cards are shuffled. One at a time each player turns over a card and places it on the ordinal number corresponding to the cardinal number of the set of green bottles shown. A player who at any stage turns over a number already covered on their strip returns the card to the pack. The first player to get three consecutive numbers covered, as, for example, shown in Figure 2.9, wins the round.

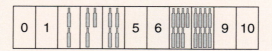

Figure 2.9   *Relating cardinal and ordinal numbers in Activity 2.5*

Summary of key ideas

1 The concept of a number involves a network of connections between the number symbol (the numeral), the number name, pictures (such as the number line) and concrete situations (such as sets of counters).

2 There is a potential danger in continually reinforcing just one particular link in the network of connections constituting a mathematical concept (such as numbers as being sets of things) at the expense of equally important connections (such as numbers as points on a number line), particularly if the connection emphasized is of limited long-term significance.

3 The idea of a number as representing a set of things (for example, three ducks, five fingers, ten counters) is called the cardinal aspect of number.

4   Sometimes numbers are used purely as labels (for example, a number 9 bus). This is called the nominal aspect of number.

5   The idea of number as a label for putting things in order (for example, page 9, room 9) is called the ordinal aspect of number.

6   The ordinal aspect of number, particularly as pictured in the number line, is the notion onto which we can more readily build extensions to our understanding of number, such as negative numbers.

7   Zero does not represent just an empty set (that is, nothing or an absence of something), but also has, for example, important ordinal meanings, such as a significant point on the number line or freezing point in a temperature scale.

8   Important pre-counting experiences are sorting and categorizing, informal use of 'another one' and 'one more', and recognizing at a glance small numbers of items (subitizing).

9   Key principles in learning to count are: in counting the numbers are in a fixed order; one object is matched to one number name; the ordinal number of the last number counted is the cardinal number of the set; counting is an abstraction, so the actual objects counted are irrelevant to the process; the order of the objects is irrelevant; the arrangement of the objects is irrelevant; each number name is matched to a symbol (the numeral); the next number is always one more; the patterns in counting enable counting to continue to a hundred and beyond; numbers go on for ever.

10 Children also have to learn that there are numbers other than those we use for counting.

11 The set of natural numbers consists of those numbers used for counting: 1, 2, 3, 4, 5, ... going on for ever.

12 The set of integers comprises all whole numbers, positive, negative or zero: ..., −4, −3, −2, −1, 0, 1, 2, 3, 4, ... going on for ever in both directions. The set of integers includes the set of natural numbers.

13 The set of rational numbers consists of all numbers that can be expressed as the ratio of two integers (that is, all the integers themselves plus all types of fractions, including decimal fractions).

14 A real number is any number representing a point on a number line. The set of real numbers includes the rationals. It also includes irrational numbers, like $\sqrt{2}$ (the square root of 2), which cannot be written down exactly in our number system, but that nevertheless represent real points or real lengths.

15 As the concept of a number develops – through the sets of naturals, integers, rationals, reals – the properties of number change. For example, the cardinality of number is lost in moving from naturals to integers, and the nextness (or successor) property is lost in moving from integers to rationals.

Suggestions for further reading

Chapters 1–3 of Anghileri (2006) draw on the author's extensive and practical knowledge of young children's ability to learn and the processes of counting and coming to know numbers.

The excellent review of research into children's understanding of mathematics by Nunes and Bryant (1996) provides in Chapters 1–3 some fascinating insights into the early stages of number and counting.

Chapter 4 of Ryan and Williams (2007) discusses the development of number concepts and provides practical examples to reduce the likelihood of mathematical misconceptions developing.

Well worth reading are Sections 2 and 3 of Thompson (2008); a variety of authors offer a range of interesting insights into young children's beliefs and learning about counting, including the contributions of play and experiences at home.

Mosley (2004) is a very practical resource that helps teachers to foster children's understanding of numbers and the number system, particularly through the use of number lines.

In Chapter 16 of Moyles (2010), Maulfry Worthington, writing about multi-modality play and children's mark-making in mathematics, provides some fascinating insights into children's early mathematical thinking and their use of graphics to support their developing understanding of number.

Chapter 8 of Gifford (2005) focuses on number and counting, including useful sections on subitizing, counting for a purpose, and the use of number stories, songs and games.

For practical suggestions for games and practical activities for children in the early years of schooling, aimed at developing understanding of number, counting and many other elementary mathematical concepts, have a look at Hansen (2012).

In Chapter 0 of Cockburn and Littler (2008), entitled 'Zero: understanding an apparently paradoxical number', Anne Cockburn and Paul Parslow-Williams provide suggestions on how this elusive number might best be introduced to young children.

Also in Cockburn and Littler (2008), for those who would like to learn more about number systems we can recommend Chapter 7 by Carlo Marchini and Paola Vighi. It is a fascinating read but not for the faint-hearted!

Alex's Adventures in Numberland (Bellos, 2010) is an engaging and popular book about mathematics. Chapters 0 and 1 are about numbers and counting.

If you are interested in finding out more about 'how maths illuminates our lives' and those around us, we recommend Daniel Tammet's accessible and fascinating book *Thinking in Numbers* (Tammet, 2012).

CHAPTER 3

UNDERSTANDING ADDITION AND SUBTRACTION

AN INSIGHTFUL MOMENT

Mark, a Year 3 child, was trying to calculate the number of drinks we would have to provide so that each player in the football team could have three drinks. Suddenly he announced what seemed to him a surprising discovery: 'You can use adding for this! I reckon that's why we learn it, so we can use it for things!'

Mark's insight here was that he could connect the symbols and formal language of addition that he had used in school mathematics lessons with a practical situation in the real world. (Later, we hope that he will be able more efficiently to connect multiplication with this particular situation.) Before reading this chapter, the reader is invited to reflect upon these questions:

- What other kinds of real-life situations will Mark have to learn to connect with the language and symbols of addition?
- And in what kinds of real-life situations might he say, 'You can use subtracting for this!'?

In this chapter

In this chapter we identify the network of connections between various kinds of concrete situations, pictures, language and symbols for each of addition and subtraction. We see that for both these operations, but especially for subtraction, there are differently structured situations and a variety of pictures and language, all of which have to be connected with the same symbols. For example, we see that subtraction is much more than taking away and finding how many are left. We are not concerned in this chapter with how to do addition and subtraction calculations – that will be covered in Chapters 5, 6 and 7.

What is addition?

In this section we identify two main structures for addition and illustrate them with examples of 'stories' written by teachers and children.

Addition Structure 1: the union of two sets

What stories might go with the symbols 12 + 3, for example? We asked this question to some of the teachers we worked with. Table 3.1 gives some examples of the kinds of stories they wrote to begin with.

Table 3.1   *Stories for 12 + 3 using the union of two sets structure*

A	I've got 12 red pens and 3 blue pens. How many altogether?
B	There are 12 girls and 3 boys. How many children?
C	John ate 12 cakes. His sister ate only 3. How many cakes did they eat altogether?

Responses like those in Table 3.1, clearly interpreting the numbers in the cardinal sense as sets of things, share a common *structure*. This structure refers to situations in which objects in two sets are collected together in some way. In each of the stories given in Table 3.1 two distinct sets of objects, with no members in common, are brought together to form what is called the *union of the two sets*, and the cardinal number of this new set is computed. This structure is illustrated by the picture shown in Figure 3.1, where two discrete sets are combined into one set.

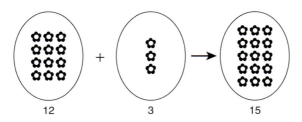

Figure 3.1   *Addition: union of two sets*

The union of two distinct sets into one set is an important structure that has to be linked with the symbols and language of addition; it forms part of the network of connections that constitutes the concept of addition. It is first experienced by children through the process of physically forming the union of two sets, such as so many fingers on one hand combined with so many on the other, so many blue counters and so many red counters collected together, or so many boys and so many girls put into a group; they then connect this experience with the language 'How many altogether?' and count up how many there are in the two sets combined. Later this idea of addition will extend quite easily to include situations where things other than sets are combined: putting two lengths end to end; combining two prices to find the total cost; combining two weights, two quantities of liquid, and so on. In such measuring contexts often the question asked is 'How much altogether?'

Addition Structure 2: counting on and increasing

There are, however, other situations that share a different structure that also have to be connected with the language and symbols of addition. These are those situations that incorporate the ideas of *counting on* or *increasing*. For example: start at twelve and count on three; start with twelve and increase this by three. This idea often relates most strongly to the ordinal aspect of the numbers and is experienced most clearly in making moves on a number strip or a number line.

> My 5- and 6-year-olds get a lot of ideas about addition from playing board games with dice. When they throw two dice they get very adept at recognizing what the two numbers make together. I suppose that's like the union of two sets. But then they use counting on, when they start at one number on the board and count on a number of steps from there.

A key picture to be connected with this interpretation of 12 + 3 is the number-line diagram shown in Figure 3.2. Teachers should be aware that in this picture of

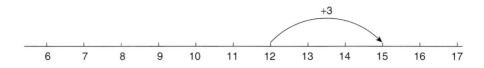

Figure 3.2   *Addition: counting on*

addition the 12 and the 3 represent different kinds of things. The numeral 12 represents a *point* on the number line, the starting point, but the numeral 3 represents three *steps* along the line. To help young children understand this structure of addition teachers find it useful therefore to connect the number line process with the language 'twelve and three more'. This encourages the child, when doing this mentally, to 'put the twelve in their heads' and then to count on three more, avoiding the common error of starting the counting at twelve (and thus finishing at 14 rather than 15). Note that the child now learns to connect with the idea of addition such language as 'increases by', 'goes up by', 'count on by', 'and so many more'. So, Addition Structure 2 involves a different set of language from that used in Addition Structure 1.

There are plenty of other situations in the contexts of money and various measures that essentially have this same structure and that are to be connected with addition. We asked the teachers in our group to come up with some examples of real situations, using the idea of 'increasing', which children might learn to connect with the addition 12 + 3. Some of the stories they wrote are shown in Table 3.2. These stories are set in the contexts of prices (D), length (E) and liquid volume (F). The reader should again note the range of language connected with this structure: *increased, has grown, a further amount, how much now.*

Table 3.2   *Stories for 12 + 3 using the idea of increasing*

D	The chocolate bar was 12p last week, but today the price went up by 3p. What is the price now?
E	The plant was 12 cm tall; but it has grown another 3 cm. How tall is it now?
F	The jar contained 12 cl of water; then we poured in a further amount of 3 cl. How much water is now in the jar?

The photograph shows a 3-year-old in a nursery class experiencing the idea of 'increasing'. She was used to checking her height against the chart on the wall. On this occasion she was playing on the 'bucket stilts' and decided to hobble over to the height chart to see how tall she was now. The teacher engaged her in talking about how much her height had increased, giving her valuable early experience of a key concept associated with addition.

From counting all to counting on

Although we have talked about two different structures of situations connected with addition, there is nevertheless a fairly straightforward and clear relationship between them. In Addition Structure 1 we have two sets or quantities being brought together to form a union or a whole. This is not hugely different perceptually from starting with one number or amount and then increasing this by the second number or amount, which we have identified as Addition Structure 2. In fact, bringing these two structures together is an important stage in the development of a child's understanding of addition. This is the point at which the child is able to apply the process of *counting on* to find out how many there are altogether in two sets – rather than *counting all* the items in the two sets starting from 1. The process of counting on using the number line, with the associated language we have discussed above, is an important facilitator in this development.

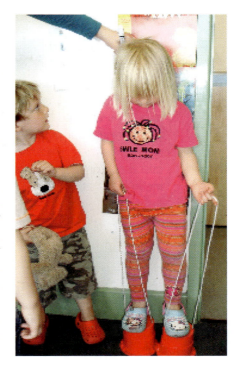

With my 4-year-olds, one of the things I do to introduce addition is to have a box with, say, 3 teddies in. We count the teddies and then close the box and say things like, 'There are three teddies hiding in the box.' One of the children then puts in, say, 2 more teddies and they have to tell me how many there are now hiding in the box. Then we open the box and see if we are right. We say something like: 3 teddies and 2 more makes 5 teddies altogether.

PAUSE TO REFLECT   Doing maths is child's play!

Reflect on why it is that teddies, toy animals, dolls and puppets are so widely used and are so clearly effective in teaching early number concepts to young children. For example, some researchers have found that young children are much more responsive and engaged if they are asked a question by a teddy rather than by an adult. Others have found that children will be much more confident and articulate

(Continued)

(Continued)

in explaining to a puppet how to do something, such as how to do '3 count on 2' on a number strip, than in explaining it to a teacher or to the other children. Think about other ways in which you might deploy such toys in teaching early number ideas. You will find it helpful to discuss this with a colleague. Here are some words and phrases that might prompt some useful reflections on this question: real-life experience, play, pretence, role-playing, humour, suspension of disbelief, making mistakes, correcting mistakes, risk-taking, non-threatening, empowering, control, meaningful situations.

What is subtraction?

In this section we identify the network of connections that should be established for an understanding of the operation of subtraction. As we have done above with addition, we identify a number of different structures for subtraction and illustrate them with examples of stories written by teachers and children. Subtraction will prove to be altogether a much more complex concept than addition.

Meg, a 7-year-old, had written down these calculations:

$$9 - 3 = 5$$
$$12 - 4 = 7$$
$$15 - 6 = 8$$
$$14 - 10 = 3$$
$$10 - 7 = 2$$

At the top of the page was a number line that she had used to do these subtractions. Her teacher (T) talked to Meg (M) about what she had done:

T.   Now, Meg, what sort of questions are these?

M.   Takes.

T.   What's this first one say then?

M.   9 take 3?

T.   9 take away 3. What's the answer for 9 take away 3?

M.   [Looking at her answer] *Five. No, that's wrong, it's 6.*

T.   Well, what about this one? 12 take away 4?

M.   Seven?

T.   [Putting out 12 cubes] *Show me 12 take away 4.*

M.   [Manipulating the cubes] *1, 2, 3, 4. That leaves 1, 2, 3, 4, 5, 6, 7, 8. Eight.*

T.   *So how did you get 7?*

M.   [Pointing to the number line] *I did it on this. Look.* [She puts her finger on the 12 on the number line and counts back 4 until it rests on the 8.] *There you are, it's 7!*

T.   [Pointing to Meg's finger resting on the 8] *Why isn't the answer 8?*

M.   *Because I've taken that one away.*

T.   *Well, show me 9 take away 3 then.* [Meg carries out the same procedure on the number line, until her finger rests on the 6.]

M.   *It's 5.* [She looks puzzled]

T.   *But why isn't it 6? You're pointing to the 6.*

M.   *No, it must be 5, because I've taken the 6 away.*

T.   *So what do you really think is the answer for 9 take away 3?*

M.   *Six.*

The above dialogue illustrates just how potentially difficult it is for children to make valid connections between some of the different structures associated with subtraction. It also highlights a significant point about the language we use for subtraction that will emerge in the subsequent analysis of this concept. Above all, it shows how teachers need to be aware of the range of situations, language and pictures that have to be connected in developing an understanding of this operation. We suggest below that there are at least five important and distinct structures to be connected with subtraction.

Subtraction Structure 1: partitioning and taking away

We start our analysis by asking to what sort of situations can subtraction be applied? What stories could we write to go with, say, 12 – 3? Table 3.3 provides examples of the first responses to this question that we had from some of the teachers we worked with.

Table 3.3   *Stories for 12 – 3 using the partitioning structure*

G	There are 12 birds sitting on a fence. Then 3 fly away. How many are still on the fence?
H	There are 12 trees in a forest and an elephant knocks over 3 of them. How many trees are left standing?
J	I had 12 chocolates and ate 3 of them. How many are left for tomorrow?

These three stories all have basically the same plot. They share what we will call the *partitioning* structure and involve *taking away*. This structure of subtraction is connected with a set diagram, as shown in Figure 3.3, in which a set of twelve objects is identified and then three of them partitioned off in some way. We find that most teachers, trainee teachers and children, when asked to write a story for subtraction, produce a version of this structure. There is a set of twelve things to start with and somehow three of them are taken away, removed, eaten, destroyed, lost, blown up, stolen, given away, or mortally wounded. Then in each case the question posed is, essentially, 'How many are left?'

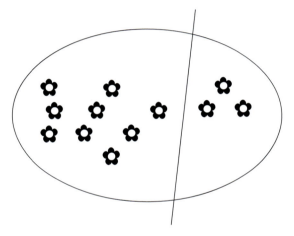

Figure 3.3   *Subtraction: partitioning*

All three of the stories G, H and J in Table 3.3 use the cardinal aspect of number, where the numbers represent sets of things. But we should note that stories with similar plots could also be written with numbers used for money or measuring. These are still examples of this partitioning structure, but now the question posed is, essentially, 'How much is left?' Table 3.4 gives some examples of situations corresponding to 12 − 3 in the contexts of money (K), liquid volume (L) and mass (M), indicating the wide range of experiences of partitioning that children have to learn to connect with subtraction.

Table 3.4   *Stories for 12 − 3 using the partitioning structure in measuring contexts*

K	I had 12p and I spent 3p. How much did I have left?
L	There were 12 litres of wine in my cellar. We drank 3 litres. How much wine is left in my cellar now?
M	We had 12 kg of compost, but we have used 3 kg. How much compost do we have left?

Subtraction is not just partitioning

As with most mathematical symbols, we find that 12 – 3 may be connected to a wide range of very different situations. Subtraction is by no means just the partitioning plot. It is not just a synonym for 'take away'. Partitioning is just one subtraction structure and, as we shall see, a very limited one at that. Table 3.5 contains stories written by children for 12 – 3. These illustrate five different structures of situations connected with subtraction. These stories, all so varied in their interpretation of the symbols, demonstrate the range of connections that have to be made to develop a fuller understanding of the concept of subtraction.

Table 3.5   *Stories written by children for 12 – 3, illustrating different structures (children's spelling and punctuation retained)*

N	There were 12 books on the pile. The teacher took 3 of them away. How many books are left?
P	If my friend is 12 and his brother is 3 how older is he?
Q	There were 12 soldiers 3 were ill how many were not ill?
R	The price of a choc bar was 12p the shop thought it was deer and took 3p off.
S	John was 3 and 9 year latter he was 12.

Story N is another example of the familiar and most frequently used *partitioning* structure, with the associated language of 'take away, how many left?' The four other structures illustrated by the stories P, Q, R and S are considered in turn below.

Subtraction Structure 2: comparison

Story P introduces a different but very important aspect of subtraction, the *comparison* structure. In this structure the basic plot for 12 – 3 is that the two numbers 12 and 3 represent quantities that are compared. In this case the story compares two ages. Similarly, a line of twelve blue cubes can be compared with a line of three red cubes, as shown in Figure 3.4(a), or the numbers of objects in two sets compared, as in Figure 3.4(b). A collection of twelve green marbles can be compared with a collection of three yellow marbles. A price of 12p can be compared with a price of 3p. A weight of 12 kg can be compared with a weight of 3 kg. Notice one significant difference between this structure and that of partitioning (Subtraction Structure 1). Both the 12 and the 3 are there right from the start. In the partitioning structure you start with the 12, and the 3 you take away is part of the 12. Here, in the comparison structure, you have the 12 and the 3 side by side and you compare them.

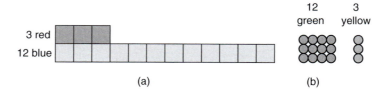

Figure 3.4   *Subtraction: comparison*

There are three versions of the punchline in stories that use the comparison plot. The child who produced story P above asked 'how older is he?' – presumably meaning 'how much older?' The question could also have been 'how much younger?' or 'what is the difference in their ages?' Similarly, when comparing two sets, as in Figure 3.4(b) we may ask 'How many *more* green?' or 'How many *fewer* yellow?' or 'What is the *difference* between the number of green and the number of yellow?'

'Difference' is used here in a technical mathematical sense. We do not mean, for example, that the difference between the red cubes and the blue cubes in Figure 3.4(a) is their colour. We should note, incidentally, that the difference between 3 and 12 is the same as the difference between 12 and 3, but 3 – 12 is not the same as 12 – 3. Notice also the picture of 'difference between' that we get on the number line, as illustrated in Figure 3.5, where 12 – 3 is represented by the gap between 12 and 3. This is a powerful image of subtraction and one that is often used in mental calculations. Many people when calculating 105 – 78 mentally, for example, would deal with it essentially by adding together the bits needed to fill the gap between 78 and 105, namely 2 + 20 + 5 (in various orders). This process is facilitated by forming a mental image of the difference between the two numbers, such as that provided by the picture of the two numbers situated on a number line.

We want to emphasize at this point how different are the actual manipulations of materials when carrying out procedures that incorporate these first two subtraction structures, partitioning and comparison. For example, using cubes, in Subtraction Structure 1, you put out a set of twelve cubes and take three of them away. But in Subtraction Structure 2, you put out a set of twelve cubes and a set of three cubes and compare them. Yet both manipulations represent the same subtraction and correspond to the same symbols, 12 – 3. Comparing two sets or quantities to find out how many more or how many fewer is just as valid and important an interpretation

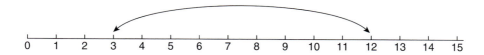

Figure 3.5   *The difference between 12 and 3*

of subtraction as taking something away from a set or quantity and finding out how many are left.

The language of comparison

The language of comparison merits some special consideration. When we make a comparison between two quantities, using subtraction, there are always two equivalent ways of stating the relationship; there are two sets of language available. Mathematically this is expressed by the statement:

$$A > B \text{ is equivalent to } B < A$$

In words, this reads: '*A* is greater than *B*' is equivalent to '*B* is less than *A*'. Hence, we could either make a comparison statement using the language that focuses on the larger quantity, such as that in the left-hand column in Table 3.6, or we could make an equivalent statement using the language that focuses on the smaller quantity, such as that in the right-hand column. Table 3.6 indicates only some of the very wide range of contexts in which children have to use comparative language and in which they might therefore meet the comparison structure of subtraction.

Table 3.6 *Some language of comparison*

A is greater than *B*	*B* is less than *A*
A is more than *B*	*B* is fewer than *A*
A is larger (bigger) than *B*	*B* is smaller than *A*
A is longer (taller) than *B*	*B* is shorter than *A*
A is higher than *B*	*B* is lower than *A*
A is further than *B*	*B* is nearer than *A*
A is wider than *B*	*B* is narrower than *A*
A is fatter than *B*	*B* is thinner than *A*
A is heavier than *B*	*B* is lighter than *A*
A holds more than *B*	*B* holds less than *A*
A costs more than *B*	*B* costs less than A
A is dearer (more expensive) than *B*	*B* is cheaper (less expensive) than *A*
A takes longer than *B*	*B* takes less time than *A*
A is later than *B*	*B* is earlier (sooner) than *A*
A happens after *B*	*B* happens before *A*
A is older than *B*	*B* is younger than *A*
A is faster (quicker) than *B*	*B* is slower than *A*
A is hotter (warmer) than *B*	*B* is colder (cooler) than *A*

We feel constrained to comment on the distinction between the words 'fewer' and 'less'. It is a strange quirk of the English language that we should use 'fewer' when we use the plural verb 'are' and use 'less' when we use the singular 'is'. For example, there *are fewer* vehicles and there *is less* traffic. This rather unnecessary distinction is disappearing from common usage; although we have pedantically adopted it in this book. Interestingly, there is no corresponding distinction with the word 'more': we would say both that there are more cars and that there is more traffic.

Three stages in developing the use of the language of comparison can be identified. For example, when comparing the line of twelve blue cubes with the line of three red cubes shown in Figure 3.4(a), in the first stage the child would note simply that 'there are more blue than red'. They would, of course, be encouraged to use the equivalent statement that 'there are fewer (or less) red than blue'. No actual numbers are involved in these statements. The second stage is to note that 'there are nine more blue than red' and 'there are nine fewer (or less) red than blue', actually specifying the numerical difference. The third stage is to make the abstracted statements, 'twelve is nine more than three' and 'three is nine less than twelve'. It is these last observations that connect the comparison situation with the subtraction written in symbols as $12 - 3 = 9$.

- I find it's really hard to get the children in my reception class to say that something is less than something else. They get the idea of 'more' quite easily, like 'can I have one more?' or 'he's got more than me', but they don't naturally seem to use the language of 'less' when they're comparing two amounts.
- Some children find it hard to accept that they are shorter than someone else when they compare heights. They like to be the biggest. I always tell them that good things come in small packages.

It is an interesting observation that, in practice, when we make comparisons, there is a tendency in most situations to use language from the left-hand column in Table 3.6. We tend to use the language that makes the greater quantity the subject of the sentence. As the teacher above observed, a child will complain 'It's not fair, he's got more than me!' but rarely 'I've got less than him!' Inevitably, the one with more becomes the focus of attention. In order to build up connections with the full range of language, teachers asking children to make comparisons need, therefore, to make a conscious effort to use 'more' no more than they use 'less'; or, to put it another way, to use 'less' no less than they use 'more'. In fact we would advocate a teaching principle that whenever children make a comparison they should be encouraged to make the two equivalent statements. So if they have observed that a pencil costs 3p more than a ballpoint, they should immediately be encouraged to make the equivalent observation that the ballpoint costs 3p less than the pencil. If measuring leads to the discovery that Reuben is 3 cm taller than Rachel, then the children are also encouraged to report that Rachel is 3 cm shorter than Reuben.

There is a subtle problem built into the notion of 'less than' that makes it considerably more difficult for a child to handle than 'more than'. This is illustrated by the following account of an interaction with a 7-year-old:

> I put two sweets in my hand and five in Clare's. She seemed to understand that she had more than me. I asked how many more did she have. She said she had five more. That seemed a reasonable response – although not the one I was looking for – since she did have five and she did have more. We did the obvious thing of laying our sweets out on the table and matching them, so that the three more in her pile could be identified. She quickly cottoned on to the idea that she had three more than me. We did a few more examples like this and she handled 'more than' with considerable success. I then put two sweets in her hand and five in mine. With a bit of prompting she managed to say that she had less than me. I then asked her how many less. This completely defeated her, even when we laid out our sweets and matched them. The best she could manage was, 'I've got two more less than you.' I then realized what a difficult task I had set Clare. I wanted her to look at the two sweets in her hand and make a statement beginning with the words 'I've got three …' I wanted her to say 'I've got three less than you.' But she didn't have those three sweets. I had them!

The point to note here is that when we use subtraction in this comparison structure to make statements of the form 'three is nine less than twelve' we appear to be making a statement about the three, since we begin with the words 'three is …'. But in fact the nine is actually part of the twelve, not part of the three. If someone says that they have £9 less than you, the odd thing about the structure of the language used here is that they don't have the £9 in question. You have it! These examples underline the importance of establishing the equivalence of two statements such as 'I have 9 more than you' and 'You have 9 less (or fewer) than me.'

Subtraction Structure 3: the complement of a set

Story Q in Table 3.5 on page 71 has what we call the *complement of a set* structure. This is illustrated in a set diagram in Figure 3.6. The basic plot of the story for 12 − 3 in this structure is that there is a set of twelve things, three of which have some attribute. The question posed is how many do *not* have this attribute? The word 'not' is usually central to the punchline of stories with this structure.

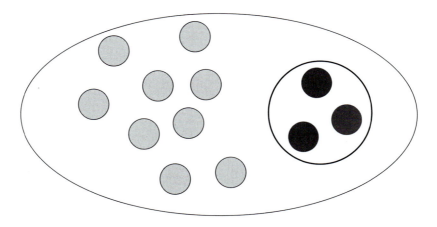

Figure 3.6   *Subtraction: complement of a set*

Subtraction Structure 3 is very similar to Subtraction Structure 1 (partitioning) and it would seem to be not too difficult for children to learn to connect the same symbols and arithmetic processes with these two different kinds of situations. We identify it as a separate structure mainly to make explicit the need to associate questions containing the phrase 'how many are not' with subtraction.

Subtraction Structure 4: reduction, counting back

Story R in Table 3.5, about a shopkeeper taking 3p off the price of a 12p chocolate bar, has what we call the *reduction* structure. The process of reduction involved here is clearly the opposite of that involved in Addition Structure 2, discussed earlier in the chapter, in which an addition represents an increase. In Addition Structure 2 'add 3' is interpreted as 'count on 3'; and in Subtraction Structure 4 'subtract 3' is interpreted as 'count back 3'.

The basic plot for 12 – 3 in the reduction structure is therefore that you start at the twelve and count back or reduce the quantity by three. Examples of this structure might be a 12-stone person losing 3 stones of weight after some serious dieting, a temperature of 12 degrees shown on a thermometer scale falling by 3 degrees, or a £12 article in a store being reduced by £3. The most important picture of this subtraction structure – and therefore an important experience for children – is counting back (or down) along the number line. This is shown in Figure 3.7.

The same problem occurs here as in using the number line for counting on (see the discussion around Figure 3.2). Children doing 12 – 3 on a number line will be helped by using the language 'twelve, then three less' or 'twelve, then count back three' to avoid the error of starting the counting with twelve and finishing on ten

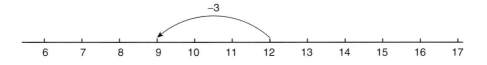

Figure 3.7   *Counting back on the number line*

rather than on nine. The associated mental strategy is to say, 'Put the twelve in your head and then count back three, before counting down, eleven, ten, nine, using your fingers.'

Subtraction Structure 5: the inverse of addition

Finally, in this section, we identify a fifth category of situations associated with subtraction, illustrated by story S in Table 3.5, where the implied question is 'How many years does it take for a 3-year-old to become a 12-year-old?' We call this the *inverse of addition* structure. In many ways this would appear to be the most important and fundamental subtraction structure. As was seen in Chapter 2, from a mathematical point of view subtraction is actually defined as the inverse of addition. In this structure the plot for 12 – 3 is essentially 'What must be added to three to make twelve?' The remarkable thing about story S is that it actually begins with the three. The child who made up this story has clearly interpreted 12 – 3 as meaning that you start at the three and add on until you get to twelve, as illustrated on the number line in Figure 3.8.

Subtraction Structure 5 is undoubtedly the most difficult of the five structures we are considering here for children to connect with subtraction. This is probably related to the fact that the language involved signals addition rather than subtraction. For example, consider these two word problems:

- I have £37 and I want to buy a radio costing £49. How much more do I need?
- The radio cost £37 last week and £49 this week. By how much has the price gone up?

Many children will pick up the wrong cues from the words 'more' and 'gone up' – words signalling addition – and respond by adding the numbers 37 and 49. Further examples of such miscues in word problems are discussed later in this chapter.

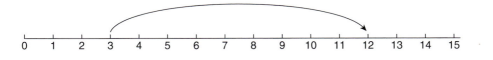

Figure 3.8   *Subtraction: inverse of addition on the number line*

Some of the structural apparatus that we might use with young children provides concrete experience of procedures that incorporate the idea of subtraction as the inverse of addition very clearly. For example, using materials such as coloured number rods, the subtraction 12 – 3 can become a question of finding which rod has to be added to the 3-rod to make a train the same length as the 12-rod (see Figure 3.9).

Figure 3.9   *Inverse of addition with structural apparatus*

Once again we want to emphasize how significantly different from some of the other structures is the manipulation of materials involved in this subtraction structure. Earlier we were putting out a set of twelve cubes and taking away three (Subtraction Structure 1). Then we were putting out sets of twelve cubes and three cubes and comparing them (Subtraction Structure 2). But now we would be putting out three cubes and adding on further cubes until we have reached a total of twelve. Yet all these – partitioning, comparison, inverse of addition, as well as complement of a set and reduction – are examples of situations and the associated language to which the subtraction symbol has to be connected. They are all part of the complex network of connections that constitute the concept of subtraction. This is a most challenging example of the way in which one symbol is used in mathematics to represent many different and varied situations.

Overemphasis on 'take away'

When we discussed the cardinal aspect of number in Chapter 2 we indicated that there was the potential problem of this one connection (the cardinal aspect) being emphasized too strongly in the early years of schooling, at the expense of other equally important connections (particularly the ordinal aspect). The same thing can be said of 'take away' in relation to subtraction. Teachers of young children may focus on the experiences of the take-away interpretation of subtraction (Subtraction Structure 1) almost to the exclusion of situations with the other structures. As we have seen, partitioning is only one subtraction structure, and a very limited one. Yet when teachers in Key Stage 1 set out to demonstrate a subtraction question to children they almost invariably put out a set of objects and take some away. The comparison and inverse of addition structures are, in the long run, much more significant, yet too many children (and teachers) seem fixated on the partitioning structure and the associated language of 'take away'. When we discussed this with the teachers in one of our groups some of them responded as follows:

- I think I've just seen the light! I always used to think that the subtraction symbol (−) just meant 'take away'. But it doesn't, does it? It means lots of other things as well.
- But we always say 'take away' when we write the symbol down. Should we?
- I must admit I will find it difficult to think of it as meaning anything other than 'take away'.

Of course, subtraction is sometimes 'take away', and when this is so it is appropriate to use this language. But there are two levels of language involved here: the formal language that goes with the concept, such as 'twelve subtract three'; and the informal language appropriate to the physical situation. This informal language might be 'twelve take away three', but it might be 'twelve count back three', or 'what's the difference between 12 and 3?' or any of the language of comparison in Table 3.6, and so on. The problem that Meg encountered in the dialogue discussed earlier would appear to be related to the fact that she is saying and thinking 'take away'. But she is not using the partitioning structure for which the language of 'take away' is appropriate. She is using the reduction structure and should be talking about 'counting back'.

Later in their mathematical careers, children will encounter calculations like 6 − (−3). With the proper foundation of the network of connections associated with subtraction that has been outlined above put in place in the early years, there is no need for subtraction with negative numbers like this to be such a mystery for them as it often seems to be. This is an extract from a conversation with two of the teachers we worked with:

D. *What do you make of this question, six subtract negative three?*
M. *I know the answer's nine, but I don't understand why.*
C. *It's because two minuses make a plus.*
D. *Why do you smile when you say that?*
C. *I suppose it's because I know it's no explanation really. It's just a trick or a rule someone taught me. I've no idea what it means or why it works!*

Most people feel very uneasy about a statement like 6 − (−3) = 9. This is not surprising in view of the dominance of 'take away' in our understanding of subtraction. If you say to yourself 'six take away negative three' then you will probably imagine a pile of six objects and wonder what on earth taking away negative three of them could mean. Of course, it is meaningless. So how do we make sense of subtracting a negative number? We must assume, of course, that −3 itself has some meaning for us. Let's connect it, for example, with a temperature (or your bank balance, whichever is closer to your experience). Now connect the symbols 6 − (−3) with a temperature situation, using the comparison structure. Does this suddenly make sense? If the temperature inside is 6 degrees and the temperature outside is −3 degrees, then … how much hotter is it inside? How much colder is it outside? Or connect the symbols with the number line, using the inverse of addition structure. If you start at −3, what do you have to add to get to 6? This is not difficult mathematics, once the symbols are connected to the appropriate structures.

The network of connections for understanding subtraction

We can now summarize what we see as the teacher's task in developing children's understanding of subtraction. It would appear to be a question of helping the child to:

- build up a network of connections between the symbols and the various structures that have been outlined in the above analysis – partitioning, comparison, complement of a set, counting back/reducing, inverse of addition;
- use these with a range of concrete and real situations, such as sets of objects, coins, prices, lengths, ages;
- experience various subtraction procedures using the picture of number in the number line;
- then connect all this with the language of subtraction, both the formal word 'subtract' and the range of language appropriate to the various actual physical situations, with a particular focus on the extensive language of comparison.

And how will understanding of subtraction be recognized? By the child:

- demonstrating that cognitive connections between the concrete situations, symbols, language and pictures of subtraction are being established.
- showing us, for example, what the symbols 12 − 3 mean in terms of a set of counters, or two sticks of cubes placed side by side, or on a number line.
- being able to make up number stories using more than one subtraction structure, like the stories N, P, Q, R and S, cited in Table 3.5.
- knowing what calculation to perform for a take-away situation, for finding out how many are not, for counting back or reducing, for comparing two numbers to find out how many more or how many less, and for determining what must be added to one number to give another.

That's quite an agenda! And we have not even considered the problems of doing the actual calculations by a range of oral/mental and written methods.

PAUSE TO REFLECT   Spot the difference

We suspect that, for many readers, this chapter will have been a bit of an eye-opener. Did you have any idea, for example, that subtraction could come in quite so many guises?

Changing our deeply-embedded ideas can be extremely challenging, especially if we have held them for many years. This is true in many walks of life. If you pause for a few minutes we suspect you can come up with several examples of where you have had to change your view of someone or something in the light of new information or different experiences. For example, consider your early understanding of the concept of 'foreigner' and then how your understanding of this concept might have had to be modified later to accommodate the experience of going overseas and discovering that now you were the foreigner!

In discussing subtraction in this chapter we have linked it with situations involving comparison of two numbers or quantities and finding the difference between them. One of the easiest ways to visualize this idea of subtraction is to imagine two points on the scale of a thermometer and the size of the gap between them. For example, we can regard the difference between 4°C and 10°C on a thermometer scale as a picture of '10 − 4'. Similarly, we could think about the difference between −4°C and 10°C on a thermometer as a picture of '10 − (−4)'. Make up some stories that might go with the pictures shown in Figure 3.10. For example, a

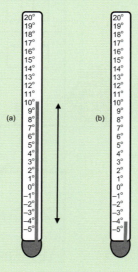

Figure 3.10   *'Difference between' on a thermometer scale*

(Continued)

(Continued)

story for Figure 3.10(b) might begin: 'At midnight last night, the temperature had dropped to −4 degrees, but by noon today …'.

Or you might prefer to make up some stories involving a block of flats with several underground car parks and a lift that can stop at any floor. See Figure 3.11. For example, invent a story about someone using the lift between floor −2 and floor 5 that involves finding the difference between 5 and −2, and how this is a picture of 5 − (−2) = 7. There are many stories you can make up that involve finding the difference between the numbers for different floors in this building − this is a multi-story building.

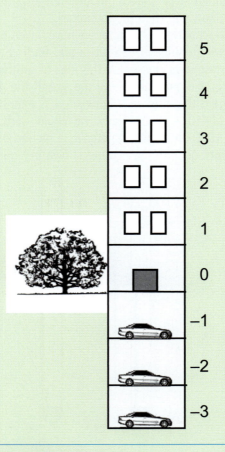

Figure 3.11   *A multi-story building!*

Verbal miscues

In discussing the inverse of addition structure above (Subtraction Structure 5), we highlighted the way in which children can respond incorrectly to particular cues in a word problem that signal addition, even though the underlying structure of the problem requires a subtraction. There is a similar point to make about the language of comparison. When children encounter language related to the greater quantity (such as 'more than', 'longer than', 'heavier than') in a word problem, these particular words can often signal addition rather than subtraction. For example, consider this word problem: John has £58 and Helen has £37. How much more than Helen does John have? Some primary-school children, rather than engaging with the logical structure of the problem, will simply respond to the cue given by the word 'more' by adding the numbers 58 and 37.

There are also plenty of word problems that require addition where the language used in the problem miscues the idea of subtraction. In Table 3.7, for example, we have deliberately generated situations corresponding to 12 + 3 that contain 'subtraction' words, such as 'spent' (T), 'takes' (U), 'less than' (V), and 'difference' (W). In spite of the language used these are actually examples of various addition structures. All these questions require the calculation 12 + 3 = 15, but we are fairly confident that many primary-school children would subtract the 3 from the 12 and give the answer 9 to most of these rather complex questions.

We can also cite other variations of subtraction structures that have this potential for verbal miscues. These are problems that do not fall neatly into the five main categories we have outlined in this chapter. In Table 3.8, for example, we have deliberately generated situations corresponding to the subtraction 12 – 3 that contain 'addition' words, such as 'earned' (X) and 'more than' (Y and Z). In spite of the language used these are actually examples of various subtraction structures. All these questions correspond to the calculation 12 – 3 = 9, although we would predict fairly confidently that many primary-school children would add the 3 and 12 and give the answer 15 to these questions.

Tables 3.7 and 3.8 contain problems with contrived and complex logical structures. But they are given here to illustrate the potential problem of children responding merely

Table 3.7   *Stories for 12 + 3 using language that might suggest subtraction*

T	John spent £3 this afternoon and now he has £12 left. How much did he have this morning?
U	Anne has some marbles. Derek takes 12 of them and now Anne has only 3 left. How many marbles did Anne have to begin with?
V	Helen has 12 pencils, which is 3 fewer than Gill. How many does Gill have?
W	Model A costs £12 more than Model B and £3 less than Model C. What is the difference in cost between Model A and Model C?

Table 3.8   *Stories for 12 – 3 using language that might suggest addition*

X	John earned £3 this afternoon and now he has £12. How much did he have this morning?
Y	Helen has 12 pencils and this is 3 more than Gill. How many pencils does Gill have?
Z	Model A costs £12 more than Model B and £3 more than Model C. How much more than Model B is Model C?

to the verbal cues in a situation, rather than grasping its structure. Analysis of the way children will misinterpret verbal cues reinforces the principle that our teaching must enable children to recognize the structure of situations, not just to respond like automatons to key words. Our message therefore is that the main focus of our work with children should be on developing understanding, by establishing the connections between the symbols for subtraction and the associated language, pictures and concrete situations.

RESEARCH FOCUS   Early addition and subtraction

In the previous chapter we discussed the importance of talking to children. Here we start by referring to a seminal work that develops this theme with particular reference to addition. We then suggest some interesting research developments related to young children learning mathematics in the Czech Republic and in the Netherlands that the reader will find worth following up.

In 1986 Martin Hughes's influential book *Children and Number* was published. We strongly recommend reading this. In the Foreword Margaret Donaldson wrote that it felt like she was '... reviewing a good detective story' (p. vi). We, as she, '... must be careful not to reveal too much of the plot' (p. vi), but the following conversation between Hughes and 4-year-old Patrick (Hughes, 1986, pp. 47–8) will give you a flavour of some of the research findings discussed.

Hughes starts by asking Patrick, 'How many is two and one more?' to which he gets the response, 'Four'. Having noted that the child does not answer this question correctly, he then asks a sequence of questions putting this addition of 'one more' into various contexts, before asking the abstract question again:

MH	Well how many is two *lollipops* and one more?
Patrick	Three
MH	How many is two *elephants* and one more?
Patrick	Three
MH	How many is two *giraffes* and one more?
Patrick	Three

MH	So how many is two and one more?
Patrick	Six

Why does Patrick give the answer 'six' to the final abstract question when in the previous questions set in various real-life contexts he seems to recognize that 'two and one more' gives 'three'? Of course, neither Hughes nor we know what Patrick was thinking when he responded 'six'. But in the light of our earlier discussions we might make two observations. The first is that Patrick might be at the stage where he needs to visualize concrete objects before he can use correctly this kind of number relationship; 'two and one more' is simply too abstract for him and without being attached to 'things' the numbers and the process of adding on seem to have no real meaning for him. The second is that Patrick may have picked up the pattern in the three questions about lollipops, elephants and giraffes, but then not see the final question as part of the pattern. Rather, he may be thinking, 'Well, this question is different from the previous ones, so I had better give a different answer!' How might Hughes have gained more insight into Patrick's thinking? What further questions might he have posed?

More recently, Milan Hejný and his colleagues in the Czech Republic have been doing some interesting research in the earliest years of schooling which encourages children to act out simple stories and problems in order to develop their understanding of the processes of addition and subtraction. In Hejný (2008: available online through *Google Scholar*), for example, Milan describes the 'Walk Environment'. He explains how simple whole-class sessions with 5–6-year-olds taking steps forwards and backwards can help their understanding of number ordering, addition and subtraction with natural numbers, and even give them an early appreciation of negative numbers – as, for example, when a child is asked to take 2 steps forwards and 3 steps backwards. As we write this we realize that it may not sound very exciting, but, we can assure you that, when presented in an appropriate manner, Hejný's ideas are very appealing to children and the signs are that they are enhancing the mathematical understanding of young children in Prague and beyond. The reader will find it worthwhile following this up.

Also, have a look at Emergent Mathematics and Realistic Mathematics Education (RME), which are child-centred approaches that are very popular in the Netherlands at the moment. There is a growing body of research on both. Bert van Oers (2010) reviews a range of studies which demonstrate that, with the appropriate support, children's play can be an effective and enjoyable way in which to develop their understanding of mathematical concepts. Similarly, Marja van den Heuvel-Panhuizen and Sylvia van den Boogaard (2008) show how picture books that might be used for language and literacy development can be used for encouraging mathematical discussion. In a small-scale study of four 5-year-olds being read one story, they concluded, 'Surprisingly, almost half the utterances were mathematics-related. The findings of the study support the idea that reading children picture books without explicit instruction or prompting has large potential for mathematically engaging children' (van den Heuvel-Panhuizen and van den Boogaard, 2008, p. 342).

(Continued)

(Continued)

In a climate when the curriculum for mathematics sessions may be fairly prescribed, teachers will be encouraged to note the evidence that stories and play prove to be important and effective ways of enhancing young children's appreciation of mathematical concepts.

Some activities to use with children

The following are some examples of activities that can be used with groups of children in the Foundation Stage and Key Stage 1, to develop their understanding of addition and subtraction. The focus here is on developing key language, understanding the operations and making connections, rather than on the development of skills in manipulating numbers.

ACTIVITY 3.1 Teddies on the Bus	3–4	4–5	5–6	6–7	7–8
	☐				

Objective

To help young children make the transition from 'counting all' to 'counting on'.

Materials

A supply of teddies and a toy bus or some other vehicle in which the teddies can be placed.

Method

Put, say, 5 teddies on the bus, engaging the children in counting them as you do this. Say, for example, 'These 5 teddies are going to the seaside.' Then get one of the children to drive the bus away out of sight. Ask the children how many teddies have gone to the seaside on the bus.

Then tell them that soon the bus is going to come back with the 5 teddies on it and then 3 other teddies are going to get on it as well and they are all going to the shopping mall. How many teddies will be going on the bus to the shopping mall? The children are now in a position where they cannot physically count all the teddies, because 5 of them are out of sight, and can be encouraged to count on from 5. Get the children to join in: (a) 'On the bus there are one, two, three, four, *five* teddies. When these get on there will be ... (pointing to them in turn) six, seven, *eight*.' Then: (b) 'So on the bus there are *five* teddies, and these three will make ... (again pointing) six, seven, *eight*.' Then the bus is brought back and the three teddies are put on the bus, with the children again counting six, seven, eight. The bus is driven off to the shopping mall.

Repeat the story with different small numbers. Eventually drop stage (a).

ACTIVITY 3.2 Staircase and Zero-Mat	3–4	4–5	5–6	6–7	7–8
		☐			

Objective

To provide experience of addition and subtraction by counting up and counting down.

Materials

A bag of wooden cuboid blocks and a blank strip of card the same size as one of the oblong faces of the blocks. The blocks are used to construct a staircase with four or more steps, as shown in the photograph; the piece of card represents a mat at the bottom of the stairs. The mat will be called the 'zero-mat'. One or more toy people/animals to stand on the mat and then to climb up and down the stairs – or any other suitable items you wish to use to liven up the activity.

Method

This activity can be done with one child or a small group. Start by allowing the children to build the staircase and put the mat in place. To begin with, get the children to count up and down as the toy person climbs from the zero-mat to the top of the stairs and back down again: zero, one, two, three, four … four, three, two, one, zero. The activity works particularly well if it is incorporated into a story. Thus, for example, in the photograph, Mr Black – Arthur's toy builder – is having a rest on step 2 as he makes his way up to step 4, which requires some repair work. How many steps more does he have to climb? As the toy climbs up, the child counts on from step 2: two … three, four. When he arrives at step 4 he realizes that he needs some more nails, which he left on the zero-mat. How many steps does he have to go down to collect them? As the toy climbs down the staircase the child counts down from step 4: four … three, two, one, zero!

ACTIVITY 3.3 Comparative Language	3–4	4–5	5–6	6–7	7–8
	☐	☐			

Objective

To lay the foundation for later experience of the comparison structure of subtraction by developing the language of comparison (see Table 3.6).

(Continued)

(Continued)

Materials

The children; a bag of coloured cubes and some corresponding coloured discs; some toy cars and a ramp; a jumper and some building blocks; and potentially many other things.

Method

Generate lots of situations in which the children can answer questions using some of the language in Table 3.6. Here are some examples. Each one is repeated enough times for all the children to have a turn and for the language patterns to be established.

1 The children stand in a circle. Two children are chosen to step forward and to stand back to back in the middle. Establish this pattern of questions and answers:

Teacher: *Who is shorter?*
Children: *Tom is shorter than Meg.*
Teacher: *Who is taller?*
Children: *Meg is taller than Tom.*

2 A long line is marked on the ground, with a number of coloured discs placed randomly along it. All the children assemble at one end of the line. Then two children in turn choose a coloured cube from a bag and go and stand on the corresponding disc on the line. Again, the same pattern of questions and answers is used:

Teacher: *Who is nearer?*
Children: *Tom is nearer than Meg.*
Teacher: *Who is further away?*
Children: *Meg is further away than Tom.*

3 Two children are chosen to pick a toy car and on a signal from the teacher they let them roll down a ramp. The questions and answers follow a similar pattern. *Whose car is faster? Whose car is slower?*
4 Two children are chosen to do two tasks, such as one putting on a jumper and the other stacking some wooden blocks. The questions and answers follow a similar pattern. *Which takes longer? Which takes less time?*

	3–4	4–5	5–6	6–7	7–8
ACTIVITY 3.4 In My House and in Your House			□		

Objective

To draw on data from the child's home to develop the comparison structure of subtraction.

Materials

A survey sheet for children to take home, along the lines of the example shown in Table 3.9. The teacher will be careful to avoid requests for personal data that might be regarded as being in any way sensitive.

Table 3.9   Survey sheet for children to complete at home

	In my house	In your house	How many more or less?
People living there	5	----	----
Children	3	----	----
Pets	0	----	----
Telephones	3	----	----
Chairs	16	----	----
Pairs of scissors	8	----	----

Method

The teacher explains that the first column is what she (he) has in her (his) house. The children take the survey sheets home and, with the help of an adult, write in how many in their house, and how many more or less this is than the teacher's. For example: Pairs of scissors: 8 (in the teacher's house); 5 (in the child's house); 3 less. The children's own data is then used back at school (sensitively) in a question and answer session on difference, more than, and less than. The benefits of making this a home-based activity are that children are motivated by genuine data about themselves, it makes the connection between mathematics learnt in school and their real lives, and it promotes talk with the parent/guardian that uses key mathematical language.

ACTIVITY 3.5   Stories (Add, Subtract)

3–4	4–5	5–6	6–7	7–8
			□	

Objective

To help children connect the symbols for addition and subtraction with a wide range of situations and language.

Method

Read the children some examples of stories for addition statements, such as 3 + 5. For example: 'One day Henny Penny laid 3 eggs and Turkey Lurkey laid 5 eggs. How many eggs is that altogether?' Get them to make up their own stories, for examples like 4 + 8. Use larger numbers if appropriate.

(Continued)

(Continued)

Children should share and discuss their stories with one another and with the teacher. Repeat this with subtraction statements such as 9 − 3.

To encourage the use of different structures and contexts, give specific words or phrases to be included in the story, such as more than, less than, increased, reduced, younger, older. Alternatively, give the children the start of the story and ask them to complete it. For example, for 9 − 3: 'Meg had 9 marbles, but Tom …' Or ask them to make up a story for 9 − 3 about someone going shopping with 9p to spend.

 ACTIVITY 3.6   Swaps (Add, Subtract)

3–4	4–5	5–6	6–7	7–8
			□	

Objective

To develop connections between language, symbols, concrete experience and pictures, for the concepts of addition and subtraction.

Materials

Coins, such as 1p and 10p; base-ten materials (ten-rods and units); number lines; blank paper; a collection of simple stories for addition and subtraction; cards with the following words written on them: story, number line, picture, symbols, coins, blocks.

Method

A small group of children is given a starting point and a selection of cards indicating a sequence of swaps to be achieved. When they have completed all their swaps, they report to the teacher on what they have done.

Figure 3.12 shows an example with a story given as the starting point, and a challenge to swap this for coins, then for a number line drawing, and finally for symbols. The children might respond to this challenge by putting out 8p and a further 4p to make the 12p required; then drawing an arrow on a number line from 8 to 12; and finally writing on their piece of paper the symbols 8 + 4 = 12 or 12 − 8 = 4. The starting point may be a story, a number-line diagram, a sum written in symbols or a picture, with the sequence of swaps varied appropriately.

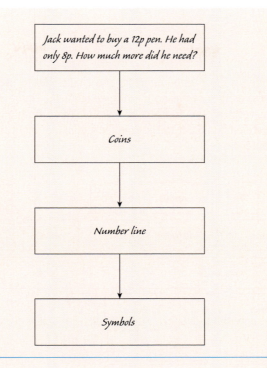

Figure 3.12 *Swaps*

ACTIVITY 3.7   Sentences (Add, Subtract)

3–4	4–5	5–6	6–7	7–8
			☐	

Objective

To develop language patterns for addition and subtraction.

Materials

Several sets of strips of card with the following words or phrases written on them: add, subtract, and, take away, more than, less than, the difference, between, makes, leaves, is, equals; several sets of cards with appropriate numerals written on them; counting materials; a number line.

(Continued)

(Continued)

Method

A small group of children is given three numbers and challenged to use the cards to make up as many different sentences as they can using these three numbers. Figure 3.13 shows some examples of what might be achieved with the numbers 3, 4 and 7. The counting materials and number line are used to give concrete embodiment to the children's thinking about the numbers and to enable them to check their sentences.

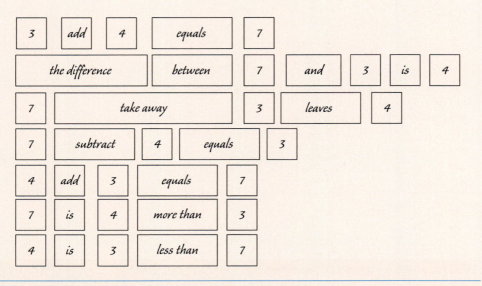

Figure 3.13   *Sentences for 3, 4 and 7*

ACTIVITY 3.8   I Have, Who Has? (Add/Subtract Stories)

3–4	4–5	5–6	6–7	7–8
			☐	☐

Objective

To provide practice in using a range of structures and associated language for addition and subtraction.

Materials

Prepare a set of 16 cards with various situations described on one side and the corresponding calculations on the other side, using the same cyclic scheme as explained in Activity 2.4, with the question on one card answered on the reverse side of the next. In this version use as questions a wide range of situations with different structures and associated language for addition and subtraction. Make sure that there are no duplicate calculations. Here are some suggestions for situations for a pack of 16 cards, with the corresponding calculations in brackets after each one:

1   Start at 7 and count on 4. (7 + 4)
2   John has 3 apples, Peter has 8. How many more than John has Peter? (8 − 3)
3   Gill had 8 apples. She ate 5. How many are left? (8 − 5)
4   Twelve subtract seven. (12 − 7)
5   The difference between 4 and 7. (7 − 4)
6   Eight add four. (8 + 4)
7   A plant 7 cm tall grows by 5 cm. How tall is it now? (7 + 5)
8   A 12p chocolate bar was reduced by 5p. What does it cost now? (12 − 5)
9   I want to buy a book costing £7. I have £3. How much more do I need? (7 − 3)
10 John is 4, Jack is 8. How much younger is John? (8 − 4)
11 Start at 12 and count back 8. (12 − 8)
12 There are 12 children. If 4 are going on a school trip, how many are not going? (12 − 4)
13 One sweet costs 4p, another costs 3p. How much for them both? (4 + 3)
14 The sum of 12 and 4. (12 + 4)
15 I am 12. How old was I three years ago? (12 − 3)
16 How many less than 8 is 7? (8 − 7)

Method

The cards are shuffled and dealt between three players, with the remaining card placed in the centre of the table. The game is then played in exactly the same way as in Activity 2.4. To simplify the game, use fewer cards with a narrower range of language and structures, and smaller numbers. Or to extend it, use more cards, a wider range of language and structures, and larger numbers.

Summary of key ideas

1   The two most important categories of situations to which the language and symbols of addition can be connected are: (a) the union of two sets with no members in common, where the child counts and calculates how many altogether (Addition Structure 1); and (b) increasing, where the child starts at one number and counts on by another (Addition Structure 2).
2   Five key categories of situations to which the language and symbols of subtraction can be connected are: partitioning, involving the idea of take away and how

(Continued)

(Continued)

many left (Subtraction Structure 1); complement of a set, finding how many are not (Subtraction Structure 2); reduction and counting back (Subtraction Structure 3); comparison, to find how many more or less (fewer), or the difference between (Subtraction Structure 4); and inverse of addition, where the question is what must be added (Subtraction Structure 5).

3   Particularly important in understanding subtraction is the extensive language of comparison (see Table 3.6).

4   For any comparison statement that makes the greater quantity the subject of the sentence there is an equivalent statement that makes the smaller quantity the subject. Teachers should encourage children always to make both statements and to develop both sets of language.

5   Subtraction is not just 'take away'. This language applies only to partitioning (Subtraction Structure 1). Since this is only one of a number of subtraction structures it should not be overemphasized at the expense of the other languages of subtraction.

6   The partitioning structure and the language of 'take away' cannot, for example, be used meaningfully in situations involving negative numbers. Subtraction in these situations is normally either comparison or inverse of addition.

7   When tackling word problems children often respond incorrectly to words that cue addition in situations that actually have a subtraction structure, and vice versa.

 ## Suggestions for further reading

In Chapter 7 of Haylock (2010) Derek explains in further detail the various structures and associated language of addition and subtraction.

Clements and Sarama (2009) provide in Chapter 5 an analysis of the development path for young children's understanding of addition and subtraction, including their own framework of addition and subtraction problem structures.

In the book by Hughes (1986) that we have referred to in the Research Focus above, Chapter 3 provides an analysis of children's understanding of the concepts of addition and subtraction in the early years of schooling.

In Chapter 6 of an important book in the field of mathematics education, Nunes and Bryant (1996) provide a detailed and research-based analysis of children's understanding of addition and subtraction structures.

In a chapter entitled 'Understanding subtraction through enhanced communication' (Cockburn, 2007) Anne discusses subtraction activities tried and tested in Germany and the Czech Republic.

CHAPTER 4

UNDERSTANDING MULTIPLICATION AND DIVISION

A PUZZLING MULTIPLICATION

This little puzzle might alert you to the possibility that the operation of multiplication, like addition and subtraction, has more than one structure.

Professor Conundrum has invented an amazing bank machine that multiplies by four everything that is fed into it. One day he feeds into the machine two £5 notes. What notes would you expect to come out?

- What does your answer suggest about how you have interpreted 'multiplies by four'?
- Is there another answer you might have given?

In this chapter

In this chapter we explore the meaning of multiplication. We see that it is indeed the case that multiplication has more than one structure. We then see that the same is true for division. Again our focus is on the network of connections that constitutes understanding of each operation.

Some of the material in this chapter goes beyond the mathematics that would normally be taught to children in the age range 3 to 8 years. This is because we

(Continued)

(Continued)

think that it is important for teachers of young children to have a clear overview of the network of connections that children will eventually have to establish in order to understand these operations. To help in this analysis we use stories written by children aged 9 to 11 years for various multiplication and division statements. Although the children are older than those we are focusing on in this book, we hope that the reader will find that their stories provide a number of significant insights into the misconceptions that might arise from the ways in which younger children first encounter the language and symbols of multiplication and division.

Understanding multiplication

We have given the multiplication puzzle at the start of this chapter to a number of primary school teachers. Their first responses tend to be one of two of the several possible answers to the question. First, there is the answer: eight £5 notes. The idea of multiplication by four that lies behind this response is that the set of two notes has been reproduced four times. We get four sets of two notes, that is, eight notes. We refer to the structure used here as repeated addition. Then, second, there is the answer: two £20 notes. The idea of multiplication by four that lies behind this response is that the value of each note has been made four times larger. So each £5 note is scaled up by a factor of four to become a £20 note. We refer to this as the scaling structure. So, we see from this puzzle that there is potentially more than one structure for multiplication. In this section we explore the different categories of situations and pictures to which the language and symbols of multiplication can be connected; we see that the network of connections to be established for understanding multiplication is a complex one. The fact there are a number of different kinds of situation to which the same symbols can be attached is sufficient to make multiplication a difficult concept for children to understand. But when we analyse children's stories for multiplication we find that there are other inherent difficulties in the concept, which we consider first.

Children's difficulties in understanding multiplication

Some children aged 9 to 11 years were asked to write a story that goes with '9 × 3'. Table 4.1 provides some of their responses.

Table 4.1   *Children's stories for 9 × 3 showing problems with multiplication*

A	9 and 3 stood in a shop they said please could we have a times sign. He said yes so they walked along with the times sign in the middle.
B	9 said to 3 lets multiply together and see what it makes.
C	9 children were writing an essay and 3 more children joined them. That made 27 children altogether.
D	The boy had 9 pens and the teacher asked him what would 9 × 3 be. He said 27 and the teacher said that's right.
E	I had 9 footballs and I lost 3 footballs, then I got back 3 footballs, so I had 9 footballs × 3 footballs.
F	The army had 9 tanks and the navy had 3 ships. When they timesed them together they were the biggest army in the whole world.
G	John had 9 cars and his brother had 3 cars, so his dad asked him what was 9 times 3 and he told him 27.
H	There was a boy at school and he was given some sums to do but when he got to number five he could not do it. The sum was 9 × 3.

A quick look at the stories in Table 4.1 reveals the difficulty that many children have in making sense of multiplication in real terms. Stories A and B are amusing, but they reveal the problem that many children have in making any real-life connections with this particular mathematical operation. This is even the case when the children apparently know their tables and can recall multiplication facts like 9 × 3 = 27 with confidence, as is shown in stories C and D. Each of these stories starts with a set of nine things (nine children, nine pens), but then the child is clearly at a loss to imagine any way in which multiplying by three could be applied to these.

This highlights one of the inbuilt difficulties in interpreting multiplication in concrete terms, namely that the two numbers must normally represent different sorts of things. (Multiplying two lengths to obtain an area is an example of an exception to this rule.) So, for example, if the 9 in 9 × 3 represents nine children (as in story C) then the 3 would have to represent something other than children: for example, nine children each had three pencils. If the 9 represents pens (as in story D) then the 3 must represent something other than pens: for example, the boy has nine pens and they cost £3 each. This idea that the two numbers usually have to represent different kinds of things clearly throws some children, as illustrated further in stories E, F and G. Story E tries to multiply footballs by footballs and story F tries to multiply tanks by ships, neither of which makes any sense whatsoever. In story G the child gives up trying to write a realistic story, realizing presumably that you cannot multiply cars by cars.

For many children multiplication seems to be only something you do with numbers in mathematics sessions in school; it is not connected with any confidence to the real world. A multiplication statement appears to be just a set of marks made on a piece of paper or an instruction to recall the appropriate response. This is something that you get either right or wrong (as in story D), or something you either can or cannot do (as in story H).

Given this task, only a few children produce valid stories, such as 'I had nine cats and they each had three kittens'. Analysis of hundreds of these stories for multiplication written by children aged 9 to 11 years shows that only a small proportion of them seem to have clear structures in their mind that they can connect with multiplication. Children seem to lack any kind of picture of what is going on when two numbers are multiplied together. If this is the case, then our contention is that those who introduce multiplication in the earlier years of primary schooling have a responsibility to lay down a foundation of experience and to provide images to which the language and symbols of multiplication can be connected.

Multiplication Structure 1: repeated addition

We asked some of the teachers we worked with how they interpreted a multiplication like 9 × 3. The following responses raise some significant ideas.

> C.   *I just think of it as 9 times 3, something you do with numbers.*
> M.   *It's nine sets of three, isn't it?*
> E.   *Or is it three, sets of nine?*
> M.   *No, surely that would be 3 times 9?*
> A.   *I don't think it matters. It's both, isn't it?*

Certainly one important category of situations to which multiplication must be connected is that to which one of the teachers here is alluding: the idea that the multiplication sign means 'sets of'. So, one of the most obvious ways of interpreting the symbols 9 × 3 is by imagining situations where we have nine sets of three things. These situations have what we will refer to as the repeated addition structure. It is called repeated addition simply because nine sets of three, for example, can also be written in symbols as 3 + 3 + 3 + 3 + 3 + 3 + 3 + 3 + 3. We should note that the language of 'so many sets of so many', which is central to this structure, implies that we are dealing here with situations involving cardinal numbers – where the second number is the number of objects in a set and the first is the number of these sets.

The commutative principle (multiplication and addition)

The responses of the teachers to how they interpret 9 × 3 raise a question that causes some confusion. Does 9 × 3 mean 'nine sets of three' or should it be 'three

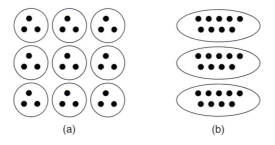

Figure 4.1   *(a) Nine sets of three (b) three sets of nine*

sets of nine'? Which of the pictures (a) or (b) in Figure 4.1 should be connected with these symbols?

The first thing to note is that it is by no means immediately obvious that nine sets of three objects and three sets of nine objects come to the same result. The two diagrams in Figure 4.1 do not immediately strike us as necessarily representing the same number. The fact that they do is an instance of the property of multiplication known as *commutativity*. In essence, the property is that when two numbers are multiplied together it does not matter which one comes first. Because of the commutative property of multiplication we know that seven sets of six children and six sets of seven children contain the same number of children altogether; that 12 items at 29p each will cost the same as 29 items at 12p each; that five 10-g masses will weigh the same as ten 5-g masses; and so on.

The other operation for which commutativity holds is addition. When two numbers are added together, it does not matter which one comes first. For example, four added to five is the same as five added to four. Commutativity of addition and commutativity of multiplication are two of the fundamental principles of arithmetic that are the focus of Chapter 5.

There is a stage in their development of understanding of addition in which young children gradually get hold of the idea that a set of five objects combined with a set of four objects is the same as a set of four combined with a set of five. This may not seem a huge step, but it is a highly significant one. With addition there does not appear to be much perceptual difference between, say, holding up four fingers on your left hand and five on your right hand, and holding up five fingers on your left and four on your right. Although there is a transformation involved between the two situations, the equivalence is easily demonstrated.

Eventually most children are able to switch freely between, say, 5 + 4 and 4 + 5. But grasping this principle is more of a hurdle for multiplication. The equivalence between 'five sets of four' and 'four sets of five' is not clearly apparent. Now, strictly speaking, the words 'nine times three' mean that you have 'nine, three times', in other words, 'three sets of nine', as shown in Figure 4.1(b). Similarly, the formal language 'nine multiplied by three' also refers to the picture in Figure 4.1(b): a set of nine is reproduced three times. So, in this strict interpretation, 9×3 would represent $9 + 9 + 9$, whereas 3×9 would represent $3 + 3 + 3 + 3 + 3 + 3 + 3 + 3 + 3$.

We would not wish to be as pedantic as this. In fact, it would seem to us to be appropriate that the commutative property of multiplication be established *before* the introduction of the formal representation in symbols. So when the multiplication sign is introduced it really would be the case that both 9×3 and 3×9 could represent either nine sets of three or three sets of nine; because the children already know and understand securely that nine sets of three and three sets of nine are equivalent.

Rectangular arrays

In order to establish commutativity in multiplication it is most helpful if considerable attention is given to connecting one particular picture of multiplication into the network of experiences associated with this concept. This is the picture of a *rectangular array*, as shown in Figure 4.2(a) and (b).

It is our contention that pictures such as these should form a major component of the child's understanding of 9×3. One of the reasons for this emphasis on the notion of rectangular array is that this picture of multiplication makes the commutative property transparent. So Figure 4.2(a) can be talked about as being both 'nine rows of three dots' (going across the page) and 'three rows (or columns) of nine dots' (going down the page). Clearly, in this case, nine threes and three nines are the same. In the same way, Figure 4.2(b) can be talked about as being both 'three rows of nine dots' (going across the page) and 'nine rows (or columns) of three dots' (going down the page). Later on, then, both 9×3 and 3×9 can be used as symbols to represent either of these diagrams.

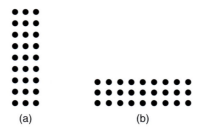

(a)   (b)

Figure 4.2   *Rectangular arrays for 9 × 3*

Children in my reception class often put things, including themselves, in pairs and they quickly pick up the idea of numbers as so many pairs. So they will see 4 as 2 pairs, 6 as 3 pairs and so on. Sometimes I get, say, 10 children to line up in pairs and we count the pairs.

Then I get the two lines to separate and we count the children in each line. So they get to see the 10 children first as 5 pairs of children and then as 2 lines of 5 children. That's an early experience of seeing multiplication in rectangular arrays.

Young children, before they start recording multiplication facts like 3 × 4 = 12 formally, can be encouraged to identify rectangular arrays in their environment – the world is full of them – and to record their observations with a diagram and an appropriate comment, as in Figure 4.3.

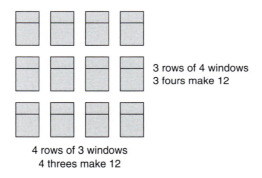

3 rows of 4 windows
3 fours make 12

4 rows of 3 windows
4 threes make 12

Figure 4.3   *Recording arrays*

A network of connections for multiplication

We are beginning to see again that understanding of a number operation is about the establishment of a network of connections. Understanding multiplication involves connecting the language of 'multiplied by', 'times', and 'so many sets of so many', to concrete situations such as repeated sets of objects, the symbols for multiplication statements and the important picture of the rectangular array. With this picture forming a major component of the multiplication network, the child has a strong image to which to connect later experiences in mathematics, such as multiplying with two- and three-digit numbers and finding areas of rectangles using multiplication. One further important picture to be built into the network of connections for multiplication is that of repeated steps on the number line. In this image, children learn to connect the symbols 9 × 3 with 'three steps of nine' or 'nine steps of three' along the number line, as shown in Figure 4.4. Before commutativity is firmly established it is quite a surprise when these two different procedures lead to the same point!

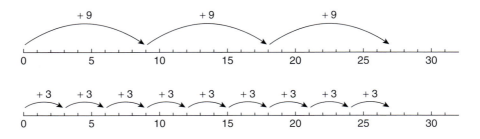

Figure 4.4   *Three steps of nine and nine steps of three on a number line*

Contexts for repeated addition

We encounter operations with numbers not just when dealing with sets of things, but also in the context of money and in a variety of measurement contexts. Consequently, a major part of the development of the child's understanding of number operations is the establishment of connections between the symbols and language associated with the operation and the various structures of the operation as they are met in a wide range of real contexts.

Having discussed the idea of multiplication as 'so many sets of so many', we asked some of the teachers we worked with whether they could recall other situations in which multiplication is the appropriate operation – other contexts in real life in which we might press the multiplication key on the calculator if the numbers involved were much larger.

> M.   *We use it a lot when we're shopping, don't we? When you're working out the cost of three things at 9p each, for example.*
> E.   *But isn't that just three sets of nine again?*
> D.   *Not really. Nine pence isn't necessarily a set of nine things.*
> A.   *And what about 3 lengths of 9 cm, or 3 periods of 9 minutes, or 3 buckets each containing 9 litres?*

From this discussion we can see first that the repeated addition structure of multiplication, which has so far been thought of as repeated sets, can be extended quite naturally to other contexts, such as money, length, weight, capacity, time, and so on. Each of the ideas suggested in the conversation above in these various contexts is connected with 9 × 3 or 3 × 9. This is a not too difficult extension of the repeated addition structure: from 'three sets of nine' to 'three lots of 9 cm' or 'three lots of 9 minutes', and so on. But we should note that now only one of the numbers is a cardinal number and the other number is used for measuring a length or a value or a weight, and so on.

Multiplication often arises in two different contexts simultaneously. We have already hinted at this problem in discussing multiplication earlier in this chapter, when we noted that the two numbers involved in a multiplication statement have to represent different sorts of things. This contrasts with addition and subtraction where the two numbers involved usually represent the same sort of thing; we add a set to a set, a price to a price, a length to a length, and so on. But if we consider possible contexts to be, for example, sets, money, length and distance, weight, liquid volume and capacity, and time, then numbers occurring in any *two* of these might produce a possible real situation in which multiplication has some application and meaning.

We can illustrate this observation with a number of examples of situations that might correspond to the calculation 9 × 3. For example, putting the 9 into the context of money (£9) and the 3 into the context of weight (3 kg), we might encounter the repeated addition structure of multiplication when finding the cost of 3 kilograms of salmon at £9 a kilogram. Using the two contexts of money and liquid volume we would encounter the same structure when calculating the cost of 9 litres of wine at £3 per litre. Using the two contexts of time and distance we might be calculating how far we would get in 3 hours if we cycle at 9 miles per hour. We would argue that this process of bringing together into one operation numbers from two different contexts is one of the most difficult features of multiplication, and one that contributes to its complexity as a concept to be learnt and used with understanding.

Multiplication Structure 2: scaling

There is a further structure associated with multiplication to be considered, in which a quantity is *scaled* by a factor. Not surprisingly, we call this the *scaling* structure. This is the structure of the following story written by a 10-year-old to go with the symbols 9 × 3: 'I have three pens. My friend has nine times as many. How many has she got?' At a casual glance the reader may well think this is no different from the repeated addition structure. But we should note that we are not dealing here with 'nine sets of three pens'. The story is about *two* sets of pens. One is a set of three pens, the other is 'nine times as many' and is to be calculated as a set of 27 pens. The 'nine times as many' is used to express a relationship between the two sets involved in the story. So, multiplication can also be understood as a process of enlargement, of scaling up by a factor; a process of making a quantity 'so many times bigger'.

This scaling structure is an important component of the network of connections for multiplication because of later mathematical experiences that involve this idea of scaling. So, for example, it will be encountered when calculating a percentage increase, or when dealing with scale factors in mapwork and scale drawings. Children get an early experience of the scaling structure of multiplication in the process of doubling, which is using a scale factor of 2. The word 'twice' is connected with this structure: 'I have twice as many marbles as you.' This then leads on to other scale factors and various measuring contexts, using language such as 'three times as many', 'three times as long', 'four times as much', 'ten times as heavy', and so on.

We should mention that it is still multiplication if the scale factor is less than 1 (for example, multiplying by 0.2) and the process of scaling makes the quantity smaller. For example, in a 1:5 scale drawing of the classroom each actual length can be multiplied by 0.2 to get the corresponding length in the drawing. This is one of several reasons why we should avoid children developing the idea that multiplication always results in a bigger number than the ones you started with. The idea of 'ten times greater' is particularly important in understanding place value (see Chapter 7), where a digit written in one place in a numeral is worth ten times as much as it would be if written in the next place to the right.

PAUSE TO REFLECT   Multiple multiplications

We have seen that of all the operations multiplication is the one that people find most difficult to visualize. But this does not mean that multiplication is something that is not part of our everyday experience. Whether you are keen on mathematics or not it is likely that you use multiplication several times a day. This may be consciously, but it may not.

For example, imagine that two of you are having some friends over for a meal. To decide whether it is cheaper to buy two bottles of good wine or three bottles of inferior wine on special offer will involve you in some basic multiplication. Because you will be cooking for six rather than two you will have to adjust your usual recipes accordingly, scaling up by a factor of three. If you get some multiplications wrong everything could, on the one hand, end up too salty, too spicy, too sweet or too much; on the other hand, it could all end up being pretty tasteless or too little.

When it comes to the meal itself, you will be sitting at a multiplication table! Think about the seating. Can you visualize three sets of your normal two chairs round your circular table? As you sit round the table for the meal look out for lots of numbers of things that have been multiplied by three for the occasion: cutlery, glasses, people. There are normally only four feet under your table; how many are there today?

That's just one illustration of how we might experience multiplication in our everyday lives. Take a few minutes to reflect on what you have already done today and think about any experience of multiplication that might have been involved.

And have a look around you, wherever you are as you read this, and see if you can spot any rectangular arrays that could be connected with multiplications? Derek, for example, has just spotted four rows of three buttons on the telephone on his desk; that's a picture of $3 \times 4 = 12$.

Understanding division

What image comes most readily to our minds when we see the symbols 12 ÷ 3? The following conversation with some of the teachers in one of our groups raises some important points about language and shows that there are at least two different structures associated with division:

D. *If I put twelve cubes on the desk what would you expect me to do with them to demonstrate 12 ÷ 3?*

L. *I expect you to share them into three piles. One for you, one for you, and one for you. And so on. Until they're all shared out.*

D. *So the answer is how many in each pile. What do you say when you have done this?*

L. *Twelve shared by three is four.*

C. *Twelve shared between three is four each, surely.*

D. *Or, what about twelve shared equally between four is three each?*

L. *I think I sometimes just say twelve share three is four, but I don't think it's right to say that.*

C. *I was thinking of something different. I had in mind putting the twelve cubes into piles of three.*

D. *And if you do that where's the answer?*

C. *It's the number of piles you finish up with. Four piles.*

D. *So twelve divided by three is also how many threes in twelve?*

L. *I'd never think of it like that. I'd only think of it as sharing between three.*

Division Structure 1: equal sharing between

We are back on familiar ground. The elementary mathematical operation of division, represented by the symbol ÷, appears to represent more than one type of situation, as has been the case with all the mathematical symbols we have analysed so far. On the one hand, the symbols 12 ÷ 3 are connected to the idea of sharing twelve equally between three. A set of twelve objects would thus be arranged into three groups, as shown in Figure 4.5(a), and the answer is the number of objects in each group. Division situations of this kind have what we call the *equal sharing* structure. The key language associated with this structure is 'share equally between'. It is important to note that 'sharing' is an experience of division only if it is 'sharing equally between'.

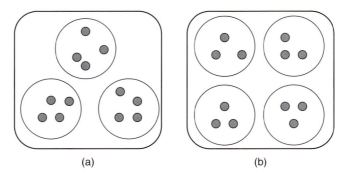

(a)   (b)

Figure 4.5   *Interpretations of 12 ÷ 3: (a) equal sharing between (b) inverse of multiplication*
(grouping)

Division Structure 2: inverse of multiplication (grouping)

But just as valid is to interpret 12 ÷ 3 as 'how many threes make twelve?' In this case the twelve objects are arranged into groups of three, as shown in Figure 4.5(b), and the answer is the number of groups. Division situations of this kind have what we call the *inverse of multiplication* structure. Because this structure involves finding out how many groups of a given size can be obtained, it is also sometimes referred to as 'grouping'. So the first thing to emphasize in our analysis of division is that teachers must be explicitly aware that the symbol for division has at least these two distinct and different meanings.

> M.   *I'm not sure I ever really realized that division could mean two different things like that! I always think of it as sharing.*
> D.   *What's 72 divided by nine?*
> M.   *[After some thought] Eight.*
> D.   *What went on in your mind when you worked that out?*
> M.   *I was trying to remember how many nines make 72.*
> D.   *So, you were using the inverse of multiplication structure!*
> C.   *How did we become teachers without knowing this?*

Children's stories for division statements give us some very interesting insights into their understanding of the operation. Most stories use Division Structure 1 (equal sharing between), as in stories J, K and L shown in Table 4.2, written to go with the division, 12 ÷ 3. Stories such as these, in which the twelve is shared equally between three piles or three people, are by far the commonest response, indicating presumably that 'sharing' is what teachers emphasize most in explaining division to children.

Table 4.2   *Children's stories for 12 ÷ 3*

J	There was a boy and he had 12 stones so he shared them out into 3 piles. How many stones were there in each pile?
K	There were 12 dolls. If there were 3 girls how many dolls would each girl get?
L	The father won £12 on the lottery and shared it between his 3 children.
M	Tom had 12 butterflies and he wanted them in sets of 3. How many sets?
N	On a class outing 12 children were going. The head dived (*sic*) 3 children in each car. How many cars did he need?
P	I had 12 chocolates and I put 3 on each plate and I used 4 plates.
Q	One day in class the teacher asked Ben the answer to 12 shared by 3. Ben didn't know and he got an essay.
R	12 ÷ 3 = 4 and the King of Norwich did not know what it meant.

However, some children do successfully interpret the division symbol in terms of Division Structure 2 (the inverse of multiplication). Each of the stories M, N and P in Table 4.2, for example, uses the idea of putting the twelve into groups of three and finding out how many groups. There are, of course, those children for whom division is just something you do in school without any apparent meaning or purpose other than satisfying the teacher. This is demonstrated in stories Q and R. We can infer that the writer of story R and the King of Norwich were in the same position as far as understanding division goes!

Overemphasis on sharing

In our experience, it seems that teachers of young children tend to emphasize the first division structure, equal sharing between, when introducing this operation to young children. This is presumably because we perceive 'sharing' as an everyday concept with which children are familiar. There is a tendency therefore for the words 'shared between', 'shared by' or even just 'share' to be attached very strongly to the symbol, as though this is exclusively what division means. We would argue therefore – just as we argued in Chapter 3 that subtraction is not just 'take away' – that division is not just 'sharing'. In Chapter 3 we saw that the partitioning (take away) structure of subtraction was a limited aspect of less long-term significance than, say, subtraction as comparison or the inverse of addition. Similarly, we should note that the sharing structure of division (Division Structure 1) is a limited view and of less significance in the long term than the inverse of multiplication structure (Division Structure 2).

Consider, for example, a division statement like 6 ÷ 0.25. You can happily press the appropriate keys on your calculator and get the answer 24, but what might this mean in concrete terms? It certainly could not mean '6 cakes shared between 0.25 of a person makes 24 each'! However you might want to calculate 6 ÷ 0.25 if you needed to find out how many articles costing 25p each could be bought for £6. So, in this sense, 6 ÷ 0.25 means 'how many amounts of 0.25 make 6?' In other words, these symbols make meaningful sense in a situation that has the inverse of multiplication structure.

Division in money and measuring contexts

When division is extended into contexts other than just sets of things, such as the money context example given above, both structures may be encountered. But Division Structure 1 makes sense only when the second number is a cardinal number, that is, a positive whole number representing a set of things – normally the number of people receiving a portion or the number of portions being measured out. For example, we might encounter this sharing structure in the context of liquid volume if we have 750 ml of wine to share out into 5 equal portions (750 ÷ 5). Or we might meet it in the context of money if we have £220 to share equally between 4 people (220 ÷ 4).

For Division Structure 2, on the other hand, the second number does not have to be a whole number, as we have seen in the discussion of 6 ÷ 0.25 above. For example, we would encounter this inverse of multiplication structure of division if we needed to find out how many 0.125 litre (125 ml) glasses could be filled from a 2-litre (2000 ml) bottle. Using millilitres, the corresponding division statement is 2000 ÷ 125. Using litres, the corresponding division statement is 2 ÷ 0.125. Likewise, in the context of money, familiar problems such as 'how many articles costing £1.25 each can be bought with £75?' (75 ÷ 1.25) have the structure of division as the inverse of multiplication.

A key feature of Division Structure 2 to note is that the two numbers in the division represent the same kind of thing. See, for example, stories M, N, and P in Table 4.2, which use this structure. The 12 and the 3 both represent numbers of butterflies in story M; they both represent numbers of children in story N; and they both represent numbers of chocolates in story P. So, using this structure you would divide a price by a price, a weight by a weight, a time by a time, and so on.

But division in the sense of 'equal sharing between' (Division Structure 1) will often occur with numbers from two different contexts. We will consider some examples of pairs of contexts in which 12 ÷ 3 might have an application and meaning. For example, putting the 12 into the context of money (£12) and the 3 into the context of weight (3 kg), 12 ÷ 3 would be the division involved when finding the equivalent price per kilogram of a 3 kg pack of some material costing £12. It is as though the 12 pounds of cost are shared equally between the 3 kilograms. The two contexts of distance and time involve division when calculating average speed. For example: What is my average speed if I walk 12 miles in 3 hours? Here it is as though the 12 miles is being shared equally between the 3 hours. And the two contexts of money and time would produce division problems such as calculating your rate of pay if you have earned £12 in 3 hours. In this case the 12 pounds of money are being shared equally between the 3 hours.

Rectangular arrays and division

It will help children to make the connections between the two structures of division we have discussed so far if they are encouraged to associate rectangular arrays with the idea of division, as well as with multiplication. A child could be given, for example, twelve counters and challenged to find different ways of arranging them in a rectangular array. Figure 4.6, showing one such possible arrangement, could then lead to discussion both about how many counters are in each of the three rows across the page and also about how many columns of three there are coming down the page. Hence, looked at one way this array answers the question 'what is twelve shared equally between three?' (Division Structure 1) – the answer is provided by the fact that each of the three rows has 4 counters. Looked at another way it answers the question 'how many threes make twelve?' (Division Structure 2) – with the answer provided by the fact that there are 4 columns of three counters.

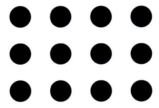

Figure 4.6   *One way of arranging twelve counters in an array*

Division Structure 3: repeated subtraction

The idea of division as the inverse of multiplication leads to a further interpretation. Since one structure of multiplication is repeated addition, it follows that a possible structure for division is *repeated subtraction*. In this interpretation 12 ÷ 3 might be thought of as: 'How many times can I take three away from twelve until there is nothing left?' This is clearly very similar to the question: 'How many threes in twelve?' So even though we give this as a different structure it is really just another way of thinking about grouping (Division Structure 2), and it seems likely that there will not be much difficulty in learning to connect the same symbols with both questions. The number line picture helps to connect these ideas together. In Figure 4.7,

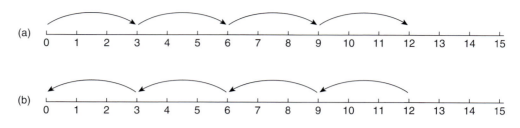

Figure 4.7 *Dividing 12 by 3 on a number line*

12 ÷ 3 is experienced in two different ways: (a) using a procedure based on the idea of the inverse of multiplication, we can start at zero and move forward in steps of three until twelve is reached – this answers the question 'how many threes make twelve?'; or (b) using a procedure that incorporates the idea of repeated subtraction, we could start at twelve and move down in steps of three until zero is reached. Both of these experiences on the number line are important components of the network of connections for division.

It is important that teachers give children experience of both ideas: building up to the target of twelve in threes and taking away threes from twelve until nothing is left. This is because, later on in the primary years, when children come to do calculations involving division, particularly by mental and informal methods, these two ideas are often the basis for the most effective strategies.

For example, to calculate 616 ÷ 28, a common strategy that many children in upper primary classes are taught is to keep adding groups of 28 until they reach the target of 616:

$$
\begin{array}{rcr}
10 \text{ lots of } 28 & = & 280 \\
10 \text{ lots of } 28 & = & \underline{280} \\
& & 560 \\
1 \text{ lot of } 28 & = & \underline{28} \\
& & 588 \\
1 \text{ lot of } 28 & = & \underline{28} \\
& & 616 \\
\end{array}
$$

So 616 ÷ 28 = 10 + 10 + 1 + 1 = 22.

But an alternative approach is to start with the 616 and to subtract groups of 28, until there's nothing left, as follows:

$$
\begin{array}{rcl}
 & & 616 \\
10 \text{ lots of } 28 & = & \underline{280} \\
 & & 336 \\
10 \text{ lots of } 28 & = & \underline{280} \\
 & & 56 \\
2 \text{ lots of } 28 & = & \underline{56} \\
 & & 0
\end{array}
$$

Altogether we have subtracted 10 + 10 + 2 = 22 lots of 28. So 616 ÷ 28 = 22.

Division Structure 4: ratio

A more difficult aspect of division arises from the inverse of the scaling structure of multiplication. This is the *ratio* structure of division. In this structure, 12 ÷ 3 might be thought of as meaning something like: 'How many times bigger than three is twelve?' This is using division to make a *comparison* between two quantities. If, for example, A earns £12 an hour and B earns £3 an hour, there are, in fact, two ways of comparing their earnings. We could, on the one hand, use the *comparison* structure of *subtraction* – as discussed in Chapter 3 – and conclude that A earns £9 more than B (or B earns £9 less than A). In this way we would be considering the *difference* between the two quantities. On the other hand, we could consider the *ratio*, using this structure of *division*, to conclude that A earns *four times as much as* B – because 12 ÷ 3 = 4.

Which of these two ways of making the comparison (difference or ratio) should be used will depend on the context, although it is often a matter of subjective judgement. It is interesting to note, for example, that there was a time when teams in the English Football League table with the same number of points were ranked according to goal ratio. So a team with 12 goals for and 6 against would be ranked above a team with 17 goals for and 10 against, since the goal ratio of the first team is 2 (that is, 12 ÷ 6), whereas that of the second team is only 1.7 (that is, 17 ÷ 10). Nowadays goal difference is used, so that the two teams would be ranked in the reverse order since a goal difference of 7 is better than a goal difference of 6. Teachers will be familiar with this question as it applies to salary increases. A pay award in which all members get the same flat-rate increase is seen by some as being fair because it maintains the existing *differences* in salaries, but is seen by others as being unfair because it does not preserve the existing *ratios* between salaries. The latter would favour a pay award in which all get the same percentage increase because this preserves the existing ratios. This is a nice example of the way in which some mathematical transformations (the salary increases) preserve some equivalences and destroy others (that is, the existing salary differences or salary ratios).

Experiences of sharing that do not correspond to division

Children begin to understand and to use the idea of 'sharing' in a social context, such as sharing toys and sharing sweets, from about the age of 3 – albeit, at times, somewhat reluctantly. Willingness to take turns and to share are seen by parents and teachers as key social skills for development around this age. As they get older children will have many more experiences of sharing, but most of them are nothing like the process we expect them to do when we give them, say, 12 ÷ 3. Some of the stories that children write for 12 ÷ 3 suggest that we might be deceiving ourselves in thinking that sharing, in the way intended when doing division in school, is an experience with which children are very familiar. We can identify at least four examples of sharing experiences that are not actually division in the mathematical sense. These are illustrated by the stories in Table 4.3.

Table 4.3   *Stories for 12 ÷ 3 showing misunderstanding of sharing*

S	Tim had 12 cakes he shared them out with 3 of his friends.
T	The girl had 12 pens and her friends borrowed 3. Her other 2 friends had 1 each. How many did she have left?
U	The boy had 12 sweets and he ate one and gave 2 away to his friends. How many left?
V	I had 12 cars. I shared 3 of them.
W	One boy had 12 conkers the other had 3 conkers. When they shared the conkers they had equal amounts and they threw the remainder conker away.

First, story S reminds us that it is most unlikely that any children would share their twelve cakes between three friends and not have any for themselves. The child's familiarity with the experience of *sharing with* rather than *sharing between* would seem to be the reason for the misunderstanding shown in this story. Parents and teachers share things out *between* children and seem happy to exclude themselves, but children share *with* their friends. Teachers should be alert to the subtle difficulties involved in mastering the use of prepositions such as 'between' and 'with' in the context of mathematical statements and language patterns.

Second, sharing *equally* is a peculiarly mathematical process, not always reflected in the sharing experiences of everyday life. This is shown in story T in Table 4.3 and is certainly an example of sharing. It is also an example of sharing between three. But it is not 'sharing *equally* between three', which is the language that must be connected with the symbols in the equal sharing structure of division.

Third, children experience sharing when they are told to share their possessions with another child. For example, the child might have twelve items and agree to share three of them. In story U this is what the child with twelve sweets is doing: disposing of three of them! This invalid interpretation of division is no doubt prompted by the unhelpful language pattern 'twelve share three'. Story V shows most clearly the kind of misunderstanding that can arise from this sloppy use of mathematical language. Again, we emphasize that the correct language pattern that children need for the equal sharing structure is 'twelve shared equally between three'.

Finally, two children with unequal numbers of possessions might sometimes agree to share them by a process of pooling their resources. This is another way in which children understand sharing that is sometimes wrongly associated with division. This misunderstanding occurs in story W in Table 4.3.

PAUSE TO REFLECT   The great divide

We have argued in this chapter that children do not often experience division in their everyday experience of sharing, because this experience is rarely 'equal sharing between'? What do you think? Consider all the occasions in the everyday life of a 7-year-old when they might engage in sharing. How many of these are actually 'equal sharing between'? On the other hand, we would argue that children have lots of experiences of being put into groups of 2, groups of 3, or groups of 4, and so on; or of dividing up a collection of objects into groups of a given number. Can you think of a number of situations where this might be the case? Do you agree with us that children should find 'How many groups of 3 in 12?' to be a more familiar and meaningful experience of 12 ÷ 3 than 'Share 12 equally between 3 people, how many each?' If this is the case why is it that, for example, division by 3 is so strongly associated with sharing between 3?

The language of division

So, in summary, we are suggesting that 'sharing equally between' is actually a more sophisticated and abstract idea than we might imagine, and that it is not in the long term the most important structure of division. This then raises the question of the language that we as teachers use when we write the symbol. Now, of course, in real situations division is sometimes 'sharing equally between'. When this is the actual concrete situation being attended to, then it is appropriate to use this language. However, we must take note of the distinction between 'sharing equally between' and the other possible interpretations of sharing described above that are not what we want to connect with division. Children will need specific help in getting this complex pattern of language established: 'twelve shared equally between three is four each'.

But again there are two levels of language here, as was the case with subtraction. First there is the formal language that goes with the concept, such as 'twelve divided by three'. But then there is the language appropriate to the physical situation. This might be 'twelve shared equally between three' (Division Structure 1), but it might equally well be 'twelve shared into groups of three' (Division Structure 2), depending on what we are actually doing with the counters on the table in front of us. So, in general terms, we will say 'twelve divided by three' and talk about the operation of 'division' and the process of 'dividing one number by another'. But in specific situations we will happily use the informal language appropriate to what we are actually doing in concrete terms.

Conclusion

The conclusion we come to then is that understanding of multiplication and division once again involves the building up of complex networks of connections. The child has to make connections between the symbols, the language, both formal and informal, and the pictures associated with the operations, particularly rectangular arrays, but also steps up and down the number line. And the language and symbols have to be connected further with the surprising variety of concrete situations, the range of contexts and the combinations of contexts in which multiplication and division arise.

RESEARCH FOCUS   Division

Before you read this section, write down a story in a real-life context that corresponds to '15 ÷ 3'.

   A theme that is emerging in this book is the need to take into account children's experiences and perspectives when endeavouring to develop their mathematical understanding. As we have discussed in this chapter, this is particularly the case with the concept of 'sharing'. When adults think of division they tend to think of dividing a quantity or a number of items, into equal parts, or sharing equally between a number of people. We have suggested above that teachers should be alert to the fact that this is not necessarily the way children will interpret sharing (likewise, in our experience, some adults!). Imagine, for example, that you are with two friends and you happen to have six chocolate peppermint creams: might there be a temptation to give them each one, eat one yourself and quietly keep three 'for later'? This tendency for children to interpret sharing in a variety of ways that suit their purposes is confirmed by the research of Desforges and Desforges (1980). To develop the idea of 'sharing equally between' they asked thirty 4–6-year-olds to share mints between a number of dolls in a way that was 'fair'. They found that by making the child the distributor of the items rather than one of the recipients in the sharing process the children were able to apply the correct mathematical concept of division. The 6-year-olds had no difficulty in completing the task successfully and many of the younger children were able to do so as well.

Margaret Brown's (1981) research revealed – over 30 years ago – that 11-year-olds appeared to find it relatively easy to connect the symbol for division with both the 'equal sharing between' structure and the inverse of multiplication or 'grouping' structure. Before we reveal her further results, have a look at the story for '15 ÷ 3' that we asked you to write down at the start of this section. Did you come up with a sharing story? Something about 15 items or units being shared equally between 3 individuals? Or did you come up with a grouping story? Something about 15 items or units being put into groups of 3 and finding the number of groups? Interestingly, Brown observed that ten times as many 11-year-olds presented a sharing situation rather than a grouping one when asked to write a story for a division like this. When a division statement was met in symbols and was to be interpreted as a concrete situation, the idea of division as sharing was found to be dominant.

More recently, Dina Tirosh, Pessia Tsamir and Sara Hershkovitz (2008) observed a teachers' professional development group in Israel. In much the same manner as Margaret Brown's 11-year-olds, the 12 teachers in the group were presented with the task of writing word problems for a range of number statements, including '2 ÷ 16' and '5 ÷ 0.25'. One of the teachers, Dan, wrote the following suggestion on the board for 2 ÷ 16:

> *Sixteen friends bought 2 kilograms of cheese. If the cheese was equally shared, how much did each get?* (p. 62)

What do you think of this story? Reading Dan's response to the second task might give you some insight into his choice of the above problem. He explained that he could not write a 'sharing' problem for 5 ÷ 0.25 as '0.25 is not a whole number'. So, instead, his response for 5 ÷ 0.25 was:

> *Peanuts are packed so that there are 0.25 kilograms in a box. How many boxes can be filled with 5 kilograms of peanuts?* (p. 62)

Dina and her colleagues explain that, when asked to divide, people tend to share rather than group. It is likely that this reflects the way that the language of sharing is emphasized in learning division in schools. This can result in a number of misconceptions, such as: (a) you can only divide by a whole number; and (b) you must always divide a smaller number into a bigger one.

Some activities to use with children

As in the previous chapters, the suggestions here are examples of the kinds of activities that aim to develop understanding. In this case the focus is on establishing the connections between the language, pictures, concrete situations and symbols of multiplication and division. Clearly, these kinds of activities would have to be supplemented, at an appropriate stage, by others that focus on computational skills.

ACTIVITY 4.1   Sharing Equally Between

3–4	4–5	5–6	6–7	7–8
☐	☐			

Objective

To provide younger children with experience of 'sharing between' that will form the basis for later development of the concepts of division.

Materials

Toys such as dolls and teddies and objects that can be shared equally between them.

Method

In addition to all the emphasis on sharing toys and other resources *with* their friends, ensure that children in the Foundation Stage get some experience of sharing *between*. This is best done in role play with toys. For example, on the theme of the Goldilocks story, give the child three toy bears and a suitable number of toy cakes. Tell them that Goldilocks has eaten all their soup so we are going to give them some cakes to eat. And it's not fair if one bear gets more than the others. Ask the child to sit the bears around a table and then to share the cakes between the three bears, so they each get the same number of cakes. Teach them the process of 'one for you, and one for you ...' and stress the key phrases, 'sharing between' and 'the same number'.

ACTIVITY 4.2   Home-based Multiplication

3–4	4–5	5–6	6–7	7–8
		☐	☐	

Objective

To connect the language and structure of multiplication as repeated addition with children's lives at home.

Materials

Give the children the following to complete.
   At John's house he has:

- 6 forks and each one has 3 prongs
- 4 stools and each one has 3 legs
- 2 children and each one has 10 toes.

Write down what you have at your house.

At my house we have:

- .... and each one has ....
- .... and each one has ....
- .... and each one has ....

Method

Challenge the children to find three different examples from their home following the same pattern as the given examples. Use the children's examples at school to set up multiplication statements for discussion with the class.

 ACTIVITY 4.3   Swaps (Multiply, Divide)

3–4	4–5	5–6	6–7	7–8
				□

Objective

To develop connections between language, symbols, concrete experience and pictures, for the concepts of multiplication and division.

Materials and method

The same as Activity 3.5, but using stories with multiplication and division examples. For example, a possible starting point might be the story: 'How many £16 chairs can my Mum buy with £48?'; this could then be swapped for coins, symbols, a number line drawing and a drawing of a rectangular array (three rows of 16 pound coins).

 ACTIVITY 4.4   Sentences (Multiply, Divide)

3–4	4–5	5–6	6–7	7–8
				□

Objective

To develop language patterns for multiplication and division.

Materials

Several sets of strips of card with the following words or phrases written on them: *divided by, multiplied by, times, shared equally between, makes, is, equals, sets, of, altogether, each*; several sets of cards with appropriate numerals written on them; counting materials; a number line.

(Continued)

(Continued)

Method

As in Activity 3.6, a small group of children is given three numbers and challenged to use the cards to make up as many different sentences as they can that use these three numbers. Figure 4.8 shows some examples of what might be achieved with the numbers 3, 4 and 12.

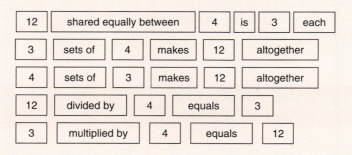

Figure 4.8   *Sentences for 3, 4 and 12*

⊠⊠		3–4	4–5	5–6	6–7	7–8
⊠⊠⊠	**ACTIVITY 4.5 Stories (Multiply, Divide)**					
⊠⊠						□

Objective

To help children to connect the symbols for multiplication and division with a wide range of situations and language.

Method

Give children some multiplication and division statements (such as 8×3 and $15 \div 5$) and ask them to write stories to go with them. This is handled in the same way as Activity 3.4. Encourage children to use the different models and contexts for multiplication and division, by giving the beginnings of some stories.

For example, children could be asked to write a story for 8×3 beginning 'Chocolates are 8p each …'. Or they could write a story for $15 \div 5$ beginning 'Meg had £15 to spend on CDs …'.

Another approach is to specify contexts, for example by asking children to write a story for 8×3 that is about a farmer who sells potatoes; or a story about $15 \div 5$ that is about a person who walks for 15 miles.

ACTIVITY 4.6   I Have, Who Has? (Multiply/Divide Stories)

3–4	4–5	5–6	6–7	7–8
				□

Objective

To experience all the different structures for multiplication and division and to practise the range of language.

Materials

Prepare a set of 16 cards with questions on one side and the corresponding answers on the other side, using the same cyclic scheme as explained in Activity 2.4 and Activity 3.7, with the question on one card answered on the reverse side of the next. In this activity use as questions a series of statements or stories covering a wide range of situations with different structures and language associated with multiplication and division. Again, ensure that there are no duplicate answers. Here are some suggestions, with the corresponding answers in brackets after each one:

1   Four times three. (4×3)
2   How much for 4 apples at 5p each? (5×4)
3   Debbie shared 12p between 4 people. How much each? ($12 \div 4$)
4   How many sets of 3 make a set of 12? ($12 \div 3$)
5   20 divided by 4. ($20 \div 4$)
6   20 multiplied by 4. (20×4)
7   John has 4 sets of 12 stamps. How many altogether? (12×4)
8   How many times longer than 3 cm is 15 cm? ($15 \div 3$)
9   How many times can 5p be taken from 15p until there's nothing left? ($15 \div 5$)
10   4 rows of 15 seats. (15×4)
11   John is 12 years old. His Mum is 3 times as old as he is. How old is John's Mum? (12×3)
12   How many 5p coins make 20p? ($20 \div 5$)
13   20 add 20 add 20. (20×3)
14   Three fives. (5×3)
15   Half of 20. ($20 \div 2$)
16   Two people shared 12 sweets. How many each? ($12 \div 2$)

Method

The game is played as in Activities 2.4 and 3.7.

Summary of key ideas

1   One category of situations to which the language and symbols of multiplication can be connected is repeated addition (Multiplication Structure 1). This structure is most clearly seen in the context of sets (so many sets of so many), but extends naturally to repeated steps along the number line and to measuring contexts.

2   Multiplication (like addition) is commutative. This means that the order of two numbers in a product (or a sum) makes no difference to the result. For example, $3 \times 15 = 15 \times 3$ (just as $3 + 15 = 15 + 3$).

3   The commutative property of multiplication is most clearly seen in a rectangular array. This image, together with the associated language, is an important component in the network of connections for understanding multiplication and division.

4   Strictly speaking, in the repeated addition structure 9×3 means 'three sets of nine'. But once commutativity is established both 9×3 and 3×9 can be connected with either 'three sets of nine' or 'nine sets of three'.

5   Another category of situations to which the language and symbols of multiplication can be connected is scaling (Multiplication Structure 2).

6   The first experience of scaling is doubling. This leads on to relationships such as 'twice as many', 'three times as much' and 'ten times as heavy'.

7   Four categories of situations to which the language and symbols of division can be connected are equal sharing between (Division Structure 1), inverse of multiplication, also called grouping (Division Structure 2), repeated subtraction (Division Structure 3), and ratio (Division Structure 4).

8   Teachers tend to overemphasize sharing in division. In the long run the most important structures of division are the inverse of multiplication and ratio.

9   Ratio and difference are two ways of comparing quantities, using division and subtraction respectively.

10 Children have many other experiences of sharing that do not correspond to the equal sharing structure of division.

11 Multiplication and division often arise in situations involving two different contexts, such as money and weight, or distance and time.

Suggestions for further reading

Julia Anghileri has written extensively on the development of children's understanding of multiplication and division. In a chapter entitled 'Uses of counting in multiplication and division', in Thompson (2008), she explores young children's early experiences of these two operations. In a chapter entitled 'Making sense of symbols' in Anghileri (1995) she considers the meaning of multiplication and division and methods of teaching them to avoid later confusion. Anghileri (2006) also includes an interesting chapter on multiplication and division, combining the work of researchers with her personal knowledge of schooling.

Chapter 8 of Haylock (2010) considers in detail the structures and associated language of multiplication and division.

We would refer the reader again to Nunes and Bryant (1996): Chapter 7 of this research into children's understanding of mathematics deals with multiplication and division structures.

Wright et al. (2006) provide strategies for assessing children's understanding of multiplication and division, and suggestions on how to develop their understanding of these operations.

CHAPTER 5

UNDERSTANDING THE PRINCIPLES OF ARITHMETIC

A SILLY QUESTION

Tom, aged 6, was learning to subtract a 2-digit number from 100. One of the authors (D) asked Tom what was 100 take away 50?

T. That's easy. 50.
D. How do you know that?
T. 50 and 50 is a hundred. Ask me a hard one.
D. OK, what's 100 take away 49?
T. Are you sure you want to ask me that?
D. Why?
T. Because it's easy as well. 51.
D. How did you know that?
T. Because 100 take away 50 is 50. So 49 is 51.
D. OK, so 100 take away 49 is 51. What's 100 take away 51?
T. 49, silly!

- What strategy does Tom use in connecting the subtraction of 49 to the subtraction of 50?
- What is the principle that Tom has grasped that makes the final question so easy for him?

In this chapter

In this chapter we make explicit some of the most fundamental principles of arithmetic and show how these underpin the different ways we carry out calculations. Tom's confidence with calculation illustrates how important is our grasp of such principles. Two of the key ideas discussed in this chapter lie behind Tom's reasoning in the conversation above: compensation and the principle of complements. In Chapter 4 we identified the important commutative principles of addition and multiplication and showed how a grasp of these is essential in understanding the operations. In this chapter we aim to strengthen the teacher's own understanding of the early years of learning to calculate by exploring a number of such fundamental ideas. For the sake of completeness, in covering these principles in relation to all four operations – addition, subtraction, multiplication and division – we must inevitably go a little beyond the mathematics taught in the age range on which this book focuses. Our conviction is that, by engaging with the rather formal but fundamental mathematical ideas in this chapter, teachers will be become more alert to the significance of some of the mathematical experiences they might provide for young children.

Commutativity

The commutative properties of addition and multiplication, which we discussed in Chapter 4, are expressed in general terms as follows:

for any two numbers, a and b,
$a + b = b + a$ (commutativity of addition)
$a \times b = b \times a$ (commutativity of multiplication)

As we have seen in Chapter 4, these mean that in practice the order in which you write down the two numbers in a sum or a product makes no difference to the result. These fundamental principles of commutativity are important in terms of understanding the structure of the operations of addition and multiplication, but they also make certain calculations more accessible. For example, teachers of young children usually teach them that a good strategy for adding two numbers is to start with the larger number. For example, given $5 + 88$ children would learn to change this to $88 + 5$, so that they can start with the 88 and add on 5. This is much easier to conceptualize than to imagine starting with the 5 and adding on 88. It is also much easier to perform practically by counting on with your fingers, since it is rather difficult to get hold of 88 fingers! Likewise, if we needed to find the value of 5 × 46 some might find it easier to think of it as '46 fives' rather than '5 forty-sixes', because 2 fives make 10 and so 46 fives is equivalent to 23 tens (= 230).

We should note, however, that the operations of subtraction and division are *not* commutative. In general, for any two numbers a and b, $a - b$ does not equal $b - a$, and $a ÷ b$ does not equal $b ÷ a$. (We say 'in general' because these are equal if a and b happen to be the same number!) These are clearly important and fundamental principles that children must understand and get into their mental structures for manipulating numbers. When they start doing subtraction calculations with larger numbers (for example, 243 − 125) they will have to realize that you cannot deal with the 'three subtract five' in the units position simply by regarding it as being the same as 'five subtract three'. With division, they should learn eventually, for example, that it makes a big difference whether you enter 28 ÷ 4 on a calculator or 4 ÷ 28.

The principle of complements

Subtraction and division do satisfy, however, what we call the *principle of complements*. We have already introduced the idea of a complement of a set in Chapter 3, as one of the important subtraction structures – in Figure 3.6, for example, with a total set of 12 counters, subsets of 3 and 9 are complements of each other. We shall now refer to numbers such as 3 and 9 that sum to 12 as complements of each other with respect to 12, or twelve-complements.

The principle of complements in subtraction

The concept of complements is an important one underpinning many calculations. Young children usually first learn about complements with respect to 10. These are pairs of numbers that add up to 10, such as 1 and 9, 6 and 4. We will see in Chapter 6 how important ten-complements and hundred-complements are in calculations. An obvious area where knowing about these complements is important is in handling practical calculations with coins, where you often need to know what to add to make a sum of money up to the next ten or hundred. Similarly, we use sixty-complements (such as 25 and 35) in telling the time; for example, switching freely between 35 minutes after an hour and 25 minutes to the next hour.

> I get my 5-year-olds to use ten-complements by putting my hands behind my back and asking questions like, 'I've got four fingers folded down, how many am I holding up?' They work it out on their own fingers, and then I show them my hands and we count the fingers to see if they're right.

If these children find out that there are 6 fingers held up when 4 are folded down, they should also learn that there are 4 held up when 6 are folded down. The correspondence between these two results is what we call the *principle of complements*. In terms of subtraction, in general, this principle of complements is expressed as follows:

> for three numbers, *a*, *b* and *c*,
> if $c - a = b$, then $c - b = a$.
> *a* and *b* are complements of each other with respect to *c*.

For example, knowing that $200 - 37$ is 163, we could deduce by this principle that $200 - 163$ is 37. This is because 163 and 37 are complements with respect to 200. In the dialogue with Tom at the head of this chapter, the 6-year-old shows a clear grasp of this principle in immediately connecting $100 - 51 = 49$ with $100 - 49 = 51$. In this case 49 and 51 are complements with respect to 100.

Table 5.1 contains some examples of how this works. It is important that teachers of young children recognize the significance of a simple principle like this and take opportunities to exploit it specifically in question-and-answer sessions with children.

Table 5.1   *Examples showing the principle of complements for subtraction*

$10 - 4 = 6$ and $10 - 6 = 4$	4 and 6 are ten-complements
$60 - 48 = 12$ and $60 - 12 = 48$	48 and 12 are sixty-complements
$100 - 24 = 76$ and $100 - 76 = 24$	24 and 76 are hundred-complements
$200 - 147 = 53$ and $200 - 53 = 147$	147 and 53 are 200-complements

The principle of complements in division

There is a similar pattern of relationships for division, which is explored here briefly for completeness and to deepen the reader's awareness of the underlying patterns in numbers and number operations. A number that divides exactly into another number is called a *factor*. So, for example, 3 is a factor of 12 and 4 is also a factor of 12. But these two factors (3 and 4) are what might be called *complementary factors*, because $12 \div 4$ is 3 and $12 \div 3$ is 4. Table 5.2 provides a number of examples of what we are referring to here.

Table 5.2   *Examples showing the principle of complements for division*

$12 \div 4 = 3$ and $12 \div 3 = 4$	3 and 4 are complementary factors of 12
$28 \div 4 = 7$ and $28 \div 7 = 4$	7 and 4 are complementary factors of 28
$90 \div 5 = 18$ and $90 \div 18 = 5$	18 and 5 are complementary factors of 90
$17 \div 1 = 17$ and $17 \div 17 = 1$	17 and 1 are complementary factors of 17

Significantly, this principle makes a connection between the equal sharing and the inverse of multiplication structures of division, which were discussed in Chapter 4, as illustrated below.

> I asked 7-year-old Jack to share out twelve counters equally between three. He sorted the counters into three equal piles and said, 'that's four each'. That was 12 ÷ 3 = 4, using equal sharing. Then I asked him how many sets of four can you make from twelve counters? Looking at what he had done he said, 'I just did that – three.' Now he was doing 12 ÷ 4 = 3, using inverse of multiplication! So, the same arrangement of counters gave him both 12 ÷ 3 = 4 and 12 ÷ 4 = 3, but using the two different structures of division.

In terms of division, in general, the principle of complements is therefore expressed as follows:

> for three numbers, *a*, *b* and *c*,
> if *c* ÷ *a* = *b*, then *c* ÷ *b* = *a*.
> *a* and *b* are complementary factors of *c*.

Compensation

In the dialogue at the head of this chapter Tom also used a principle known as *compensation* in his successful calculation of 100 − 49 by making the connection with 100 − 50. In subtracting 49, he first subtracts 50 and then compensates for the fact that he has taken away one more than required. This kind of genuine mathematical thinking is so much more important – and more impressive – than the rote memorization of rules and procedures, because it is clearly rooted in the understanding of principles.

The principle of compensation in the addition of two numbers is illustrated in Figure 5.1. Starting at the number *p*, you can add a little more than is required, but then compensate by subtracting the extra bit that was added on. The reason for doing this would be that the first step can make the calculation more friendly. For example,

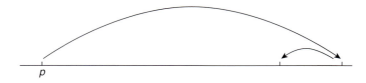

p

Figure 5.1   *Compensation in addition*

to find 26 + 18: starting at 26, add 20 (which is 2 more than required) to get to 46, then compensate by subtracting the extra 2, giving the result 44.

The principle of compensation in subtraction is illustrated in Figure 5.2. Starting at the number p, you can subtract a little more than is required, but then compensate by adding back again the extra bit that was subtracted. Again, the purpose would be to make the mental calculation easier. For example, to calculate 47 – 19, start by subtracting 20 (1 more than needed) to get to 27, and then add back on the extra 1, to get the result 28.

Figure 5.2   *Compensation in subtraction*

Associativity

Complements are also often used in mental calculation of simple additions. For example, to add 7 to 28, many of us start by adding 2 (the ten-complement of 8) to get to 30, and then we add the remaining 5. What we have done here is to transform 28 + (2 + 5) into (28 + 2) + 5.

The brackets mean 'do this bit first'. So, 28 + (2 + 5) is 28 + 7; and (28 + 2) + 5 is 30 + 5. We used this procedure because 30 + 5 is an easier addition than 28 + 7. This is, incidentally, another example where a transformation is applied to a mathematical situation and an equivalence emerges – one of the themes we discussed in Chapter 1.

We wish now to make explicit the mathematical principle behind this transformation. This is the principle of *associativity*, which, like commutativity, applies to addition and multiplication but not to subtraction and division.

Associativity of addition

In relation to the example above, the principle asserts that the 2 can be 'associated' with either the 28 on the left or the 5 on the right and it makes no difference to the answer: 28 + (2 + 5) = (28 + 2) + 5. It is this principle that we assume whenever we teach children to break up a number being added to do an addition in two (or more) steps. For example, a younger child calculating 8 + 6 by adding on first 2 and then 4 is breaking the 6 up into 2 + 4 and then transforming 8 + (2 + 4) into (8 + 2) + 4. Similarly, an older child calculating 34 + 25 might split the 25 mentally into 20 + 5 and then transform 34 + (20 + 5) into (34 + 20) + 5.

The associative principle for addition is expressed in general terms as follows:

for any numbers a, b and c,
$$a + (b + c) = (a + b) + c$$

Readers should convince themselves that the associative principle does not apply to subtraction. For example, $10 - (5 - 3)$ is *not* equal to $(10 - 5) - 3$. Remember that the brackets are an instruction to do that bit first.

For addition, this principle of associativity, like commutativity, is not difficult to grasp. As Figure 5.3 demonstrates, it is really quite apparent that, say, 'a 3-rod' on one side combined with 'a 7-rod and a 4-rod' on the other side gives you the same arrangement of rods as 'a 3-rod and a 7-rod' on one side and 'a 4-rod' on the other. Figure 5.3 also shows that the principle allows us to write $3 + 7 + 4$ without specifying which two of the three numbers have to be added first. When used along with the principle of commutativity, associativity allows you to write a string of numbers to be added without brackets and to combine them in any order you like. The fact that most children pick up this short cut fairly easily supports the suggestion that the principles of commutativity and associativity in addition are fairly self-evident.

Figure 5.3   *The principle of associativity shown with rods*

Associativity of multiplication

The same pattern of associativity seen in addition also applies to multiplication. For example, $(3 \times 4) \times 5$ gives the same result as $3 \times (4 \times 5)$. For multiplication, the principle of associativity is expressed generally as follows:

for any numbers a, b and c,
$$a \times (b \times c) = (a \times b) \times c$$

Like the principle of commutativity, associativity is by no means an obvious principle when it comes to multiplication. It would seem not to be self-evident or inevitable that $(3 \times 4) \times 5$ should give the same answer as $3 \times (4 \times 5)$. Figure 5.4 provides a concrete embodiment of the principle which can be used to show why these are equal. The rectangular block in Figure 5.4(a) is made up of 5 layers each of which is a 3×4

 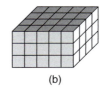

(a)   (b)

Figure 5.4   *Showing associativity in multiplication: (a) (3 × 4) × 5; (b) 3 × (4 × 5)*

rectangle of cubes. This represents (3 × 4) × 5. But the rectangular block in Figure 5.4(b) is made up of 3 layers each of which is a 4 × 5 rectangle of cubes. This represents 3 × (4 × 5). Clearly the two blocks have the same number of cubes – because they are actually the same block but standing with a different face uppermost.

As with addition, once established, the principle of associativity for multiplication combined with commutativity allows you to write a string of numbers to be multiplied without brackets and to combine them in any order you like. This is a useful trick. For example, 5 × 7 × 4 is probably easier if transformed into 5 × 4 × 7 (using commutativity to change the order) and then (by choosing to associate the 4 with the 5 rather than the 7) to 20 × 7.

Readers should convince themselves that the associative principle does not apply to division. For example, 24 ÷ (6 ÷ 2) is not equal to (24 ÷ 6) ÷ 2.

Identities

Zero and one

Zero (0) and one (1) are arguably the two most important numbers in the whole number system. Because of its special properties in relation to addition, zero is sometimes referred to as the *additive identity*. This refers to the observation that if you add zero to any number the result is identical to what you had to start with. 'Add 0' means 'do nothing'. The same thing applies to subtracting zero, of course. Similarly, the number one (1) is sometimes referred to as the *multiplicative identity*, because multiplying by 1 leaves a number unchanged. So, 'multiply by 1' also means 'do nothing'. And, of course, the same is true of dividing by 1. For example, 7 ÷ 1 = 7. Because these two identities are the foundation on which all numbers are built it is particularly important to learn their properties. In summary these are the four basic properties of 0 and 1 acting as identities, expressed as generalizations, for any number a:

$$a + 0 = a$$
$$a - 0 = a$$
$$a \times 1 = a$$
$$a \div 1 = a$$

Multiplication and division with zero

Zero also has some tricky properties in relation to multiplication and division that take a little thought. Explaining $7 \times 0 = 0$ and $0 \times 7 = 0$ is not too difficult – thinking of these as 'seven sets of zero items' or 'zero sets of seven items', using the repeated addition structure of multiplication, is straightforward enough. But children do need to think these through and discuss them, otherwise they will wrongly apply the additive-identity principle to multiplication, giving, for example, the answer 7 for 7×0. This error arises from applying the (incorrect) assumption that 'multiply by 0' means 'do nothing'.

Divisions involving zero are rather more puzzling. What do you make of $0 \div 7$ and $7 \div 0$? The first can be understood using the equal-sharing structure of division: a set of zero items shared between seven people results in each person getting zero items. So $0 \div 7 = 0$. However, $7 \div 0$ makes no sense in terms of equal sharing – you cannot envisage sharing 7 items between no people! However, we can interpret it as 'how many sets of zero items make a total of seven items?' Well, you can go on accumulating sets of zero items as long as you like and you will never reach a total of seven. For example, we have put two thousand sets of zero elephants inside these brackets: [ ] – and we're still nowhere near to getting seven elephants! The conclusion of this line of reasoning is that you just cannot do $7 \div 0$. It is a calculation without an answer. Mathematicians say that division by zero is not allowed. So does any calculator: try it and see. (You may have heard somewhere that $7 \div 0$ is equal to infinity – there is a branch of number theory that uses that kind of language, but please do not think that there is a real number called 'infinity'.) So, in summary, for any number a, the following generalizations can be made for multiplications and divisions involving zero:

$$a \times 0 = 0$$
$$0 \times a = 0$$
$$0 \div a = 0 \text{ (provided } a \text{ is not zero)}$$
$$a \div 0 \text{ cannot be done}$$

The concept of an identity is encountered more widely in mathematics than just in number operations. For example, a rotation of an object through an angle of 0° leaves it unchanged; and an enlargement of a picture by a scale factor of one leaves it unchanged. These are examples of identity transformations.

Inverses

Finally, in our review of some fundamental properties of number operations we summarize the idea of *inverses*. In general, most mathematical operations have an inverse operation. An inverse operation 'undoes' or reverses the effect of the first operation.

We asked some of our teachers for examples of operations or actions that young children might encounter where one undoes the effect of another. Their responses show that the idea of inverse operations is very basic to our experience:

- Going up and coming down some stairs.
- Standing up and sitting down.
- So many steps forward and then the same number of steps back.
- Turning left and turning right.
- Moving clockwise and moving anticlockwise.

More advanced mathematical examples might include finding the square root of a number (for example, 6 is the square root of 36), which is the inverse operation of finding the square (36 is the square of 6). Or, scaling a diagram by a factor of 3 (enlarging it) is the inverse of scaling it by a factor of one-third (reducing it).

Applied to the four basic operations with numbers, we have already seen (in Chapters 2 and 3) that addition and subtraction are inverses. So, for example, 'subtracting 5' undoes the effect of 'adding 5'. We shall see in Chapter 6 that this inverse relationship is reinforced by movements on the number line and on the hundred square. For example, on a number line, adding 5 is modelled by moving 5 steps to the right; and subtracting 5 is the reverse process, five steps to the left. Similarly, on a hundred square, adding 24 is achieved by 2 steps down and 4 along; and subtracting 24 is the reverse process, 2 steps up and 4 back.

In Chapters 2 and 4 we described the operations of multiplication and division as inverses. So, for example, 'divide by 2' undoes the effect of 'multiply by 2'. In other words, halving is the inverse of doubling.

Table 5.3 provides some examples of inverse relationships in addition and subtraction and in multiplication and division. At appropriate points in their learning about these operations, we would recommend that children discuss and articulate the pattern in examples such as those shown here, so that the inverse relationships are identified explicitly.

Table 5.3   *Examples of inverse operations*

$3 + 4 = 7$	$7 - 4 = 3$	subtracting 4 is the inverse of adding 4
$15 - 8 = 7$	$7 + 8 = 15$	adding 8 is the inverse of subtracting 8
$57 + 24 = 81$	$81 - 24 = 57$	subtracting 24 is the inverse of adding 24
$3 \times 4 = 12$	$12 \div 4 = 3$	dividing by 4 is the inverse of multiplying by 4
$56 \div 7 = 8$	$8 \times 7 = 56$	multiplying by 7 is the inverse of dividing by 7
$23 \times 5 = 115$	$115 \div 5 = 23$	dividing by 5 is the inverse of multiplying by 5

In summary, we can generalize the principles illustrated in Table 5.3 as follows:

for any numbers a, b and c,

if $a + b = c$ then $c - b = a$ (subtraction is the inverse of addition)

if $a - b = c$ then $c + b = a$ (addition is the inverse of subtraction)

if $a \times b = c$ then $c \div b = a$ (division is the inverse of multiplication)

if $a \times b = c$ then $c \div b = a$ (multiplication is the inverse of division)

PAUSE TO REFLECT   Quote, unquote

Here are some famous quotations about mathematics for you to reflect on. Do any of these resonate with your own perceptions of the subject? Encourage you? Enlighten you? Amuse you?

'Do not worry about your difficulties in mathematics, I assure you that mine are greater.' (Albert Einstein, 1879–1955)

'The laws of mathematics are not merely human inventions or creations. They simply "are"; they exist quite independently of the human intellect. The most that any(one) ... can do is to find that they are there and to take cognizance of them.' (Maurits Escher, 1898–1972)

'One cannot escape the feeling that these mathematical formulas have an independent existence and an intelligence of their own, that they are wiser than we are, wiser even than their discoverers.' (Heinrich Hertz, 1857–94)

'Mathematics is the art of giving the same name to different things.' (Henri Poincaré, 1854–1912)

'Beauty is the first test: there is no permanent place in the world for ugly mathematics.' (G.H. Hardy, 1877–1947)

'The chief forms of beauty are order and symmetry and definiteness, which the mathematical sciences demonstrate in a special degree.' (Aristotle, 384–322 BC)

'I used to love mathematics for its own sake, and I still do, because it allows for no hypocrisy and no vagueness ...' (Stendhal, 1783–1842)

'Mathematics may be defined as the subject in which we never know what we are talking about, nor whether what we are saying is true.' (Bertrand Russell, 1872–1970)

RESEARCH FOCUS   Inverses

Terezinha Nunes and her colleagues, Peter Bryant and Anne Watson, have produced very clear and comprehensive reviews of recent research in mathematics education under the global heading of *Key Understandings in Mathematics Learning* (2009). They report on a range of studies that demonstrate that '... by the age of six or seven children understand quite a lot about number...' (p. 22) and, having read our previous chapters, we hope you are beginning to develop an idea as to what this might be. They discuss the importance of learners appreciating that addition and subtraction are reversible processes, but they point out that research on the issue has not always provided insight into young children's understanding of this principle.

They describe the work of Piaget and Moreau (1977, trans. 2001) in this respect as, '... ingenious, but rather too complicated...' (Nunes, Bryant and Watson, p. 22). They also report on a study by Siegler and Stern (1998), which details how, over seven training sessions, 8-year-olds became more proficient at solving problems involving the inversion principle. When the group was given a mixture of tasks at their final meeting, however, they observed that the children over-generalized, using an inversion strategy when it was unnecessary or inappropriate to do so, as in the case of a problem that only involved addition. Teachers will be familiar with this kind of behaviour in children, for whom learning sometimes seems to be more about guessing what the teacher wants them to do than seeking to understand what they are doing. For example, if you teach children a new strategy for doing some subtraction questions (like compensation, as explained in this chapter) and then give them a mixed bag of calculations to do, you may well find that they try to use the newly-learnt strategy in every question, regardless of how appropriate it might be.

Nunes et al. (2009) observe – as we have discussed previously – that part of the difficulty when working with young children is finding appropriate tasks to gain insight into their thinking processes. Those considered above (Piaget and Moreau, Siegler and Stern) involved the researchers presenting problems either verbally or in written form without the benefit of concrete materials. By way of contrast, Bryant, Christie and Rendu (1999) ran a series of experiments on understanding inverses with 38 five- and six-year-olds; some of these involved plastic bricks, others 'invisible' items, a third type were based on story problems (such as Christmas trees and presents) and there were also conventional abstract problems such as, 'What is 11 and 5 more, take away 5?' (p. 200). There was an intriguing further dimension to the tasks. In some cases – which were called 'identity problems' (p. 197) – the *same* bricks were added to a tower, for example, and then taken away. In others – 'quantity problems' (p. 197) – a number of bricks were added (for example, to one end of a column) while the same number of bricks, but *different* ones,

(Continued)

(Continued)

were removed (from the other end). Which do you think the children found easier and why? Bryant et al.'s study provides fascinating insight into ways of unravelling young children's mathematical understanding and we would recommend that you track it down. On the issue of inversion, suffice it to say that they conclude that '... children as young as 5 years understand and frequently use the inversion principle and that they can do so in a genuinely quantitative way' (p. 210), but that it should be noted that these young-sters may not be able to explain their thinking explicitly.

To complete this section we draw your attention to a further piece of research by Gilmore and Papadatou-Pastou (2009). They identified studies that focused on the inversion prin-ciple involving participants who were under 18 years of age. This resulted in a meta-analysis of 14 investigations, which involved a total of 357 boys and 388 girls. They found that there appear to be children who have a good understanding of the principle of inversion and good calculation skills – this is no surprise. And there are others who do not appear to understand inversion and have poor calculations skills – again no real surprise. But there also seems to be a third group who demonstrate a good understanding of inversion but have poor calculation skills. We leave you with their conclusion:

> ... when describing how children develop understanding of mathematical concepts, it is important to consider multiple ways in which children may come to this understanding. The challenge for theorists from both cognitive psychology and mathematics education is to account for the variety of ways in which children might discover and integrate conceptual knowledge with their knowledge of mathematical procedures. (p. 38)

Some activities to use with children

The classroom application of the material covered in this chapter will be mainly in teaching calculation strategies, many of which are discussed in Chapter 6. So we pro-vide here just a few examples of how some of the big mathematical ideas we have discussed can be experienced in practical ways even in the Foundation Stage.

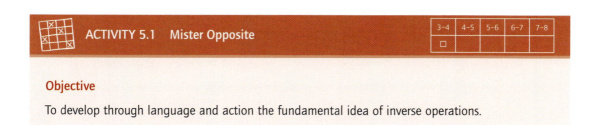

	ACTIVITY 5.1 Mister Opposite	3–4	4–5	5–6	6–7	7–8
		□				

Objective

To develop through language and action the fundamental idea of inverse operations.

Method

The children spread themselves out in a large space. One child plays the part of 'Mister Opposite' (or Miss) who undoes everything the teacher says. For example, the teacher calls out, 'Go forward two paces!' and the children all do this. Mister Opposite calls out, 'Go back two paces!' and the children move accordingly. The teacher comments on the fact that they've all gone back to where they were! She then calls out, 'Sit down!' and the children do so. Mister Opposite undoes this with, 'Stand up!' And so the game continues, with other commands, such as 'Raise one hand!' or 'Turn to the left!' or 'Jump backwards!' and so on.

		3–4	4–5	5–6	6–7	7–8
ACTIVITY 5.2	Filling the Gap	☐	☐			

Objective

To introduce the commutative principle practically using two lengths of wood.

Materials

Various lengths of wood in a pile in the playground.

Method

This can be developed within a building story theme, such as Bob the Builder. The teacher draws pairs of short parallel lines on the playground floor, such that the gap between them is exactly the combined lengths of two of the pieces of wood. The builders have to find the two lengths of wood needed to fill the gap, as shown in Figure 5.5. The teacher then asks them to swap over the two lengths and see if they still fill the gap. The children discuss what they discover with the teacher.

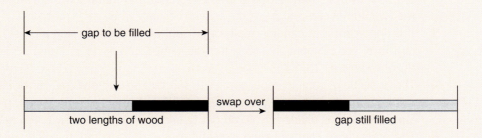

Figure 5.5   *Swapping the two lengths in Activity 5.2*

		3–4	4–5	5–6	6–7	7–8
ACTIVITY 5.3 Commutativity on Paving Stones			☐	☐		

Objective

To introduce the commutative principle practically through young children taking steps on paving stones.

Materials

An area paved with square stones, such as in the playground. Two giant numbered dice, say, one blue and one red.

Method

Two children stand side by side on the paving stones. The teacher has previously taught them how to move forward a certain number of steps, one paving stone at a time. The two dice are thrown. The children will move forward on the paving stones by first one number shown and then by the other. But one child always starts with the blue number and the other with the red. They make their first moves separately and the teacher asks the class who they think is going to win. They then make their second moves – and should finish up together! Keep playing the game until the children can predict the outcome.

Summary of key ideas

1   The foundation for confidence in calculation is the learner's understanding of the key principles that underpin arithmetic procedures.

2   One of these is the principle of commutativity in addition and multiplication: $a + b$ is always equal to $b + a$, and $a \times b$ is always equal to $b \times a$, whatever the two numbers a and b.

3   It is important that children realize that subtraction and division are not commutative. For example, $3 - 15$ is not the same thing as $15 - 3$; and $3 \div 15$ is not the same as $15 \div 3$.

4   The principle of complements applies to subtraction and division. For example, if 3 is subtracted from 10 you get 7; and if 7 is subtracted from 10 you get 3. Similarly, if 24 is divided by 4 you get 6; and if 24 is divided by 6 you get 4.

5   The principle of compensation is useful in mental calculation, when you can make an addition or subtraction more friendly by increasing the number being

added or subtracted by an extra little bit. In addition you then have to compensate by subtracting the extra bit added on. In subtraction you compensate by adding back the extra bit that has been subtracted.

6   When three numbers are to be added or multiplied together, the one in the middle can be associated with either the number on the left or the one on the right. This is called the associative principle. Addition and multiplication are associative. This principle can be exploited in mental calculation by choosing the association that makes the calculation more friendly. For example, (16 + 4) + 13 is easier than 16 + (4 + 13), and (4 × 5) × 7 is easier than 4 × (5 × 7).

7   Subtraction and division are not associative.

8   The two most important numbers in arithmetic are the additive identity (0) and the multiplicative identity (1). It is particularly important to learn the properties of these special numbers. The concept of an identity extends into other areas of mathematics.

9   Two operations in which one undoes the effect of the other, and vice versa, are called inverses. Familiar examples are: add 6 and subtract 6, double and halve, rotate anticlockwise and rotate clockwise.

Suggestions for further reading

The entry on 'Principle learning' in Haylock with Thangata (2007) discusses how principles are learnt and uses as examples some of the mathematical principles reviewed in this chapter.

Chapter 4 of Baroody and Dowker (2003) provides a review and synthesis of research into the development of additive commutativity in young children.

Check-ups 12 and 13 in Haylock (2001) provide some further discussion and practice of the commutative and associative principles.

Very relevant to our discussion here and well worth reading is Carlo Marchini and Paolo Vighi's chapter in Cockburn and Littler (2008), entitled 'Everyday numbers under a mathematical magnifying glass' (Chapter 7).

CHAPTER 6

UNDERSTANDING CALCULATIONS THROUGH PATTERNS AND PICTURES

A POWERFUL PATTERN

Sam, aged 6, had drawn a block graph showing how many children in the class had a cat as a pet and how many had a dog. He had chosen to colour in alternate squares in the columns of his graph, as shown in Figure 6.1. His teacher asked him to write about his graph. This is what he wrote:

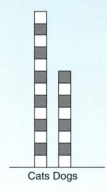

'Cats beat dogs. There are 13 squares in the cat row and only 8 squares in the dog row. There are more cats than dogs. 13 is 2 + 2 + 2 + 2 + 2 + 2 + 1. 13 is 6 twos and 1 odd one. 13 is an odd number. 8 is an even number. 8 is 4 twos and none left over.'

- In what ways does Sam show an impressive ability to articulate relationships between numbers?
- How does this appear to be linked to his recognition and use of pattern?

Cats Dogs

Figure 6.1   *Sam's block graph for numbers of cats and dogs*

In this chapter

In this chapter we turn our attention to developing understanding of the relationships between numbers and elementary calculations. As is shown by the example of 6-year-old Sam above, central to our understanding of number relationships is the notion of *pattern*. We demonstrate that this sense of pattern in number is the foundation for young children's success and confidence in handling calculations. We explore how pictures and practical experience make the patterns that underpin our manipulation of numbers explicit. The reader should note that in our discussion of number patterns in this chapter we are not considering fractions or negative numbers, so when we refer to 'a number' we mean a positive integer (whole number) or zero.

Pattern in number

Sam (above) shows the kind of grasp of number relationships and awareness of pattern in number that teachers should aim to develop as the basis for confidence and success in manipulating numbers. The spatial pattern that emerged as a result of the way he had coloured his block graph led him to see the numbers involved in terms of odd and even, and multiples of 2 (multiples of 2 are 2, 4, 6, 8, 10, 12, and so on).

Odd and even

How do we think about the concepts of 'odd' and 'even'? What ideas dominate our image of odd and even numbers? These are some responses from some of the teachers we worked with:

- Even numbers are nice. Odd numbers are a nuisance. You can't line children up in twos if there's an odd number.
- I think about the patterns that odd and even numbers make as if they were scones arranged on a tray.

(Continued)

(Continued)

- I think of even numbers as things arranged in pairs. With odd numbers there's an odd one stuck out at the end.
- I just think of even numbers as those that end in 0, 2, 4, 6 or 8, and odd numbers those that end in 1, 3, 5, 7 or 9.
- I imagine the odd numbers on one side of the road and the even numbers on the other side.
- Then there's the pattern you get when you count: odd, even, odd, even, odd, even, and so on, going on for ever.

Nearly all these comments contain visual or spatial imagery: lining up in twos, the pattern of scones on a tray, an odd one sticking out, opposite sides of a road, and so on. Even the comment about the counting pattern of 'odd, even, odd, even, odd, even' can be thought of as a spatial observation, by visualizing a line of alternately odd and even numbers arranged in order. When 6-year-old Sam looked at the 13 squares shaded alternately – in the example at the head of this chapter – the visual image immediately prompted the connection with the notions of odd and even. A strong part of his concept of 'odd' is clearly the connection between these numbers and the spatial pattern of pairs of items with an extra one added on.

Spatial patterns and visual images related to numerical patterns

We begin to see then how strong the idea of pattern is in our understanding of such simple numerical concepts as odd and even. It is significant that one of the main uses of the word 'pattern' is to refer to a spatial or geometric design, particularly one in which certain key features are repeated and linked together in a systematic fashion. It is not surprising therefore that when we talk about a 'number pattern' or make any kind of comment about patterns in the context of number, what we are doing more often than not is drawing attention to some connection between the relationships between the numbers and a visual image, a picture, or a spatial or geometric arrangement of some kind. One suspects also that for Sam, as for many children (and adults, for that matter), the aesthetic aspect of pattern in numbers, that comes through most strongly in visual imagery, is an important motivating factor in exploring, using and just playing with numbers.

Consideration of number patterns is often, therefore, another example of the importance of making connections between symbols and pictures in developing understanding. Many of the key relationships between numbers that contribute to a person having what is sometimes called a 'feel for number' are more securely understood if we make the connections with visual patterns or images. We have already done this, for example, in our discussion of understanding the principle of commutativity in multiplication in Chapter 4 (see Figure 4.2). The imagery of a rectangular array – a neatly arranged geometric pattern of dots – makes the numerical relationship transparent and contributes strongly to our understanding of the principle.

Patterns of dots for numbers

At a more elementary level, the patterns of dots that appear on dice or dominoes for the numbers zero to six (see Figure 6.2) are an important part of our feel for the various numbers. For example, many people when asked to visualize 'five' will bring to mind the spatial arrangement of dots for this number that is shown in Figure 6.2. For young children developing their understanding of elementary number relationships, this visual arrangement is very much part of what makes five the number it is and distinguishes it from other numbers. These and other such patterns of dots also help them to relate one number to other numbers. For example, the visual image of five dots makes clear how 5 is made up of two 2s and a 1, or a 4 and a 1; and, being a rectangular array, the image of six dots connects six with both two 3s and three 2s.

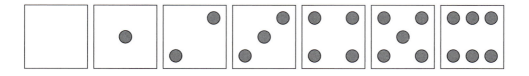

Figure 6.2   *Patterns for 0 to 6 on dice or dominoes*

Pattern in complements

In Chapter 5 we introduced the principle of complements. We now explore the idea further to show how young children learning to relate and manipulate numbers are supported by the underlying patterns involved in these complements.

Ten-complements

Because of our base-ten number system, ten-complements are particularly significant in manipulating numbers and require special emphasis when teaching young children. For example, 3 and 7 are ten-complements, because they add up to 10. The simple idea here is that of 'making a number up to 10': 7 is the number that makes 3 up to 10, and 3 is the number that makes 7 up to 10. We should aim for children to be able to recall pairs of ten-complements instantly and to use them freely.

The patterns inherent in these ten-complements are very important and play a key part in understanding the relationships involved. So, when we look at the sequence of ten-complements (0 + 10, 1 + 9, 2 + 8, 3 + 7, 4 + 6, 5 + 5, 6 + 4, 7 + 3, 8 + 2, 9 + 1, 10 + 0) we can observe the first number in each pair going up by one and the second number going down by one. But this numerical pattern is made so much stronger if it is associated with discussion of various spatial representations, such as those using blocks or shaded squares, as shown in Figure 6.3, or by a sequence of pairs of Numicon plates fitted together to make a ten.

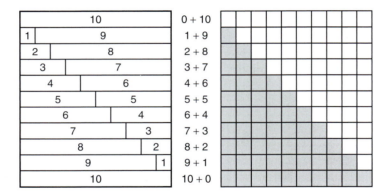

Figure 6.3   *The pattern of ten-complements using blocks or shaded squares*

The visual images of ten-complements provided by appropriate drawings on the number line also promote a deeper understanding of the relationships, as shown in Figure 6.4.

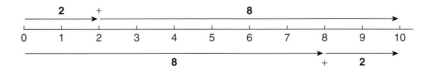

Figure 6.4   *Ten-complements shown on a number line*

Multiples of 10 and stepping stones

The visual images of ten-complements shown in Figures 6.3 and 6.4 are crucial in promoting a mental structure that facilitates the processing of operations with numbers. In the discussion of the associative principle of addition in Chapter 5 we saw how ten-complements were important in performing mental additions. For example, 8 + 7 can be transformed into (8 + 2) + 5, and 28 + 7 into (28 + 2) + 5. In each case the decision to split the 7 into 2 + 5 is prompted by knowing that 2 is what is needed to make the 8 up to 10 – or a number ending with the digit 8 up to the next *multiple* of 10 (that is, 10 or 20 or 30 or 40, and so on).

For example, children can discover this pattern for making numbers in the twenties up to 30: 21 + 9, 22 + 8, 23 + 7, 24 + 6, 25 + 5, 26 + 4, 27 + 3, 28 + 2, 29 + 1. They can usefully represent this pattern of symbols with number line drawings, or patterns of blocks or coloured squares, and discuss how it is related to the pattern of ten-complements. Figure 6.5 shows how this might be set out with blocks. It really is worthwhile allowing young children to have the time to set up and talk about patterns like this, because the patterns help them to connect pictures and concrete experiences with numerical relationships. So they are learning how numbers work.

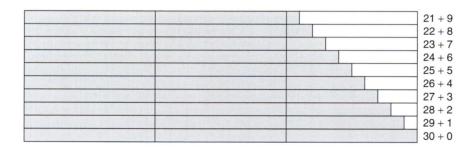

21 + 9
22 + 8
23 + 7
24 + 6
25 + 5
26 + 4
27 + 3
28 + 2
29 + 1
30 + 0

Figure 6.5   *The pattern of thirty-complements for 21 to 29*

This process of making a number up to the next multiple of 10 is the basis of an important mental strategy sometimes referred to as *bridging* through multiples of 10. We like to call it 'using multiples of 10 as *stepping stones*'. For example, to find the difference between 27 and 35, children might use 30 as a stepping stone, seeing the difference as two steps of 3 and 5. The 3, of course, is what is needed to make the 27 up to the next multiple of 10 (30). Later in this chapter we illustrate this strategy with empty number-line diagrams.

Pairs of complements for all numbers up to 20

So, knowing how to break 10 up into pairs of complements is crucial for developing ability in handling number. But to perform freely such mental manipulations of numbers as those above the child also needs to be able to recall instantly, for example, the seven-complements. When required, we want children confidently to be able to split 7 into 2 and 5, or 1 and 6, and so on. These seven-complements have the same kind of pattern as the ten-complements (0 + 7, 1 + 6, 2 + 5, 3 + 4, and so on) and, in the same way, they can be experienced, explored and discussed with appropriate visual and spatial arrangements such as blocks, colouring squares and number lines. Ideally, we need to know the complements not just for making numbers up to 10 and up to 7, but for every number at least from 0 to 20. For example, in Table 6.1 are all the pairs of numbers that sum to 0, 1, 2, 3, 4, 5, 6, 7, 8, 9 and 10, arranged in a systematic way that makes clear the extensive range of patterns involved here.

Table 6.1 *Pairs of complements with respect to numbers from 0 to 10*

0	1	2	3	4	5	6	7	8	9	10
0 + 0	0 + 1	0 + 2	0 + 3	0 + 4	0 + 5	0 + 6	0 + 7	0 + 8	0 + 9	0 +10
	1 + 0	1 + 1	1 + 2	1 + 3	1 + 4	1 + 5	1 + 6	1 + 7	1 + 8	1 + 9
		2 + 0	2 + 1	2 + 2	2 + 3	2 + 4	2 + 5	2 + 6	2 + 7	2 + 8
			3 + 0	3 + 1	3 + 2	3 + 3	3 + 4	3 + 5	3 + 6	3 + 7
				4 + 0	4 + 1	4 + 2	4 + 3	4 + 4	4 + 5	4 + 6
					5 + 0	5 + 1	5 + 2	5 + 3	5 + 4	5 + 5
						6 + 0	6 + 1	6 + 2	6 + 3	6 + 4
							7 + 0	7 + 1	7 + 2	7 + 3
								8 + 0	8 + 1	8 + 2
									9 + 0	9 + 1
										10 + 0

There are 66 number facts for young children to learn in Table 6.1! Without the strong patterns that underpin these results this would be a daunting learning task. So, we asked some of the teachers we worked with to tell us what observations about the number and spatial relationships here they would like to hear children making. Some of their suggestions were:

- The first number as you go along a row is the same for every sum, and the second number goes up by one each time.
- As you go down a column the first number goes up by one and the second number goes down by one each time.

- All the sums in any column give the same answer.
- The number of combinations in each column increases by one each time.
- And the number of combinations in each row reduces by one each time.
- So the pattern makes a triangle shape – and this would carry on if you went on to 20, or any number.

This arrangement is typical of the amazing amount of fascinating pattern inherent in number relationships that is waiting to be discovered by young children and to be built into their networks of connections. Time spent discovering and discussing patterns such as these will not be wasted. And, as you would by now expect us to say, the patterns in this table become even stronger when connected with spatial patterns of dots, or blocks or Numicon plates.

Hundred-complements

Having instant recall of the complements to any number is potentially useful knowledge. But particularly important in developing confidence in handling two-digit numbers is knowledge of hundred-complements. For example, in handling money a useful skill is to be able to make a number of pence (for example, 37p) up to £1 (100p) by recalling its hundred-complement (in this case, 63p). This is helpful when giving or checking change from £1. It also helps in mental calculations, particularly in subtraction situations with the comparison structure (see Chapter 3) – such as in finding differences in prices or lengths – when one number is less than 100 and the other is greater than 100. For example, to find the difference in height between two children of heights 123 cm and 88 cm, someone who is confident with hundred-complements might reason: we need 12 to make the 88 up to 100, and then another 23, giving 35 cm in all. This kind of reasoning is supported enormously by representations of the situation on the number line, where the gap between 88 and 123 can be seen clearly as a combination of two bits: the bit needed to get from 88 to 100 (the hundred- complement of 88) and the bit needed to get from 100 to 123. So, once again, the pictorial imagery promotes appropriate mental structures for manipulating numbers with confidence.

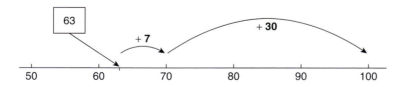

Figure 6.6   *Connecting 100 – 63 with a number-line image*

There is a common error in reasoning that occurs – with which most primary teachers will be familiar – that leads a child to write, for example: 100 – 63 = 47. This is typical of children's errors in arithmetic when they respond to the individual symbols merely as a set of marks on the paper without relating them to anything concrete or visual. For example, they might have reasoned here: 100 take away 60 is 40, … 10 take away 3 is 7 (responding to 0 as if it were 10), … 40 add 7 is 47. But if they have learnt to associate hundred-complements with the image on the number line, as shown in Figure 6.6, then they are much more likely to see 100 – 63 as 'making 63 up to 100'. Then they would use the 70 as a stepping stone and thus see 100 – 63 as 'making 63 up to 70 and then up to 100', that is, 7 + 30. It is significant that we used the word 'see' in the last two sentences. This is our main argument here. It is important that children (and their teachers) *see* numbers and number relationships – to make the connections between the symbols and the various visual images and spatial representations available.

Patterns of fives and doubles

The combinations of the numbers from 6 to 9 seem to be the trickiest of all the additions of two single-digit numbers for young children to learn: 6 + 6, 6 + 7, 6 + 8, 6 + 9, 7 + 7, 7 + 8, 7 + 9, 8 + 8, 8 + 9, 9 + 9. There are, however, two elementary patterns of relationships between numbers that are particularly useful when learning these particular number bonds. These are references to fives and doubles.

Fives

First, it seems as though many young children find it helpful to relate numbers to *five*, for example to think of 7 as 5 + 2. This is probably linked to the strong visual image of five fingers on one hand. Using this strategy, for example, 6 + 8 can be envisaged as (5 + 1) added to (5 + 3), which is then mentally rearranged – imagining the two handfuls of fingers put together to make a ten – as (5 + 5) added to (1 + 3) to give the response 14. Written down, this sounds somewhat laborious. But in practice, with the support of appropriate mental imagery or reference to fingers, the mental processing can be very rapid.

> I get two children to work together on additions like 6 + 8. One child puts up 6 fingers (one handful plus one finger), the other puts up 8 fingers (one handful plus three fingers). They then put together the two handfuls to make 10 and add on the other fingers. This makes the link between the way they manipulate the symbols and the visual image very strong.

When recording statistical data, such as how many children have cats and how many have dogs, as in the example at the head of this chapter (Figure 6.1), the process of *tallying* can be taught to capitalize on this tendency to relate numbers to five. This is shown in Figure 6.7, with the marks corresponding to the numbers of children grouped in fives. This is not just a useful skill for handling data – it also provides a strong pictorial image of numbers grouped in fives, which, as we have seen, seems to be a strategy that many children find helpful in manipulating the more difficult numbers.

Figure 6.7   *Tallying with numbers grouped in fives*

Doubles

Second, it seems as though children often pick up the *doubles* more quickly and more securely than any of the others in the list of number bonds. The reason for this is possibly that there is just less information to remember! If you are doing 6 + 6, for example, you can imagine it as (5 + 1) and the same thing again, rather than (5 + 1) and then something different, as it would be with, say, 6 + 8. The doubles also have a strong pattern – which can be made even stronger, of course, by appropriate pictorial or spatial representation with blocks or Numicon plates – of going up in twos: 1 + 1 = 2, 2 + 2 = 4, 3 + 3 = 6, 4 + 4 = 8, 5 + 5 = 10, 6 + 6 = 12, and so on. Children seem to pick up the pattern and rhythm of counting in twos fairly quickly. Whatever the reason, it seems that many children have greater fluency in instant recall of the doubles than many of the other addition bonds.

> I noticed that the children in my reception class tend to see 6 as three 2s, rather than double 3. But they always see 10 as double 5. With 6 they can visualize three pairs. But the stronger image for 10 is two lots of 5 fingers, not 5 pairs.

So, another useful strategy for many children is to relate additions to these doubles. Using this procedure many children will relate 6 + 8 to 6 + 6, transforming it mentally as follows: 6 + 8 = 6 + (6 + 2) = (6 + 6) + 2 = 12 + 2 = 14. Again the actual mental processing for many young children is more fluent than this long-winded explanation might suggest. Which strategy children use – reference to fives or reference to doubles – will depend partly on the actual sum being tackled, partly on what particular number knowledge is most secure, and very much on the picture they connect with a given number.

PAUSE TO REFLECT   Double first

In our discussion about doubles, we have drawn on the work of Constance Kamii, who, in 1985, reported that members of the first-grade class she was studying in the United States (children aged 6 to 7) learnt the following number bonds faster than any others: 2 + 2, 5 + 5 and 3 + 3. Perhaps 2 + 2 is not surprising, but it seems strange that the others came before, say, 6 + 1 and 4 + 1. Kamii also found that 4 + 4 and 6 + 6 came relatively early and, in many cases, before two plus anything. Now is it just mathematics enthusiasts like us or do most adults find it easier – and more satisfying even – to add doubles, such as 45 + 45 and 32 + 32 rather than, say, 41 + 49 or 31 + 33 which yield the same results? We are not so sure about the ease of 47 + 47 or 38 + 38 but take a minute to reflect on your own preferences – if any – and those of your friends.

Why might this be? What makes doubling easier than many other calculations? Why are children (and possibly adults) just more comfortable with doubles?

As we discussed earlier in the chapter, one suggestion is that when the child is adding a number to itself they have only one number to remember, rather than two different numbers. To support this idea, ask yourself which of these telephone numbers you would find it easier to remember: 0147259 or 014014?

Or perhaps it is that we have a natural disposition to be drawn to symmetry, and so it is the symmetry of 4 + 4 that makes us feel more comfortable with this calcula-tion than the asymmetry of 3 + 5. Many studies have shown, for example, that people tend to have a predisposition towards individuals with more symmetric faces.

A third observation is that with a double, like 4 + 4, the child does not have to decide in which order to add the two numbers, whereas with, say, 3 + 5 they have a choice between starting with the 3 or starting with the 5. What do you think?

Patterns in multiplication tables

By the end of Year 2, most children would be expected to derive and recall multipli-cation facts from 2-, 5- and 10-times tables. In Year 3 this would be extended to include a number of other multiplication tables. Whenever we talk to teachers and student-teachers about the importance of learning mathematics with understanding, as opposed to just learning by rote, we invariably get questions about learning multi-plication tables. So let us make this absolutely clear: we are definitely in favour of children eventually memorizing their multiplication tables! Obviously, the more number facts that one can recall instantly the better – and the number facts in the multiplica-tion tables (particularly up to 10 × 10) are some of the most useful to have at your fingertips. If chanting the tables helps to commit these to memory then that's fine by us. But teachers would be failing the children they teach if they did nothing more than get them to commit these results to memory. We want children to memorize them – but also to do this with understanding! This means making connections – relating the results within the tables, connecting them to concrete situations and pictures, and, above all, discovering, articulating and using the amazing amount of pattern that is built into them.

Tens, fives and twos

The most obvious patterns are those that emerge when you count in tens, fives and twos. Because ten is the base of our number system (see Chapter 7), counting in tens produces only numbers that end in zero, that is, numbers without any units: 10, 20, 30, 40, … and so on. Counting in fives produces numbers in which the last digit is alternately five and zero: 5, 10, 15, 20, 25, 30, 35, … and so on. Figure 6.8 shows how this pattern can be interpreted visually for discussion with young children, using rods representing 5s and 10s. When there is an even number of 5-rods this is equivalent to a collection of 10-rods, but when there is an odd number of 5-rods there is one extra 5-rod each time. The last digit in the number (0 or 5) is what you are left with after you have exchanged as many rods as you can for 10-rods. The same connection can be made with 5p and 10p coins.

Counting in twos produces a sequence of numbers in which the last digits follow the pattern 2, 4, 6, 8, 0, 2, 4, 6, 8, 0, 2, 4, 6, 8, 0, … repeated for ever. This is, of course, another manifestation of the set of even numbers. We do not consider patterns like this to be trivial – they are crucial for a child's developing confidence with number, and we should do all we can to make them explicit and meaningful.

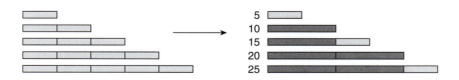

Figure 6.8   *The pattern of counting in fives shown with blocks*

Reducing the workload

In the context of learning the multiplication facts, we should mention again the importance of commutativity (see Chapter 5). This property means that if you know, say, '8 fives' (which is fairly easy because of the pattern in the 5-times table), you also know '5 eights' (which is more difficult). Clearly the ability to employ the commutativity principle strategically cuts down the number of 'difficult' results substantially.

Other potentially difficult results can be derived instantly from easier ones, by the process of doubling. Doubling is really easy if there is no carrying involved. So, if you can instantly recall, say, $3 \times 4 = 12$, you can quickly deduce $6 \times 4 = 24$, by doubling the 12. And then, because you now know $6 \times 4 = 24$, you can quickly deduce $6 \times 8 = 48$, by doubling the 24.

Figure 6.9(a) shows an alternative route to 6 eights starting from knowing 3 eights. Back in the 7-times table, 4×7 and 6×7 might cause some difficulty – so do we know simpler results that we can relate to these? Figure 6.9(b) shows how we can use 2 sevens to work out 4 sevens, and Figure 6.9(c) how we can use 3 sevens to work out 6 sevens. Learning the hundred results in the tables from 1×1 to 10×10 becomes much easier and much more based on understanding if these kinds of relationships and patterns are understood and utilized.

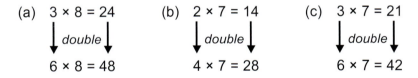

Figure 6.9   *Using doubling to get multiplication results*

The hundred square

In Chapter 2 we highlighted the importance of the hundred square (see Figure 2.3) as a picture to help understanding of the ordinal aspect of number. In this section we discuss the value of children learning to use the patterns in the hundred square to add and subtract. In the next chapter we will see how the image of the hundred square also supports children's understanding of the principle of place value and we will consider more difficult calculations with two-digit numbers.

Pattern in the hundred square

We asked some teachers what patterns they could see in the hundred square:

- All the numbers in a column end in the same digit.
- That's because you're adding 10 each time as you go down the columns.
- And you add 1 each time as you go along the rows.
- The numbers in the column on the right are the 10-times table.
- There's a diagonal line of squares starting at 9 that gives the 9-times table!
- And another diagonal line starting at 11 that gives the 11-times table!

These are examples of the way in which the hundred square can be a powerful aid for developing mental structures that support the learner's manipulation of numbers. We make explicit below some of the steps that children might go through in developing such mental strategies through calculations based on the hundred square. We start by considering addition of ones and tens, as moves on the hundred square. Then we consider the inverse processes of subtracting ones and tens.

Adding ones and adding tens

Just as with a number line, there is the obvious feature that 'adding 1' corresponds to moving 1 step along, 'adding 2' to moving 2 steps, 'adding 3' to moving 3 steps, and so on. The only difference with the hundred square is that you have to move to the beginning of the next row when you reach a multiple of 10. This might seem a disadvantage compared to working on a number line, in terms of the image of number as a continuous line going on for ever in both directions. But the hundred square has the practical advantage of being more compact than a number line labelled from 1 to 100; and, more importantly, the procedure of moving to a new line every time you reach the next ten emphasizes clearly the significance of the multiples of 10 in our counting system. Just as with the number line, children can handle 46 + 7, for example, by doing 46 + 4 to get to the end of the line (making the 46 up to the next ten) and then adding another 3.

An important pattern emerges when adding a fixed number to the numbers in a given column. So, for example, Figure 6.10(a) shows the pattern that emerges on a section of the hundred square when you add 2 to the number in the column headed by 6. Using the procedure of '2 steps along' for adding 2, children can discover, articulate and discuss the pattern that emerges: 6 + 2 = 8, 16 + 2 = 18, 26 + 2 = 28, 36 + 2 = 38, and so on.

Figure 6.10(b) shows the pattern that emerges when 7 is added to the numbers in the column headed by 6. In this case the 'move 7 steps along' procedure takes us over the end of a line each time: 6 + 7 = 13, 16 + 7 = 23, 26 + 7 = 33, 36 + 7 = 43, and so on. The patterns illustrated in Figure 6.10 make explicit key ideas in addition. They help the child to see, for example, how adding 7 to 6, or 7 to 16, or 7 to 26, or 7 to 36, and so on, is essentially the same process each time.

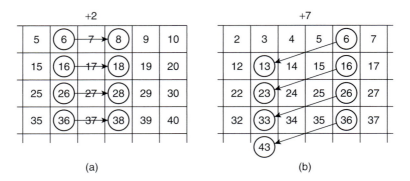

Figure 6.10   *Patterns for (a) adding 2 and (b) adding 7 on the hundred square*

A very significant pattern in the hundred square is one picked up by some of the teachers in their comments above: the adding-10 pattern. A move of one step downwards corresponds to adding 10. This then extends to adding 20 (move down 2 steps), adding 30 (move down 3 steps), and so on. So, starting at any square we choose (for example, 16), children can discover and articulate patterns like this: 16 + 10 = 26, 16 + 20 = 36, 16 + 30 = 46, and so on.

Subtracting ones and subtracting tens

Clearly, all the adding procedures described above have their inverse in subtraction procedures, where you move back along a row (rather than forwards) or move up (rather than down) the number of steps in question. The same range of patterns is there to be discovered, articulated and discussed by children. For example, there is the pattern in Figure 6.11(a) for subtracting 2 from any number in the column headed by 8, corresponding to moving 2 steps back along a line: 8 − 2 = 6, 18 − 2 = 16, 28 − 2 = 26, 38 − 2 = 36, 48 − 2 = 46, and so on. And there is the pattern in Figure 6.11(b) where

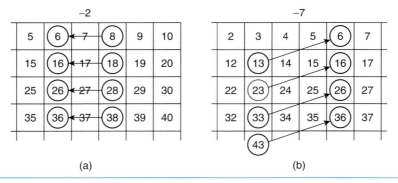

Figure 6.11   *Patterns for (a) subtracting 2 and (b) subtracting 7 on the hundred square*

7 steps back from any number in the column headed by 3 moves you to the line above: 13 − 7 = 6, 23 − 7 = 16, 33 − 7 = 26, 43 − 7 = 36, and so on. Comparison with the processes in Figure 6.10 makes clear how adding 2 and subtracting 2 (or adding 7 and subtracting 7) are inverse processes.

Subtraction also produces this kind of pattern for subtracting multiples of 10, corresponding to moving up 1 step, 2 steps, 3 steps, and so on: 86 − 10 = 76, 86 − 20 = 66, 86 − 30 = 56, 86 − 40 = 46, and so on. Once again, these kinds of activities on the hundred square provide mental structures that are helpful for the learner. With these procedures children are much more likely to see subtraction and addition as inverse processes than they are if they are using only standard written procedures for addition and subtraction.

Patterns for adding nines and eights

Other patterns in the hundred square can be helpful in developing a feeling for number and number relationships. For example, one of the teachers quoted above spotted the pattern for the 9-times table: 9, 18, 27, 36, and so on, all lying on a diagonal line. This is an instance of a more general adding-9 pattern. Adding 9 can be interpreted as moving forward 9 steps – but it can also be interpreted as moving down 1 step and back 1 step. This corresponds, of course, to adding 10 and subtracting 1. This provides the mental structure for the addition of 9 to any number. For example, 57 + 9 is transformed into 57 + 10 − 1, that is, 67 − 1. This pattern for adding 9 then extends naturally to adding 19 (add 20, subtract 1), adding 29 (add 30, subtract 1), and so on. Figure 6.12

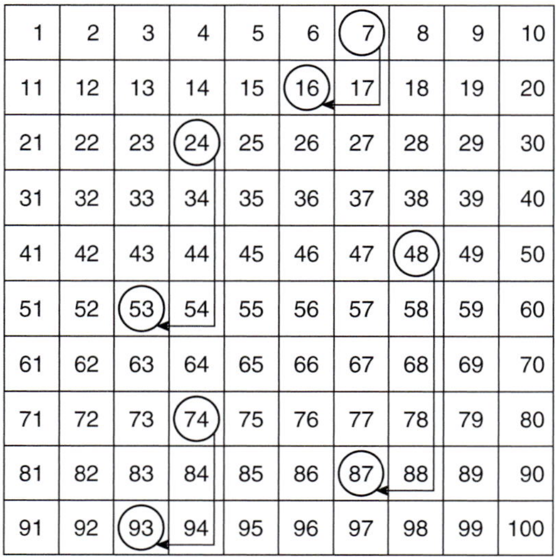

1	2	3	4	5	6	7	8	9	10
11	12	13	14	15	16	17	18	19	20
21	22	23	24	25	26	27	28	29	30
31	32	33	34	35	36	37	38	39	40
41	42	43	44	45	46	47	48	49	50
51	52	53	54	55	56	57	58	59	60
61	62	63	64	65	66	67	68	69	70
71	72	73	74	75	76	77	78	79	80
81	82	83	84	85	86	87	88	89	90
91	92	93	94	95	96	97	98	99	100

Figure 6.12   *Showing 7 + 9, 74 + 19, 24 + 29 and 48 + 39 on the hundred square*

shows some examples of these processes on the hundred square in action for various calculations.

In the same way, adding 8 can be seen as a move of 1 step down and 2 steps back, corresponding to adding 10 and subtracting 2. For example, 27 + 8 can be transformed into 27 + 10 − 2. This then extends to adding 18 (add 20, subtract 2), adding 28 (add 30, subtract 2), and so on. And, of course, the procedure for adding 9 has its inverse in subtracting 9: one step up and one step forward, corresponding to subtracting 10 and adding 1. And the procedure for adding 8 has its inverse in subtracting 8: one step up and two steps forward, corresponding to subtracting 10 and adding 2.

These movements on the hundred square for adding and subtracting numbers ending in 9 or 8 provide a powerful image to support the process of compensation that was outlined in Chapter 5. These are just the kinds of patterns that we would urge teachers to encourage children to discover, to articulate and then to use in their mental and informal calculations.

PAUSE TO REFLECT   A couple of things

(1) Multiple patterns

Use the arrays provided in Figure 6.13 to circle (a) 2 and then every 2nd number; (b) 3 and then every 3rd number; (c) 11 and then every 11th number; (d) 12 and then every 12th number. Reflect on the patterns that emerge and then try explaining to a

Figure 6.13   *Arrays for multiple patterns*

colleague *why* these patterns must be as they are. The numbers in (a) are the multiples of 2; those in (b) are the multiples of 3; and so on. Many people find that this kind of image strengthens their understanding of the number relationships involved in these sets of multiples. Does it for you?

(2) Back to square one?

Some teachers argue that we should use hundred squares starting with zero rather than 1. What would be the value in doing this? How would the experience be different? Perhaps we should use both versions? Others say we should start the hundred square with 1 (or zero) in the bottom left-hand corner, so the numbers get larger as you go up the columns. What do you think about this idea? Have you ever encountered this before? If so, in what context?

The empty number line

Throughout this chapter we have stressed the importance of children using concrete experiences such as making patterns with blocks and rods or colouring squares to make connections with number patterns and relationships. We have argued strongly the case for the development of mental processes for manipulating numbers based on visual and pictorial images, particularly the hundred square and the number line, rather than emphasizing too early standard written procedures for doing additions and subtractions. In this section we provide a few examples of the use of what is known as the *empty number line*, a powerful device for helping children to connect strategies for addition and subtraction with visual imagery.

Developing the number line

In the early stages of number young children may use a number strip to develop their skills in counting forwards and backwards and their sense of the ordinal aspect of number. Each integer is represented by an individual square. From the number strip they usually move on to using a number line, with equally spaced points marked 0, 1, 2, 3, 4, and so on. In Chapter 2 we showed in Figure 2.2 examples of a number strip and a number line. Later children learn to use number lines where only the multiples of 10 are marked (0, 10, 20, 30, and so on). See, for example, Figure 6.6, earlier in this chapter. Sometimes, as illustrated in Figure 6.6, they will use a section of the number line that does not start at zero. So, gradually they develop the image of the number line as a flexible tool for representing and manipulating numbers.

The empty number line takes this one step further: it is a number line without a scale drawn on it at all. The numbers involved in a calculation can be placed more or less anywhere on the number line, provided the order of the numbers is preserved. So, for example, points representing the three numbers 52, 60 and 100 could be placed anywhere on an empty number line, provided the 60 is positioned between the 52 and the 100. Figure 6.14 provides some examples of empty number lines used to support additions and subtractions with two-digit numbers, illustrating how all the key strategies, such as compensation and stepping stones, can be developed with this powerful aid to learning.

Additions and subtractions on the empty number line

Addition on an empty number line uses the addition structure of counting on or increasing. Subtraction can be experienced as counting back, but is often most helpfully interpreted as comparison (finding the difference) or the inverse of addition (what must be added?).

Figure 6.14(a) represents on an empty number line the addition 28 + 7. The addition of 7 is done in two steps: add 2 and then add 5. This process uses 30 as a stepping stone. The visual image and process here are readily connected with the way the same calculation is represented by moves on a hundred square (moving from 28 to 30 to 35). Similarly, Figure 6.14(b) shows the subtraction 45 − 8, counting back by 8 from 45, but in steps of 5 and then 3, using 40 as a stepping stone.

Figure 6.14(c) shows a representation on an empty number line of the more complicated calculation of 100 − 63, using 70 as a stepping stone. The subtraction here is helpfully thought of as finding the size of the gap (the difference) between 100 and 63. The key numbers in this process are 63, 70 and 100. These are the only numbers therefore that need to be put on the line. Provided they are put on in the right order it is not necessary for the gaps between them to be to scale. To calculate 100 − 63 we could start at 63 and ask what do we add to the 63 to get to 100? The diagram does this by adding on 7 to get to 70, then adding a further 30 to get to 100. So we find that 100 − 63 is equal to 7 + 30, which is 37.

Figure 6.14(d) shows an empty number line calculation of 63 − 37, using 40 and 60 as stepping stones. Notice again how the subtraction here has been interpreted as finding the difference between 37 and 63, rather than taking away 37 or counting back 37. The difference is made up of three steps: 3 + 20 + 3, which equals 26.

Figure 6.14(e) shows the use of compensation for the subtraction 52 − 29. To subtract 29 we first subtract 30, taking us to 22, and then compensate by adding 1, giving the result as 23. Similarly, Figure 6.14(f) shows the use of compensation for the addition 34 + 28. To add 28 we first add 30 and then compensate by subtracting 2, giving the result 62.

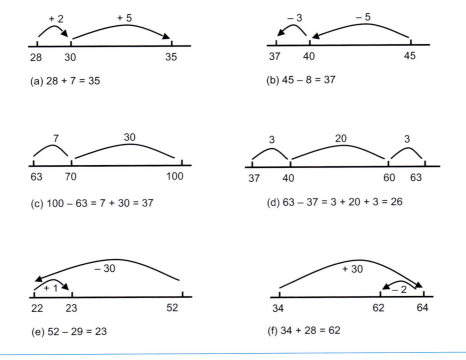

Figure 6.14   *Some additions and subtractions using an empty number line*

RESEARCH FOCUS   Empty number lines

We start this section with a heartfelt statement from Emily, a 9-year-old student who, in her earlier years at school in Australia, had been taught to add and subtract using a range of mental and informal strategies. When instructed to do a calculation using the empty number line she exclaimed, 'No one should tell me what strategy to use. I should be allowed to make up my own mind!' (Bobis, 2007, p. 410). Emily has a point and, indeed, it was enough to spur on her mother – Janette Bobis – to research the origins and purpose of the empty number line within a mathematics curriculum for younger children emphasizing mental and informal calculation strategies. Interestingly, she discovered that early experiments using it in the Netherlands in the 1970s were not as successful as anticipated. By 1994, however, Dutch researcher, Keono Gravemeijer, was advocating the use of the empty number line for a variety of reasons, including that it allows children to use it in the way that is most appropriate for their stage of understanding. He illustrated how different children might calculate, for example, 65 – 38 (see Figure 6.15). We suggest that

(Continued)

(Continued)

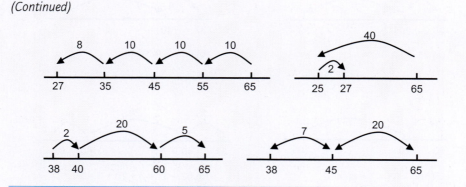

Figure 6.15   *Different strategies for 65 – 38 (Gravemeijer, 1994)*

you try to identify and put into words the reasoning behind each of the strategies used here.

This range of possible approaches to one calculation echoes Emily's response; she did not want to be tied down to one particular strategy, particularly when the empty number line proves to be such a flexible medium for doing calculations. After experimenting with the empty line, she explained to her mother that it is easier to use than more conventional paper and pencil methods, because:

- she understands how it works (it represents *her* thinking);
- it keeps a record of each step in her thinking;
- it allows her to track errors; and
- it enables her to think about what to do next when the computation is too demanding to do solely 'in her head' (Bobis, 2007, pp. 411–12)

In 2011 Carol Murphy published an article entitled, 'Comparing the use of the empty number line in England and the Netherlands'. She discovered that it was used rather differently in the two countries and that this might be due to different beliefs and approaches to the teaching and learning of mathematics. Her research is very interesting and well worth reading, should you have the opportunity. From our perspective, however, we should say that we consider the Dutch approach to be more enlightened than the English one! The following will give you a flavour of what we mean. When the children in the Netherlands were given the following problem their teacher invited them to solve it using a range of strategies – some including the empty number line: 'You weigh 37 kg and your mother 63 kg; what is the difference in weight?' As the members of the class came up with their various suggestions they were compared and contrasted by the group. In contrast, the teacher in England set the calculation 90 – 54 and the lesson proceeded thus …

> Teacher E: OK, next one, 90 subtract 54. Who can tell me what would be the first number we put on the line?
>
> Child E1:   54
>
> Teacher E: Good girl. Who can tell me what I do next?
>
> Child E2:   Put the 90 at the other end.
>
> Teacher E: Right 'cos we are going to count up to 90 aren't we? Well done ... (Murphy, 2011, p. 156)

And so it went on, with the teacher prescribing the strategy and keeping control of the discussion and direction of the children's thinking. Why do you think we might have a preference for the Dutch approach? What are your views on the matter?

Some activities to use with children

Throughout this chapter we have made suggestions for activities that might be used to enable children to build up their confidence in manipulating numbers through the development of the sense of pattern in numbers. Teachers should take every opportunity to encourage children to identify, to articulate and to use pattern in numbers, supported as much as possible by visual imagery. As we have seen, children can search for patterns in the addition and multiplication tables. They can interpret additions and subtractions with one- and two-digit numbers on a number line and on the hundred square. They can discuss how to use ten-complements and hundred-complements, and how to relate sums to fives and doubles. We also recommend that teachers give time for children to share different ideas for informal methods of doing calculations, whether these be mental, written or a combination of the two. Below we offer a few further suggestions for developing confidence with number through a greater awareness of pattern.

			3–4	4–5	5–6	6–7	7–8
ACTIVITY 6.1 Dot Patterns				□	□		

Objective

To develop children's sense of the different ways in which the whole numbers from 1 to 9 can be made up.

(Continued)

(Continued)

Materials

Each child needs a 3 × 3 square grid drawn on a square piece of card and 10 counters. They also require some sheets of centimetre-squared paper on which several 3 × 3 square grids have been drawn.

Method

Starting with, say, 5, the children make as many different patterns as they can by putting five counters on the 3 × 3 grid. They record each different pattern by drawing dots on the grids on the squared paper. Discussion about what counts as a different pattern is valuable. This could involve picking up the sheet of paper with the patterns recorded so far and rotating it – or even looking at it in a mirror. Figure 6.16 shows some of the patterns for 5. The children do this for one or two other numbers from 1 to 9. Each child then chooses his or her favourite pattern for each number. They cut these out and arrange them for display, with the appropriate numerals written underneath.

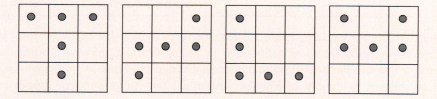

Figure 6.16   *Some dot patterns for five*

 **ACTIVITY 6.2   Rhythmic Counting**

Objective

To emphasize the rhythmic pattern of counting in twos, threes, fours, and so on.

Materials

A drum or a tambour.

Method

The class counts rhythmically in unison from 1 to, say, 50, while the teacher (or a child with a good sense of rhythm) beats in time on the drum or tambour. For counting in twos, they stress every second number: one, *two*, three, *four*, five, *six*, ... and so on. When this is mastered they do the same thing again, whispering the numbers that are not being stressed; and then once again not saying them at all, but still maintaining the same rhythm. Then move on to counting in threes, stressing every third number, then counting in fours, stressing every fourth number. Use the rhythmic beating only if the children are confident in counting in the chosen range; otherwise be more relaxed over the timing. The children can also join in with a physical action such as clapping for each stressed number.

 ACTIVITY 6.3   How Many Trains?

3–4	4–5	5–6	6–7	7–8
		☐	☐	

Objective

To connect number combinations with visual images.

Materials

A collection of coloured rods for 1 to 9; a similar collection of Numicon plates.

Method

The children take one of the rods and find all the ways they can of making up a train of rods of the same length, using first two rods, then three rods, and so on. For example, they could make a train of length 5 with $2 + 3$ or with $1 + 1 + 3$. Children should be encouraged to be systematic and to look for and use pattern. Discussion of whether, for example, $1 + 1 + 3$ is the same as $1 + 3 + 1$ involves informally the principles of commutativity and associativity. This would lead to only six possibilities for the number 5. The same patterns can then be explored using the Numicon plates. This activity provides a rich opportunity for children to talk about the patterns they observe and use in their explorations.

 ACTIVITY 6.4   Oddtown and Eventown

3–4	4–5	5–6	6–7	7–8
			☐	

Objective

To reinforce the concepts of odd and even.

(Continued)

(Continued)

Materials

Red and white (or any two colours of) Lego bricks, or similar materials that click together and can be used to build towers; small model cars numbered from 1 to 10; model people.

Method

As part of their learning about the patterns of odd and even in number, a group of younger children assemble two model towns. In Oddtown all the buildings are made from an odd number of bricks and in Eventown from an even number. They might be encouraged to use red and white bricks alternately in their buildings, so, for example, a building with seven bricks will be made from four red and three white. They might decide to put cars in the two towns according to whether they are odd-numbered or even-numbered. They could put a group with an odd number of model people in Oddtown and a group with an even number in Eventown. This can then be continued by adding other items that can be classified as odd or even – leave this to the creativity of the children. The children are then given an opportunity to show their model towns to others in the class and to talk about how the various components are odd or even.

	ACTIVITY 6.5 Board Games on the Hundred Square	3–4	4–5	5–6	6–7	7–8
					□	□

Objective

To practise the procedures for addition and subtraction on the hundred square.

Materials

A hundred square drawn on card; coloured counters; various dice.

Method

There are numerous variations of board games using a hundred square, all of which are helpful for developing children's facility with number. *Snakes and Ladders* is one of the best examples. Children can be given the opportunity to invent and play their own board games on a hundred square, using their experience of such games. The teacher can also devise their own variations to target particular number skills. For example, to target addition and subtraction of numbers from 0 to 10, the following game might be played by two or three children on a hundred square.

The children have two dice, with the faces labelled 0, 1, 2, 3, 4 and 5, and a coloured counter. When it is their turn each child throws the two dice, and then adds the two numbers shown to get a score from 0 to 10. They move their counter accordingly. On the first three turns they move forward, but on the fourth turn they move backwards. So, for example, a child having scored 7, 3 and 4 on the first three turns would be on the square labelled 14, effectively having started on 7, then added 3 and then 4. If the score on the next turn is 8, the child's counter moves back to 6, subtracting 8 from 14. The first child to reach or pass 100 is the winner. Any child who is unfortunate enough to go back beyond 1 just starts again.

		3–4	4–5	5–6	6–7	7–8
ACTIVITY 6.6 Age Differences						□

Objective

To provide opportunities for finding differences using an empty number line and to support key mental strategies.

Method

Ask the children when they are at home to find out the ages of four other people with very different ages, for example, members of their family, friends or famous people and then to use empty number lines to work out the age differences for various pairs. Encourage children to use the strategies that make most sense to them (see the Research Focus above). For example, Figure 6.17 shows one way in which a child might find the difference between her age (7) and that of her grandmother (63).

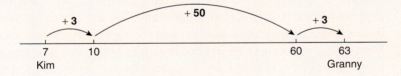

Figure 6.17 *Age difference on an empty number line*

Summary of key ideas

1 An awareness of pattern in number relationships is an important factor in developing confidence and success in manipulating numbers.
2 Many aspects of pattern in number can be understood more strongly by making connections with visual, pictorial and spatial imagery.

(Continued)

(Continued)

3 The ten-complement of a single-digit number is what you need to add to make it up to 10. Ten-complements are important for young children in developing their facility with basic addition and subtraction facts.

4 Instant recall of complements in relation to many other numbers is also very useful, especially all the numbers up to 20.

5 Being able to recall hundred-complements is important in mental manipulation of two-digit numbers.

6 Two strategies for learning basic number bonds that young children find useful are (a) reference to fives; and (b) reference to doubles.

7 Tallying is a useful skill that incorporates the idea of relating numbers to fives.

8 Instant recall of multiplication tables is an important objective for numeracy. But learning these with understanding includes recognizing and using the extensive range of patterns in the tables and the relationships between various results.

9 As well as working with concrete materials, such as base-ten blocks and coins, children will benefit from extensive use of the hundred square in the early stages of addition and subtraction calculations.

10 In a hundred square what is significant about a number is its position in relation to other numbers.

11 Additions and subtractions on a hundred square are experienced as spatial patterns of movements, forward and back, down and up. These experiences promote mental structures that support effective procedures for mental calculations and also emphasize addition and subtraction as inverse processes.

12 Mental and informal strategies for doing addition and subtraction calculations, such as compensation and using multiples of ten as stepping stones, are supported effectively by the use of the empty number line.

 ## Suggestions for further reading

Chapters 8, 9, 11 and 12 in Haylock (2010) provide detailed explanations of various mental calculation strategies, how to teach written methods with an emphasis on understanding, and further explanation of some of the fundamental principles discussed in this chapter.

A theme of Anghileri (2006) is the way in which an appreciation of pattern can enhance children's understanding of number and facility in number operations.

A chapter by Beishuizen entitled 'The empty number line as a new model', in Thompson (2010) outlines the rationale and successful experience of introducing the empty number line into mathematics teaching in primary classrooms in Holland.

Chapter 4 of Montague-Smith and Price (2012) focuses on pattern and explains its importance in early mathematics education. Plenty of helpful practical suggestions are provided.

Similarly, Pound (2006) makes a strong case for making more of pattern in the mathematics curriculum, arguing that it is crucial but frequently underrepresented in the early years of schooling.

Skinner et al. (2004) is a very practical set of three books that provide challenges to foster the addition and subtraction skills of children in Years 1 and 2.

For a fascinating account of the unorthodox but dazzling skills in calculation of Brazilian street-children, see Nunes et al. (1993). This is a book that makes the reader reassess the balance between teaching formal procedures and encouraging children to develop methods that make sense to them in real-life contexts.

For an intelligent approach to teaching calculation methods being promoted in the Netherlands, see van den Heuvel-Panhuizen (2008).

CHAPTER 7

UNDERSTANDING PLACE VALUE

A COMMON MISTAKE

Freddie, aged 7 years, had four cards with the digits 0, 2, 5 and 7 on them. He was using them to answer various questions posed by his teacher. 'Make me a number between 40 and 60', said the teacher. Freddie used the 5 and 7 to make 57. 'Now make me a number between 400 and 600', said the teacher. Freddie arranged all four cards to make the number 5027. When asked what number this was he replied, 'Five hundred and twenty-seven.'

Freddie shows good understanding of the important concept of 'between', but is led astray by his insecure grasp of place value. His mistake here, putting a 0 in 5027 to correspond to the word 'hundred', is a common error around this age (so also is writing 00, as in 50027) when children are beginning to make the connections required to understand the sophisticated principles of place value on which our number system is based.

In this chapter

In this chapter we explain the principles of place value that underpin our number system and show how children can develop understanding of place value through making connections. We consider the role of zero as a place holder and some of the difficulties this causes for children. We then show how experiencing addition and subtraction calculations with two-digit numbers on the hundred square and on the empty number line depends on and strengthens understanding of aspects of place value, as well as developing some key informal and mental strategies. Somewhat reluctantly, we explain formal addition and subtraction calculations using vertical layout, but emphasize the importance of connecting these processes with the corresponding manipulation of concrete materials, such as base-ten blocks and coins. We conclude this chapter by looking at some of the common errors associated with vertical layout for addition and subtraction.

Making sense of place value

Place value in our number system

The principle of place value is the basis of the Hindu-Arabic number system that enables us to represent numbers by using just ten digits (0, 1, 2, 3, 4, 5, 6, 7, 8, 9). The value that each digit represents is determined by its place (going from right to left), the first place on the right representing ones (or units), the second tens, the next hundreds, and so on, with increasing powers of ten. So, for example, in the numeral 3456 the 3 represents '3 thousands' because of the place in which it is written. Similarly, the 4 represents '4 hundreds', the 5 represents '5 tens' and the 6 represents '6 ones' – because of the places in which they are written. The principle of place value means that the *place* of a digit is the most significant contribution to the value it represents. Thus the digit 9 in 900 represents a value ten times greater than it does in the number 90. Clearly, some understanding of place value is essential for handling numbers and calculations with confidence.

The principle of exchange

What is involved in understanding place value? What connections between symbols, language, concrete experiences and pictures might be developed and established as part of this understanding in children up to the age of about 8 years? First, there is the principle of exchange, that when you have accumulated ten in one place in a numeral these can be exchanged for one in the next place to the left. So 10 units can be exchanged for one ten, and 10 tens for one hundred, and so on. It also works in reverse, so if you need to you can exchange one in any place for ten in the next place to the right. So a hundred, for example, can be exchanged for 10 tens. This principle is fundamental to calculations with multi-digit numbers, as we shall see later in this chapter. To understand the principle of exchange the child can experience it in a variety of concrete situations, learning to connect the manipulation of materials with the language pattern 'one of these is ten of those' or 'ten of these is one of those'. This might be, for example, working with base-ten blocks, as shown in Figure 7.1, where a flat piece can be constructed from 10 long pieces, and a long piece can be constructed from 10 units. (Note that we use 'ones' and 'units' interchangeably when discussing place value, sometimes because of the context and sometimes on a whim.)

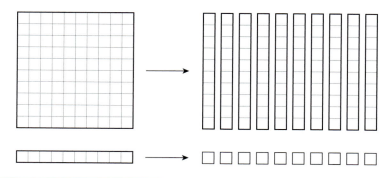

Figure 7.1   *'One of these is ten of those'*

Children would also demonstrate understanding of the principle of exchange when they reduce a collection of base-ten blocks to the smallest number of pieces by a process of exchange, using the appropriate language to describe what they are doing: 'one of these is ten of those'. In relation to our model of understanding (see Chapter 1) we recognize this as significant because the child is making connections between language and the manipulation of concrete materials.

- If you give children a collection of 1p, 10p and £1 coins they get a different experience of the same mathematical ideas. When I do this with my class we call the £1 coin 'a hundred'. So, for example, 3 pound coins, 7 ten-pences and 5 pennies stand for the number 375. Then they do lots of activities that involve going to a bank to change a ten for 10 ones, or a hundred for 10 tens, or vice versa. What works well is to give them a pile of 1p, 10p and £1 coins and ask them to exchange coins at the bank until they have as few coins as possible.
- I find children prefer working with coins, rather than blocks.
- Blocks are easier to understand, because you can actually make a ten out of ten ones, or make a hundred out of ten tens – and later a thousand block out of ten hundreds. But with coins you just have to believe that a 10p coin is worth ten 1p coins and a £1 coin is worth ten 10p coins.

Connecting materials, symbols and arrow cards

To understand place value, children must also learn to connect collections of materials with the symbols, as shown in Figure 7.2. They might demonstrate understanding of this connection by selecting appropriate base-ten blocks to correspond to any given two- or three-digit number written in symbols.

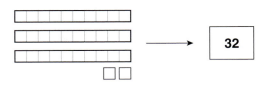

Figure 7.2   *Connecting materials and symbols*

Particularly helpful in establishing understanding of place value is the use of what are sometimes called arrow cards. These are illustrated in Figure 7.3. By placing the 2-card on top of the 30-card, the cards show how the symbol 32 is made up from the 30 represented by the 3 tens and the 2 represented by the 2 units. These arrow cards therefore provide children with a kind of picture, an image of what is going on when we write in symbols a number with more than one digit. So, with an appropriate dialogue between the teacher and the children, activities with arrow cards promote connections between language, pictures and symbols. This experience helps children to see how 32 is equivalent to 30 + 2.

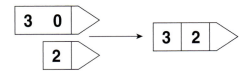

Figure 7.3   *Arrow cards to show 32 as 30 and 2*

Later in the chapter we shall see that 'partitioning' a number into tens and units, as illustrated in Figure 7.3, is a key strategy in doing calculations. (Note that this is a different use of the word partitioning from 'the partitioning structure' for subtraction, discussed in Chapter 3.) Figure 7.4 shows how the same process can be applied to partition three-digit numbers into hundreds, tens and units.

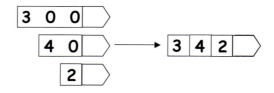

Figure 7.4   *Arrow cards to show 342 = 300 + 40 + 2*

Connecting the number names with the symbols

Understanding place value also involves learning to connect the particular ways in which we read and say out loud the names of numerals with the corresponding symbols. So, for example, the written numeral 342 is connected with 'three hundred and forty-two', spoken. The connection from the spoken form to the written form in particular is far from straightforward. Many children, like Freddie above, will write 'three hundred and forty-two' as 30042 or 3042, making a false connection between the word 'hundred' and the symbol for zero. This illustrates the need to develop understanding by making as many connections as possible. The child who makes this kind of error will be helped, for example, by connecting the spoken language and the written symbols with the concrete experience of blocks or coins and the image of the arrow cards.

> When I get the children to make three-digit numbers, like 342, using arrow cards, we talk about the way the zeros in the 300 disappear when the 40 and the 2 cards are added. But the 3 still tells us that this is 'three hundred'. The zeros are just hidden behind the other numbers.

Zero as a place holder

In some numerals, such as 206, there is a zero occupying one of the places. This use of zero as a 'place holder' is an important component of understanding place-value notation. As we have seen earlier in Chapters 1 and 2, zero is the cause of many of the difficulties that children have in handling numbers, because the connections to be established are sometimes challenging and far from straightforward. There are particular problems in making the connections between the way we say numbers and the way we write them in symbols where zero is involved. For example, in Figure 7.5, the child must learn to connect the symbols 206 and the collection of

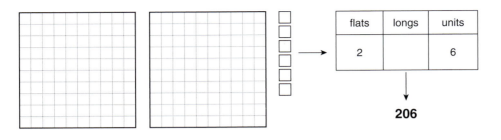

Figure 7.5   *Zero as a place holder*

materials shown, namely, 2 flat pieces (hundreds), no long pieces (tens) and 6 units (ones). The zero is needed to occupy the empty place, to show that there is an absence of long pieces (tens). So the child has to write something to represent the absence of something.

As we have seen above, children may wrongly connect the symbol for zero with the word 'hundred'. This seems to be because when they read a number like 206, they connect the symbol 2 with the word 'two', the symbol 0 with the word 'hundred' and the symbol 6 with the word 'six'. What is really difficult to grasp is to connect the symbol 2 with 'two hundred' because of the position in which it is written. Once again, constructing numbers like this using arrow cards, as shown in Figure 7.6, is effective in helping children to see that 206 is made up of two hundred (200) and 6.

> When I am teaching this idea, I write a number like 206 on the board. Then I point to the 2 and ask, 'What does this 2 say?' The children reply 'two hundred'. Then I point to the zero and ask 'What does this zero say?' The children have to put their hands over their mouths and say nothing! Then I point to the six and ask 'What does this 6 say?' and they reply 'six'. Finally we read the whole number: 'Two hundred ... (silence) ... and six'. They like the idea of 'keeping mum' when they see the zero.

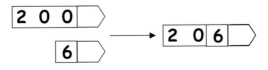

Figure 7.6   *Arrow cards to show 206 = 200 + 6*

Connecting symbols for numbers with the number line

A further aspect of understanding of place value, connecting symbols with pictures, is shown in Figure 7.7. The child learns to connect the symbols for numbers with the important picture of the number line. This might involve, for example, locating the approximate position of a given number on a number line labelled in 10s or in 100s. Then, vice versa, the child has to be able to state or write the approximate number corresponding to a given point on a number line labelled in 10s or in 100s.

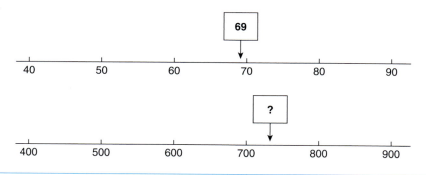

Figure 7.7   *Connecting symbols with the number line*

A developing understanding of place value

We can see therefore that much of what is involved in understanding place value can be identified as the building up of a complex network of connections between language, symbols, concrete materials and pictures. But we would not wish to imply that children have to understand all this completely before they can make progress in handling numbers up to thousands or doing additions with, say, two- or three-digit numbers. Children can get a long way in learning to add and subtract if they have confidence in:

- counting forwards and backwards from any number in tens (for example, 14, 24, 34, 44, …), and then in hundreds (for example, 728, 628, 528, 428, …);
- positioning numbers in relation to other numbers, particularly multiples of ten and a hundred, through spatial images such as number lines (see Figure 7.7 above) and hundred squares (see below);
- partitioning two-digit numbers into tens and ones (for example, 74 = 70 + 4), and then three-digit numbers into hundreds, tens and ones (for example, 253 = 200 + 50 + 3);
- using mental and informal calculation strategies.

Place value and the hundred square

The hundred square is an important image on which to build understanding of place value. Figure 7.8 shows how it might be used to connect the number 57, for example, with 5 tens and 7 ones, using base-ten blocks (tens and ones). Children place ten-blocks on the hundred square (drawn to an appropriate size to accommodate the blocks), counting in tens as they do this to show how many squares they have covered up: 10, 20, 30, 40, 50. Then they place unit blocks along the next row until they reach 57, counting on from 50: 51, 52, 53, 54, 55, 56, 57. They can then talk about how counting to 57 is equivalent to counting 5 tens and 7 ones.

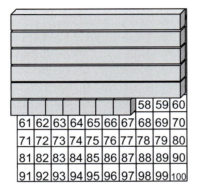

Figure 7.8   *Tens and units on the hundred square*

Additions with two-digit numbers on the hundred square

The activities on the hundred square that we described in Chapter 6 help to shape appropriate mental structures for visualizing addition and subtraction strategies. As we saw in that chapter, moving down a square adds 10, and moving along a square adds 1. This provides a basis for developing effective mental methods for the addition and subtraction of two 2-digit numbers.

- If you do something like 'add 32' it's the same move each time – down three squares and along two – wherever you start.
- So, do the 3 squares down and the 2 squares across correspond to the 3 tens and 2 ones in 32?

Yes, they do! This movement on the hundred square illustrates a key strategy for addition. This is to partition the second number into tens and ones, as we discussed above in relation to arrow cards (see Figures 7.3, 7.4 and 7.6).

So, on the hundred square to find 26 + 32, for example, we think of the 32 as 30 + 2, so the calculation is transformed into 26 + 30 + 2. To do this we start at 26, move down three steps (adding 30) and along 2 steps (adding 2). This spatial procedure should then provide children with mental structures that will enable them to carry out such calculations mentally, by the same strategy: 26, … add 30, … 56, … add 2, … 58. As we argue later in this chapter, this is so much more valuable to children than introducing them too early to formal written methods of calculation that encourage them to treat the 2 and 6 in 26 and the 3 and 2 in 32 as separate entities. In the hundred square approach, the number 26 is seen first in terms of its *position* in the ordering of numbers. And adding 32 is seen as a combination of adding 30 and adding 2.

Errors in addition are most likely to occur when children tackle an addition such as 26 + 37 by a formal written method that involves 'carrying 1' (this is explained later in the chapter). Using the hundred square procedure such errors are much less likely to arise. The child starts at 26, adds 30 (3 steps down) to get 56, and then adds 7 to this (7 steps along – possibly by first making up to 60 with 4 steps and then a further 3). Eventually this kind of activity leads to facility with the corresponding mental strategy for 26 + 37: 26, … add 30, … 56, … add 4, … 60, … add 3, … 63. The procedures on the hundred square corresponding to 26 + 32 and 26 + 37 are illustrated in Figure 7.9.

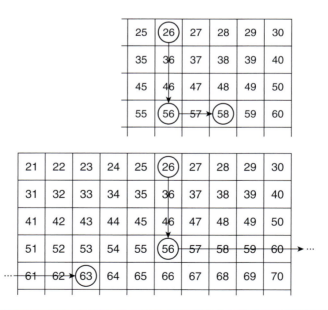

Figure 7.9   *Showing 26 + 32 and 26 + 37 on the hundred square*

Subtractions with two-digit numbers on the hundred square

Subtraction of a two-digit number can be experienced on the hundred square as the reverse process of addition, using the counting-back principle. So, to deal with 83 − 57 (a tricky subtraction), the 57 is mentally partitioned into 50 and 7. We can then interpret subtracting 57 as 5 steps up (which takes us to 33) and 7 steps back (which takes us to 26). Of course, we are assuming here that the procedures for subtracting 50 and for subtracting 7 have already been thoroughly grasped. For most children it is then an achievable step from carrying out the process on the hundred square to performing the task mentally – or informally with paper and pencil – using this kind of strategy: 83, … subtract 50, … 33, … subtract 3, … 30, … subtract 4, … 26. Again, we should note how the procedure leads the child to deal with 83 as a number in its own right defined by its position in the hundred square. The number 83 is not seen as an 8 and a 3, with a 5 and a 7 to be taken away. In this way we avoid the potential for bizarre and random combinations of 8, 3, 5, 7, little 1s and crossings-out that are so common in the formal vertical layout of subtractions like this.

But subtraction, as we have seen in Chapter 3, has a number of different structures. So, as well as dealing with, say, 83 − 57 by using the process of counting back, we can also use subtraction as the inverse of addition. In this way, the subtraction is conceived as: What must be added to 57 to get 83? On the hundred square this is often the most useful interpretation of subtraction, especially as it supports the kind of mental process for subtraction that many people find most successful. The process on the hundred square is straightforward. For example: start at 57, move along 3 steps to get to 60, move down 2 steps to get to 80, then move along 3 steps to get to 83. So to get from 57 to 83 you need to add 3 + 20 + 3, which is 26. This experience connects very strongly with doing subtraction on an empty number line. See, for example, Figure 6.14(c) and (d) in the previous chapter.

The two-hundred grid

The reader may be wondering about additions of two-digit numbers where the answer is greater than 100. How do you learn to do these using a hundred square? The answer is simple: extend it to a two-hundred grid! Figure 7.10 shows a possible layout for a two-hundred grid. As an example, we show the steps involved for the addition 76 + 57: start at 76, move down 5 steps (add 50) to 126, and move along 7 steps (add 7) to 133.

To get to the stage where this level of addition can be carried out confidently we have to extend two kinds of patterns. First, we have to be able to extend the pattern for adding 10 beyond 100. For example: 76 + 10 = 86, 76 + 20 = 96, 76 + 30 = 106, 76 + 40 = 116, and so on. Then, we have to be able to extend a sequence such as 6 + 7 = 13, 16 + 7 = 23, 26 + 7 = 33, 36 + 7 = 43, … 86 + 7 = 93, beyond 100: 96 + 7 = 103, 106 + 7 = 113, 116 + 7 = 123, and so on. Of course, in terms of movements on the

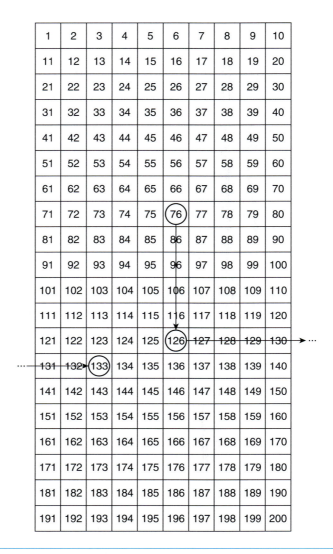

Figure 7.10   *Showing 76 + 57 on a two-hundred grid*

two-hundred grid these are not difficult extensions. With these ideas secure, we can handle the two steps of 76 + 50 and 126 + 7 that are involved in 76 + 57.

Then, of course, with the provision of a two-hundred grid, children can handle the corresponding subtractions, such as 133 − 57. This can be done either by counting back 57 from 133, or (better) by starting at 57 and adding on to get to 133. Appropriate activities on the two-hundred grid can establish patterns of results like: 133 − 10 = 123, 133 − 20 = 113, 133 − 30 = 103, 133 − 40 = 93, and so on.

Using partitioning for additions on the empty number line

An addition like 432 + 216 is very easy to do mentally, just by partitioning the numbers into hundreds, tens and ones, and then adding these in turn, starting from the left: 400 + 200 = 600, 30 + 10 = 40, 2 + 6 = 8. So the result is 600 + 40 + 8, which is 648. In this example there is no need to use the principle of exchange (ten of these is one of those). Contrast this with 476 + 283. We asked a primary school teacher how they would do this addition mentally.

> I would start with the 476, add 200, then add 80, then add 3. So, I would think, 476 add 200 is 676. Then I need 676 add 80. Mentally I break the 80 into 30 and 50, so that's 676 add 30, giving me 706, then another 50, giving me 756. Then I need 756 add 3, which is 759.

The teacher here has first partitioned the second number, 283, into 200 + 80 + 3. So the calculation is conceived mentally as: 476 + 200 + 80 + 3. The most accessible mental strategy for addition is often what is used here: to partition the second number into tens and ones (or hundreds, ten and ones) and then to add these in turn to the first number. Note that all you need to be able to do then is to count on in hundreds or tens or ones from a given number. On the way the teacher has simplified the addition of 80 by splitting it further into 30 and 50. This kind of reasoning is supported by doing additions using partitioning on the empty number line, as shown in Figure 7.11(d). Clearly, to get to this level of proficiency children would build up the processes involved through simpler examples, such as those shown in Figure 7.11(a), (b) and (c).

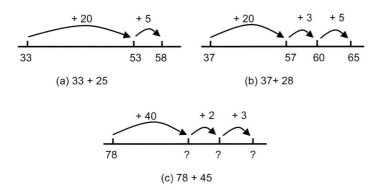

(a) 33 + 25   (b) 37+ 28

(c) 78 + 45

Figure 7.11   *Additions on an empty number line using partitioning of the second number*

Figure 7.11(a) shows the calculation of 33 + 25 on an empty number line, partitioning the 25 into 20 + 5, so the calculation becomes 33 + 20 + 5. Figure 7.11(b) shows the use of partitioning into tens and ones and the use of 60 as a stepping stone for calculating 37 + 28. The use of the empty number line shows visually how 37 + 28 can be conceived in simple steps as 37 + 20 + 3 + 5. Figure 7.11(c) shows the calculation of 78 + 45, seeing this initially as 78 add 40 add 5. The reader may find it instructive to insert the missing numbers and to reflect on the mental processes involved in getting to these.

Using place value in vertical layout addition

The reader will probably have inferred (correctly) that our preference in this age range is to focus on informal and mental calculation strategies for addition and subtraction, building on the child's developing understanding of place value, supported by the visual imagery of hundred squares and number lines. But the reader may find themselves working in a situation where the policy is to introduce formal addition and subtraction methods, even for 2-digit numbers, using a vertical layout with digits set out in columns. We feel obliged therefore to give some space to explaining how these methods might be learnt with understanding. This will require giving time to enable the learner to make connections between the manipulation of the symbols and the manipulation of base-ten materials. We will start by discussing addition, using coins to represent hundreds, tens and ones. The same principles could be experienced using base-ten blocks. Using a vertical layout is very straightforward for additions such as 43 + 26 or 123 + 345, where there is no need to call on the principle of exchange (because there is no 'carrying'; see below). You just add the units, then the tens, and then the hundreds. It gets interesting when one of these additions produces a result of 10 or more.

Addition of two-digit numbers, with 'carrying'

We start with a simple example with two 2-digit numbers. This is easier to explain verbally with actual coins or blocks than in writing, but we'll do our best! Figure 7.12 shows this process for 38 + 26. First, the two numbers are written as shown in (a), with the tens digits lined up and the units digits lined up. The numbers are represented by the coins on the left: on the top line, 3 tens and 8 ones; on the line below, 2 tens and 6 ones. To add 38 and 26 we have to combine these two sets of coins. We start by looking at the ones (units): there are 14 of these. Whenever we get ten or more of anything we do an exchange. In (b) we have shown how ten of the ones might be collected together. These are taken to the bank of coins and exchanged for a ten. This ten is then 'carried' (literally) from the bank and placed in the tens collection as

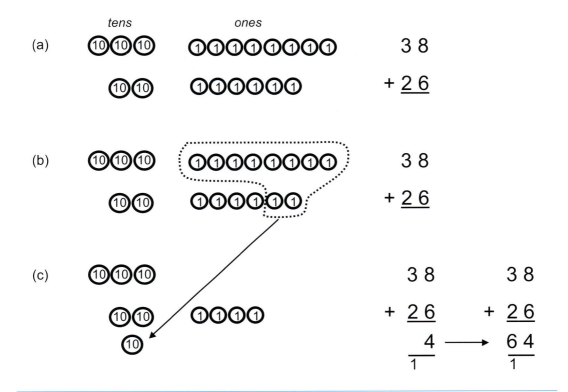

Figure 7.12 *Vertical layout for 38 + 26 illustrated with coins*

shown in (c). This is recorded as shown in (c): the 4 indicating the 4 ones left after the exchange, and the little 1 below the line indicating that a ten has been carried from the ones into the tens column. There are now 6 tens altogether, so 6 is written in the tens place in the answer, giving the result 64. Eventually, of course, the coins or blocks used here will not be required, but in the early stages they provide a concrete experience that can enable the process to be learnt with understanding, rather than as a meaningless recipe to be learnt by rote.

Addition of three-digit numbers

Figure 7.13 shows the same process applied to the addition of two 3-digit numbers, represented by pound coins (in this context referred to as hundreds), tens and ones. This example involves an exchange of 10 tens for a hundred, with one hundred carried from the tens into the hundreds column. The ones are added first, 1 + 3 = 4, and the 4 recorded in the units position, as shown in (a). Then we turn our attention to the tens.

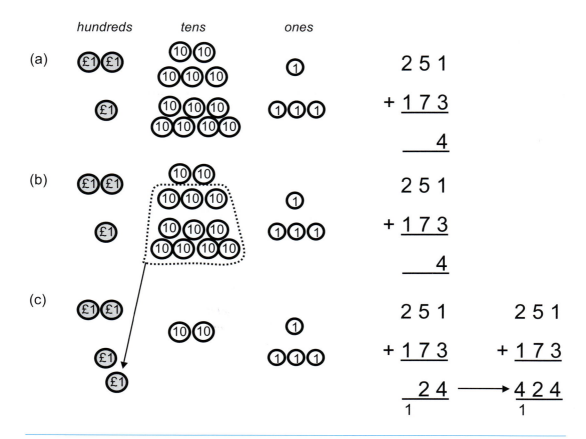

Figure 7.13   *Vertical layout for 251 + 173 illustrated with coins*

Altogether there are 12 tens, so 10 of these are exchanged at the bank for a hundred, as indicated in (b). The one hundred carried into the hundreds column is shown by the little 1 beneath the line in (c) and the number of tens remaining (2) is recorded in the tens column in the answer. Altogether there are now 4 hundreds, giving the final result of 424, corresponding to the 4 hundreds, 2 tens and 4 ones that we now have.

In summary, the process is essentially as follows:

- set out the numbers to be added so the units, tens, hundreds (thousands, and so on) are aligned in columns;
- add the numbers in the columns, starting from the units and working right to left;
- whenever you get a total of 10 or more in a particular column, exchange 10 in that column for 1 in the next;
- record the exchange with a little 1 written somewhere appropriate in the column and add this into the total in that column.

Once this process is mastered and understood with blocks or coins (or both), it can be recorded as shown in Figure 7.14. In this example, to begin with, we add the units: 8 + 7 = 15. Then 10 of these are exchanged for 1 ten, leaving 5 units in the units column of the answer and a little 1 to be added in to the total of tens. Altogether there are now 6 + 3 + 1 = 10 tens. These are exchanged for a hundred, leaving 0 tens in the tens column of the answer and a little 1 to be added in to the total of hundreds. Altogether there are now 4 + 2 + 1 = 7 hundreds; this is recorded as shown in the hundreds position in the answer, 705.

$$
\begin{array}{r}
4\ 6\ 8 \\
+\ \underline{2\ 3\ 7} \\
\underline{7\ 0\ 5} \\
1\ \ 1
\end{array}
$$

Figure 7.14   *Vertical layout for 468 + 237 = 705*

Using place value in subtraction by decomposition

Subtraction is straightforward in examples like 543 − 231, where none of the digits in the second number is greater than the corresponding digit in the first number. You can just deal with the hundreds, tens and units in turn, working from the left to the right to get 543 − 231 = 312. Subtractions like this do not need a formal method or a vertical layout. Subtractions only get tricky when one or more of the digits in the second number is greater than the corresponding digit in the first number, as in the case of 543 − 287. If children are to be expected to learn to do these using a formal method with vertical layout, then they will probably learn to use the method of decomposition.

Decomposition for subtraction with two-digit numbers

As with a formal method for addition, we think it is important that learning the method of subtraction by decomposition should involve connecting the manipulation of the symbols with the manipulation of concrete materials. We begin with a simple example, which we explain using base-ten blocks (tens and units). Figure 7.15 shows how we might tackle 63 − 27. The 63 is set out in blocks − 6 tens and 3 units. To subtract 27 we will take away from this collection 2 tens and 7 units. It is neater if you start with the units. The problem is that we do not have sufficient units to take 7 away. So, as shown in

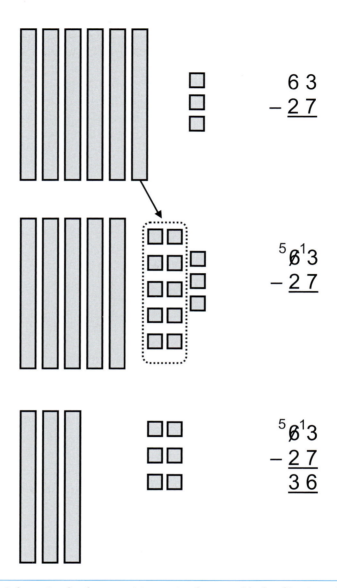

Figure 7.15   *Subtraction by decomposition, using base-ten blocks: 63 – 27 = 36*

(b), one of the tens is taken to the bank and exchanged for ten units. In the recording of this step, shown in (b), the little 5 and the crossed out 6 indicate that we now have 5 tens (not 6); and the little 1 placed in front of the 3 indicates that we now have 13 units. We can then take away the 2 tens and the 7 units required, to get the result shown in (c): 3 tens and 6 units, which is 36, as shown in the recording on the right. Note that the appropriate language to support the process here is 'exchanging one of these for ten of those'. It is not uncommon to hear teachers talking about 'borrowing one'. This expression makes no sense at all in this context and we recommend that it is not adopted.

Decomposition for subtraction with three-digit numbers

Having mastered this process for two-digit numbers children would in due course progress to examples with three-digit numbers, eventually dropping the support of the concrete materials and recording their subtractions, as shown in the examples in Figure 7.16. In the calculation of 453 − 181, shown in (a), one of the hundreds has been exchanged for 10 tens, to make possible the subtraction of 8 tens. In the calculation of 453 − 185, shown in (b), first one of the tens has been exchanged for 10 units, to make possible the subtraction of 5 units; then one of the hundreds has been exchanged for 10 tens, to enable the subtraction of 8 tens. The recording of this gets a bit messy.

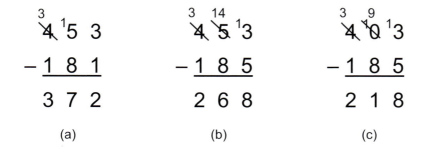

Figure 7.16 *Subtraction by decomposition: (a) 453 − 181, (b) 453 − 185, (c) 403 − 185*

Even messier is a subtraction where there is a zero in the top number as in 403 − 185, shown in (c). Here we need some more units in order to be able to subtract the 5 units, but because there are no tens we have to go across to the hundreds, exchange one of these for 10 tens and then exchange one of these for 10 units. This give us in the top line 3 hundreds, 9 tens and 13 units, from which we can subtract the 1 hundred, 8 tens and 5 units, as required. This is as far as we intend to go in explaining subtraction by decomposition. For further explanation the reader is referred to Chapter 9 of Haylock (2010).

We feel constrained to point out that although the example in (c) is really tricky to handle by this formal method of subtraction it is much simpler to do by informal methods, using, for example, an empty number line. In Figure 7.17 the difference between 185 and 403 is found very easily using 200 and 400 as stepping stones.

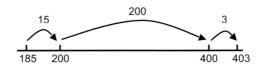

Figure 7.17 *On an empty number line 403 – 185 is seen as 15 + 200 + 3 = 218*

PAUSE TO REFLECT   For help with subtraction call 999!

We hope that we have made clear that there is no 'proper' way of doing subtractions. To demonstrate this, here's a sneaky way of doing potentially tricky subtractions, as an alternative to the method of decomposition. We thought it might amuse you, or even intrigue you!

Example 1: Calculate 406 – 158

This would be a tricky subtraction using decomposition, because of the zero in the first number.

Start by subtracting the second number (158) from 999 (giving 841). This is easy to do, because you can just do it digit by digit, working from the left, making each digit up to 9. Write down the 841 as shown in Figure 7.18(a). Then add the 406 and the 841, as shown in Figure 7.18(b). Finally cross off the digit 1 at the front of the result and add it to the final digit, as shown in Figure 7.18(c). And that's the answer! Try this with a few other three-digit subtractions.

Example 2: Calculate 83 – 47

Because the first number here has only two digits, then you subtract the second number from 99, giving 52. See Figure 7.18(d)–(f).

Example 3: Calculate 2308 – 754

In this example you need to write the second number with four digits as well, so it becomes 2308 – 0754. Then we subtract the four-digit second number from 9999 (to get 9245). See Figure 7.18(h)–(j).

Try a few more examples yourself. This method really is foolproof – we hope you don't prove us wrong in saying this! But what's going on? Because in Example 1 we add the difference between 999 and the second number to the first number, the result of the addition is 999 more than we need. How does that explain the final sneaky step with the 1s?

(a)	406 – 158	(b)	406 – 158	(c)	406 – 158
	<u>841</u>		<u>841</u>		<u>841</u>
			1247		₁247 + 1 = 248

(d)	83 – 47	(e)	83 – 47	(f)	83 – 47
	<u>52</u>		<u>52</u>		<u>52</u>
			135		₁35 + 1 = 36

(h)	2308 – 0754	(i)	2308 – 0754	(j)	2308 – 0754
	<u>9245</u>		<u>9245</u>		<u>9245</u>
			11553		₁1553 + 1 = 1554

Figure 7.18   *Sneaky subtractions*

Children's errors and vertical layout

Overemphasis on vertical layout

It is important that teachers should be aware of the potential difficulties inherent in the formal methods for addition and subtraction, using vertical layout, as explained above. In our view, there is no case for introducing children to vertical layout before they have developed a basic understanding of place value. Indeed, our experience is that the too early introduction of vertical layout can be positively harmful. It often seems that those who press most strongly for teaching these methods have a conception that writing additions and subtractions in this form is the 'proper' way to do the calculations. Such a view is misguided. Our contention is that mental strategies based on visual or pictorial images, such as movements on the hundred square or along an empty number line, should be the major priority for the development of confidence and success in handling numbers, definitely for children under the age of 9 years.

Vertical layout used too early tends to encourage children to think of the digits in, say, a two-digit number, as separate entities. They may well set out, say, 13 + 24 in the prescribed manner, with the 1 above the 2 and the 3 above the 4, add the 3 and the 4 and write down 7, then add the 1 and the 2 and write down 3, getting the correct answer – but in doing all this have no conception at all of the two numbers 13 and 24 that are being added. As far as they are concerned they may have just added 3 and 4 and then added 1 and 2 (not 1 ten and 2 tens). This kind of thinking is particularly encouraged if children are just learning procedures for manipulating the symbols without substantial experience of relating them to the concrete embodiments of place value, such as base-ten blocks or 1p, 10p and £1 coins.

Some typical errors in vertical layout

Not surprisingly then, vertical layout leads to all manner of errors, many related to the tendency to treat the digits as separate numbers and then to combine them in various ways that ignore or apply wrongly the principles of place-value. Figure 7.19 shows some of the many common errors that children make in addition and subtraction using vertical layout.

In examples (a) and (b) in Figure 7.19 the child concerned has in each case just added up the three digits in the two numbers. In example (c) the child has made a common mistake associated with failing to write the units in the same column. In example (d) the child has added the 6 and 7 to get 13, written this down, then added the 2 and 3 to get 5, without remembering to carry one. In example (e), another child has tried to apply the principle of carrying but has carried the wrong bit of the 13. In example (f) the child has worked from left to right, rather than from right to left and consequently misapplied the carrying procedure. Example (g) is the most familiar subtraction error: simply taking the smaller digit from the larger one each time. Children have many original ways of muddling up the decomposition process in subtraction. Example (h) is a case where the child has used the idea of exchanging a ten for 10 ones unnecessarily and finished up writing 12 in the units position in the answer!

Zeros in subtraction questions have huge potential for generating all kinds of errors, such as those shown in examples (i), (j), (k) and (l) in Figure 7.19. Sometimes children just ignore a zero, as in example (i). Other times they treat it like 10, as in example (j). And sometimes, because they remember that you have to apply a different procedure when there is a zero in the top number of a subtraction they will try to apply this to a zero in the bottom number, as shown in example (k). Finally, it is not uncommon for children always to write down 0 as the result whenever they have to subtract 0, as shown in example (l).

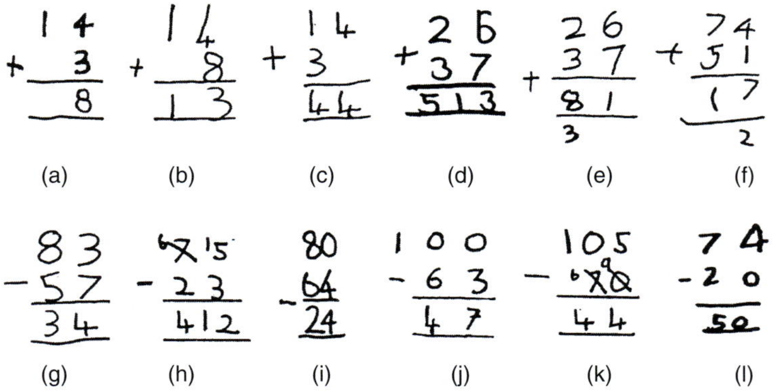

Figure 7.19   *Typical errors in vertical layout*

This is not a comprehensive analysis of all the errors that children can and do make in written calculations. But we have provided these typical examples because they are all errors that just would not arise if these children had not yet seen vertical layout. They would not have occurred if the children had been encouraged to develop mental and informal strategies based on the hundred square or the empty number line.

For example, faced with 26 + 37 the mental strategies encouraged by the use of the hundred square (26, ... add 30, ... 56, ... add 4, ... 60, ... add 3, ... 63) are unlikely to lead to answers like 513 or 81! And, given the subtraction 105 – 70, we would expect an average 8-year-old brought up on activities on the empty number line to reason along these lines: to get from 70 to 105, add 30 to get to 100, and then add another 5 ... so the answer is 35. These mental steps would be supported by images of moving along the rows of the hundred square or along a number line. Of course, children will make errors in using these mental strategies – mainly through recalling number bonds incorrectly or forgetting where they have got to – which is why they should be encouraged to make appropriate informal jottings as they go along. But they are less likely to apply a totally wrong procedure.

RESEARCH FOCUS   Ascertaining children's understanding of place value

In *Young Children Reinvent Arithmetic* Constance Kamii (1985) argues forcibly that 'premature instruction, be it in place value or other aspects of the curriculum, is injurious to children's making sense of a discipline' (p. 63). In order to test a learner's understanding of place value she devised the following procedure (see Figure 7.20).

1 Put out 16 counters. Ask the child to check the number, make a drawing of them and check that the drawing has 16 counters represented.
2 As illustrated in Figure 7.20(a), write the numeral for sixteen (16) on the same sheet.
3 As shown in Figure 7.20(b), ring the 6 in the numeral 16 and ask the child to draw a line round counters to show you this part of the number 16. Figure 7.20(b) shows a response to this.
4 Now ring the 1 in the numeral 16 and ask the child to draw a line round counters that show this part of the number 16.
5 Finally ask the child to draw a line round 'the whole thing', that is the '16'.

We suggest that you complete steps 4 and 5 using Figure 7.20(b) yourself. The procedure is a bit cumbersome to explain in words but it yielded interesting results. Typically, after step 4 above, a 6-year-old's sheet would look similar to that drawn in Figure 7.21.

(Continued)

(Continued)

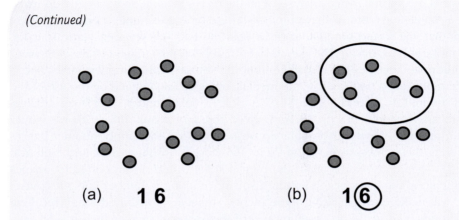

(a) **1 6**   (b) **1⑥**

Figure 7.20   *Task for assessment of understanding of place value*

How does this compare to your drawing? Having tried this task on children across grades 4, 6 and 8 in various American states, Kamii noted that, by grade 8 approximately 80% of children would draw round ten counters when asked to circle those which might represent the digit '1' in '16'. When we have tried Kamii's task we have been struck by the certainty and speed with which some individuals respond, be they correct or incorrect!

Sometimes it is relatively easy to deduce the source of a child's misunderstanding of place value from the type of error they make. For example, it has long been recognized that the reason that a child might write 'three hundred and three' as '3003' is because that is the way we say it (Dickson et al., 1984). As we have discussed already, at the start of this chapter with the example of Freddie and elsewhere, it is not difficult to link this common error with the difficulty of making correct connections between language and symbols.

Other times the reason for a child's error is not so clear. In a general article discussing the challenges involved in assessing mathematical understanding Herbert Ginsburg (2009) advocates the use of clinical interviews, illustrating their effectiveness with some examples involving place value concepts. One of the keys to such interviews is, on completion of a task, simply to ask, 'How did you do it?' An entirely reasonable suggestion, you might think – but this is a question that many teachers fail to ask. Others might ask it but pay little attention to the response, apart perhaps from assessing whether it is logical or not. But a third group might use the response to this question to analyse the degree to which the learner understands the mathematical ideas involved.

For example, Ginsburg discusses some of his earlier work (Ginsburg and Seo, 1999) where, having presented the entirely new problem of 23 × 4 to her class of 2nd graders, the teacher asked two children how they both came to the same solution, albeit using different strategies. The first child wrote a column of four 20s, added them and wrote 80. She repeated the process adding four 3s to get 12. She then added 80 and 12 and arrived at the correct answer of 92. What can you deduce of her understanding of place value? Of addition? Of multiplication? How does it compare to that of the second child who wrote down the following and then added his responses together: 4 × 20, 4 × 3, 4 × 0? Ginsburg concedes that 'the multiplication by zero is a bit of a mystery' (p. 123), but nevertheless suggests that the second child had more advanced mathematical understanding than the first. Why might this be? Finally, we would recommend that you take the time to read as much as you can about *which* mathematical misconceptions are found by researchers to be most common in children and *how* they might come about. Ball, Thames and Phelps (2008) suggest that one of the qualities of an expert mathematics teacher is the ability to break down concepts into their component parts and then to use this information to help unravel learners' thinking. In order to do this your own mathematical understanding needs to be sound – and we hope our book provides an appropriate foundation for this – but it is also extremely valuable if you have insights into the ways in which children might respond to the tasks you set *before* they do them so that you are not having to start from scratch in analysing their incorrect or muddled responses.

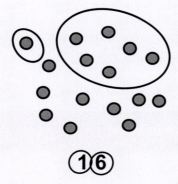

Figure 7.21   *The typical response of a 6-year-old to a place value task*

Some activities to use with children

The first half of this chapter has been about drawing on the child's developing understanding of place value to do addition and subtraction calculations, using methods supported by practical experience with materials such as arrow cards, hundred squares and empty number line diagrams. These activities would be the basis for developing confidence in such calculations. We would expect that teachers would also provide children with not just abstract calculations but with many real-life situations that provide meaningful contexts for doing addition and subtraction, both practical examples and 'word problems'. To supplement such basic mathematical experience we offer just a few suggestions below for activities focused on the development of children's understanding.

ACTIVITY 7.1   Bundling in Tens

3–4	4–5	5–6	6–7	7–8
		☐		

Objective

To provide topic-based, practical experience of the place-value principle of bundling into tens.

Materials

A Paddington Bear, pretend (or real) biscuits, packing material, and a three-minute timer with a buzzer.

Method

This could be an activity for, say, three children, as part of an ongoing project on the Paddington Bear theme. Two children package biscuits into rolls of ten at a time, while the third sets the timer going. When the buzzer sounds the third player announces that Paddington has come for his biscuits. This child, with the assistance of Paddington, counts (in tens and ones) how many biscuits each player has wrapped and awards a biscuit as a prize to the one who has packed the most. The children can take it in turns to be packers.

ACTIVITY 7.2   Connections (Place Value)

3–4	4–5	5–6	6–7	7–8
		☐	☐	

Objective

To develop understanding of place value by making connections between symbols, concrete experiences, language and pictures.

Materials

A pack of cards with the numerals 0 to 9 written on them, and strips of card with the words: *one, two, three, … nine, and twenty, thirty, forty, … ninety*; base-ten materials (tens and ones); 10p and 1p coins; a number line marked from 0 to 99 (such as a metre rule marked in centimetres); a movable pointer for indicating numbers on the number line; arrow cards for tens and units.

Method

This is a co-operative activity for a small group of children. They turn over two of the numeral cards, for example 2 and 3. They then arrange them side by side to make a two-digit numeral, for example, 23. They then have to make all the possible representations of this with the materials provided, as illustrated in Figure 7.22. (Because the 'teens' do not fit the same language pattern

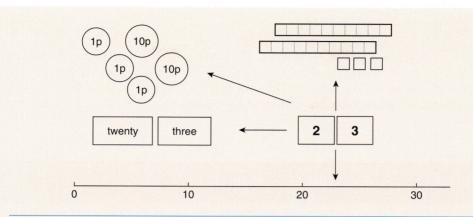

Figure 7.22 *Making place value connections*

as the subsequent numbers they should be excluded from this game – teachers should therefore arrange the cards so that one is not used in the tens position for this activity.)

ACTIVITY 7.3 Hundred Square Target

3–4	4–5	5–6	6–7	7–8
			☐	☐

Objective

To explore addition patterns on the hundred square.

Materials

A hundred square drawn on card; two coloured counters (say, blue and red).

Method

This is a game of strategy for two children. For each round, one of the children places the blue counter on a number of their choice greater than 50. This is the target. The other child then starts the game by choosing any whole number from 1 to 9, inclusive, and places the red counter on this number on the hundred square. In turn the children continue choosing numbers in the range 1–9 and moving the red counter forward each time by the number chosen. For example, if the first four numbers chosen are 7, 4, 5 and 2, then the red counter will move from 7 to 11 to 16 to 18. The child who gets the red counter to land on the target is the winner of that round.

(Continued)

(Continued)

There is a subtle strategy to discover here. Say, the target is 78. The children may discover by playing the game several times that whoever gets the counter to land on 68 (10 away from the target) must win the game. This means that whoever gets the counter to land on 58 should win the game, because they can guarantee landing on 68! And so on ...

3-4	4-5	5-6	6-7	7-8
			☐	☐

ACTIVITY 7.4   Hundred Square Addition with Blocks

Objective

To make connections between addition on the hundred square and addition using base-ten blocks.

Materials

A hundred square drawn on card, using centimetre squares; tens and units from a set of base-ten blocks, where the unit is a centimetre cube.

Method

Children explore the addition of two-digit numbers using blocks, with the twist that the blocks are placed on the hundred square. Figure 7.23 shows how this might work for the addition 47 + 25. The 47 is represented in blocks using 4 tens and 7 units, which are placed on the hundred square

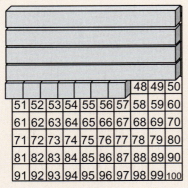

(a) 4 tens and 7 units

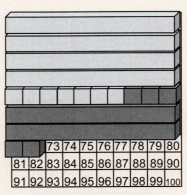

(b) add 2 tens and 5 units

Figure 7.23   *The addition 47 + 25 with base-ten blocks on a hundred square*

as shown in (a). The children are helped to observe that the blocks cover 47 cells in the hundred square, from number 1 to number 47. The child then has to add to this the 2 tens and 5 units that represent 25. This is shown in (b), where we have used a darker shading for the blocks that are added. Note how three of the units added are used to make up a ten. The children can now observe that the result of the addition is equivalent to 7 tens and 2 units, that altogether 72 cells are covered by the blocks – all the numbers from 1 to 72 – and that 47 + 25 = 72.

ACTIVITY 7.5 Equivalent Differences	3–4	4–5	5–6	6–7	7–8
				□	□

Objective

To explore an ad hoc approach to subtraction with two-digit numbers.

Materials

A measuring stick, plastic coins.

Method

Choose two children with a marked difference in height, get them to stand back to back and measure the difference in their height. Then get them to stand back to back on a table or some other secure platform and measure the difference in their heights now. Discuss with the children the way that the difference in height stays the same. Now give two children different amounts of money, using the plastic coins. Get them to work out the difference; how much more does one child have than the other? Then give each child an extra 5p. Ask them to work out the difference between their amounts of money now. Discuss how the difference stays the same.

Explain that we can do the same with numbers, and do some simple examples. For example, what is the difference between 5 and 8? Now make both the numbers bigger by 1 (so they become 6 and 9). What is the difference now? Now make these numbers larger by 4 (so they become 10 and 13). What is the difference now? See how the difference stays the same.

Apply this to doing subtractions. For example, to find 27 – 19 we need the difference between 27 and 19. If we add 1 to both numbers the difference stays the same. So, instead of doing 27 – 19 we can do 28 – 20, which is easy!

Another example: find 73 – 48. Add 2 to both numbers and this becomes 75 – 50. Continue with lots of examples, always making the second number up to a multiple of 10, by adding the same amount to both numbers. Stress the principle that if you add the same thing to both numbers the difference between them stays the same.

Summary of key ideas

1 In our number system the value of a digit in a number depends on the place in which it is written. Working from the right in a whole number the digits represent ones (units), tens, hundreds, thousands, and so on. This principle is called place value.

2 The principle of exchange is that ten in one place can be exchanged for one in the next place to the left (for example, 10 tens can be exchanged for 1 hundred); or that one in one place can be exchanged for ten in the next place to the right (for example, 1 hundred can be exchanged for 10 tens). This principle is fundamental in addition and subtraction calculations.

3 Understanding the concept of place value includes being able to move between the language and symbols used for numbers, concrete experiences with base-ten materials, and the number line.

4 Arrow cards help children to see how, for example, a three-digit number is made up from hundreds, tens and units.

5 Zero acts as a place holder in a number, indicating that this particular place is empty; for example, in 2045 the zero indicates an absence of hundreds.

6 A common error in writing three-digit numbers in symbols is to write one or two zeros for the word 'hundred'.

7 Both the hundred square and the empty number line can be used to help children understand how place value principles are used in informal addition and subtraction strategies.

8 A key strategy in addition is to partition the second number into hundreds, tens and units and to add these in turn to the first number.

9 Formal methods of addition and subtraction using a vertical layout, if taught, should be supported by connecting the manipulation of the symbols with the corresponding manipulation of concrete materials, such as base-ten blocks or 1p, 10p and £1 coins.

10 Vertical layout introduced too early can encourage a range of errors in addition and subtraction.

11 This contrasts with an approach based on the hundred square and the empty number line, which develop informal and mental strategies for addition and subtraction – with an emphasis on the whole number and its ordinal aspect, rather than on the individual digits.

12 There is no such thing as a 'proper' way to do a particular calculation.

Suggestions for further reading

A number of chapters in Cockburn and Littler (2008) explore some of the difficulties children encounter with place value in an interesting and accessible way.

Other books which have particularly useful material related to children's understanding of place value are Hansen (2011) and Cockburn (1999).

Well worth reading is Chapter 3 on children's understanding of numeration systems, in Nunes and Bryant (1996).

See also the excellent – albeit dated – book by Dickson, Brown and Gibson (1984): we suggest that you just look up 'place value' in the index and read all the relevant material. Section 3.7 of this book provides an informative summary of the problems associated with formal written methods for calculations and the kinds of errors that children make most frequently.

In a chapter in Anghileri (2001), Margaret Brown provides a historical survey of the ideological and social influences on the way in which calculations have been taught in England, tracing the variations in the emphasis on teaching standard written procedures.

Chapter 6 of Haylock (2010) provides a detailed explanation of place value and how this can be understood through making connections. Chapters 8 and 9 explain various approaches to addition and subtraction calculations in more detail than we have been able to include in this and the previous chapter.

CHAPTER 8

UNDERSTANDING MEASUREMENT

A PERCEPTUAL MISUNDERSTANDING

Amy was trying unsuccessfully to lift a box full of wooden blocks in the nursery. She announced, 'I can't lift it because it's too big.' She then tipped all the blocks on the floor and carried the box to where she wanted it!

- What might be revealed by Amy's comment here?
- How might a teacher exploit this incident as a teaching opportunity?

In this chapter

In earlier chapters we have frequently found ourselves discussing operations with numbers in various measuring contexts. We now consider the mathematical ideas involved in measurement itself. Our aim is to help those who teach young children to have a secure understanding of the various attributes of objects and events that we measure and the general principles of measurement that underpin the curriculum.

What do we measure?

Some of the comments that emerged when we raised this question with teachers set the agenda for the first part of our discussion of measurement:

- Length seems to be the most straightforward form of measurement, because the children can see what they're measuring.
- It's not quite the same when you're measuring the distance from one point to another. That's much more abstract, isn't it?
- My children do a lot with volume and capacity. But we normally only deal with measuring out stuff like water and sand, and pouring it into various containers.
- I'm never sure whether we're talking about the size of the container or the amount of water in it.
- What about mass and weight? Aren't they the same thing? Some books say you should talk about the mass and some say weight. That always confuses me, so I just ignore it and talk about weight.
- We measure time as well, but children find that very difficult. I think that's because you can't actually see what you're measuring.

In the age range that is the focus of this book, children's experiences of measuring are in the contexts of:

- length and distance,
- liquid volume and capacity,
- time of day and time intervals, and
- mass and weight.

Our experience of talking to teachers and children has made us aware that there are a number of possible confusions involved in each of these concepts.

Length and distance

To demonstrate that understanding of the concept of length is not as straightforward as might at first appear, consider some of the different types of situations to which, for example, the symbols '90 cm' might be connected.

First, we might connect '90 cm' to a straight part of some solid object, such as the edge of a table, and conclude that the table is 90 cm long, or 90 cm wide. Then we might connect '90 cm' to a straight line drawn on the floor, on the board or on a piece of paper. We sometimes connect the same symbols to an imaginary straight line running through an irregular object, such as a child – for example, when measuring the height of the child as 90 cm. We could also connect '90 cm' to an imaginary straight line passing through the air, in order to talk about the height of a table. In the last two examples, the convention is that the imaginary line must be vertical. In other circumstances, such as finding the gap between two cupboards, the convention requires an imaginary horizontal line at right angles to the edges of the cupboards. Also we might connect the same symbols to an imaginary straight line when we talk about the *distance* from one point to another. To make this connection we may have to imagine a piece of string stretched between the two points. We might also connect the symbols to other than straight lines on various objects, for example when measuring a person's waist as 90 cm. And, finally, we might connect '90 cm' to paths that are not just a straight line, for example, when we add up the lengths of the four sides of a rectangle to find that the perimeter is 90 cm, or when we find the length of a curved path from A to B to be 90 cm.

This analysis helps us to understand some of the confusions that arise in children's minds because – once again – we connect the same symbols to such a variety of situations! In Figure 8.1, for example, the question might be posed as to whether A is longer than, shorter than or the same length as B. In one sense it is true to say that A and B are the same length, if we think of B as an object and the length of it as the imaginary horizontal line passing through it. But in another sense it is true to say that B is longer than A, if we focus on the lengths of the paths.

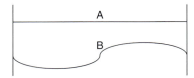

Figure 8.1   *Are A and B the same length? Or is B longer?*

Volume and capacity

These two words – volume and capacity – sometimes cause some confusion. This is not just because the word 'volume' is mostly associated nowadays with the level of sound on various electronic devices. The volume of something is the amount of three-dimensional space it occupies. Volume is normally measured in cubic units, such as cubic centimetres (symbol: cm^3). So we might say, for example, that the volume of a cuboid 3 cm long, 2 cm wide and 4 cm high is 24 cubic centimetres (24 cm^3), meaning that it occupies the same amount of space as 24 centimetre cubes.

Only *containers* have capacity. The capacity of a container is simply the volume of liquid that it will hold. Although capacity and liquid volume could be measured in the same units as volume in general, there are special units, such as litres and pints, which are usually used for measuring these aspects in particular.

Time

The importance of time in human experience is shown by the extensive language associated with the concept. Teachers of young children who recognize the importance of developing language in promoting understanding of mathematical and scientific ideas have a considerable agenda on their hands when they consider the everyday vocabulary that children have to understand and learn to use. The following list, while certainly not comprehensive, at least shows the extent of the teaching task:

how long, second, minute, hour, day, week, fortnight, month, quarter, year, leap year, decade, century, millennium, season, spring, summer, autumn, winter, weekend, term, half-term, lifetime, long time, short time, brief, temporary, for the time being, long-lasting, interval, pause, cycle, period, extra time, non-stop, never-ending, permanent, on and on, how old, age, age group, year group, teenager, young, old, elderly, middle-aged, under-age, ancient, modern, up to date, older, elder, oldest, younger, youngest, when, daytime, night-time, dawn, sunrise, morning, teatime, break-time, lunchtime (etc.), noon, midday, afternoon, dusk, sunset, evening, midnight, small hours, matinee, past, present, future, spell, then, now, before, after, next, previous, earlier, prior, following, later, afterwards, due, eventually, in the long run, in due course, never, always, once, once upon a time, one day, recent, soon, immediately, straight away, in a moment, instantly, in a jiffy, while, meanwhile, till, until, up to, not yet, in the meantime, during, nowadays, sometime, sooner or later, at the last minute, often, frequent, daily, hourly, weekly, monthly, annually, occasionally, regularly, now and again, every so often, from time to time, sometimes, hardly ever, once in a blue moon, clock, watch, sundial, timer, egg timer, meter, tick, tick-tock, dial, face, alarm, setting, hands, minute hand, hour hand, digital, (e.g.) three twenty-five, o'clock, a.m., p.m., half past, quarter to, quarter past, five past (etc.), twenty-five to (etc.), 24-hour clock, fourteen hours (etc.), timetable, zero hour, summer time, put clocks forward and back, overtime, half-time, slow, fast, on time, late, early, punctual, diary, calendar, date, Sunday, Monday, Tuesday, etc., yesterday, today, tomorrow, last week, January, February, etc., first, second, third, etc., nineteenth century, twentieth century, twenty-first century (etc.), ten-sixty-six, the year two thousand and thirteen (etc.), birth-day, anniversary, mark time, beat time, keep time, rhythm, short notice, advance notice, afterthought, postpone, put off, waste time, ...

There is one clear conclusion for the teacher: the most important activity in teaching the topic of time to young children is talking to them – and with them – aiming to focus on and to develop this extensive range of vocabulary and language patterns.

There are in fact two very different concepts associated with time that children will use and will learn to measure. First, there is the time at which something occurs. This begins as an awareness of the order in which things happen and eventually becomes the concept of *recorded time*. We use time in this sense when we consult our watch to find the time of day, or make an appointment for a particular day of the month, or recall the year in which something took place.

Second, there is the time that something takes to happen – its duration – or the time that passes between two events or between two moments of recorded time. This is the notion of a *time interval*: the time that passes from the bell signalling the start of playtime and the bell signalling its end; the time it takes to complete a train journey if the train leaves at 13:05 and arrives at 14:55. Time intervals might be measured in seconds, minutes, hours, days, weeks, months, years, decades, centuries or even millennia! Age, being the time interval from birth to the present, is one example of this rather abstract concept that children handle with surprising confidence. No doubt this is related to the fact that their age is very much part of their identity.

It suddenly struck us when we visited a school recently and spoke to some children, that the first two questions that people almost invariably ask a child are, 'What's your name?' and 'How old are you?' How old you are is as much part of who you are as a child as your name!

Teachers of young children should note that recorded time and time interval are two very different concepts. We show later in this chapter that – because they are two different types of measuring scales – they have quite different mathematical properties. We would suggest that many teachers focus too much on teaching children to tell the time – which is much better learnt in the context of real-life situations in which they need to tell the time – without giving children sufficient experience of measuring time intervals. The reader will find it a useful exercise now to go through the list of time language given above and decide which of it is associated with each of these two aspects of time.

Mass and weight

This is a tricky one. There is an important distinction in scientific terms between the mass and the weight of an object. Strictly speaking, units such as grams, kilograms, pounds and ounces are units of *mass*, not units of *weight*.

We will attempt to explain. First, we would refer to those sets of plastic shapes or pieces of metal that we use for weighing things as, for example, ten-gram masses, kilogram masses, four-ounce masses, and so on. This language convention associates the word 'mass' correctly with the units of mass, such as grams, kilograms and ounces. If an object balances against a kilogram mass, like the model car shown in Figure 8.2, then we deduce that it is also a kilogram mass.

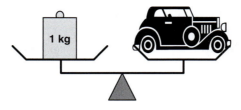

Figure 8.2   *An object weighing the same as a kilogram mass*

But what exactly is the mass of something? Well, in simple terms, the mass of an object is a measure of the amount of stuff making up the object – the quantity of matter in it – which is related to the number of atoms involved. Note that this is not the same thing as the *volume* (the amount of space it occupies), because in some objects the matter is more densely compressed together than in others.

However, when you hold an object in your hand you cannot actually experience its mass. You cannot perceive it, count it, smell it or feel it. It is the weight, not the mass, which you can feel and to which your muscles respond. This weight is the gravitational force pulling the object down towards the ground. Since weight is a force, it should be measured in the units used for measuring force. In the metric system, force – and therefore weight – is measured in *newtons*. Without being too technical, it may help the reader to know that a newton is about the weight of a small apple. On the earth's surface a mass of one kilogram has a weight of nearly 10 newtons. (More precisely, *g* newtons, where *g* is the acceleration due to gravity.)

Having seen film of astronauts on the moon, you may be familiar with the idea that if you were to take an object to the moon, where the gravitational force would be smaller, the weight of the object would be reduced. This is true – the weight would be reduced – although the object's mass is unchanged. Our one-kilogram mass would now weigh only about one and a half newtons. This is because the mass of the moon is much smaller than the mass of the earth, and therefore the gravitational pull is weaker.

This change in weight would show up if we were weighing our object on a spring-type weighing device, as shown in Figure 8.3. But it is interesting to observe that the situation in Figure 8.2 would not change if we took the balance to the moon. It appears, therefore, that the two weighing devices are measuring different things! The balance-type weighing device enables us to deduce the mass of an object, by balancing it against an equal mass. The spring-type weighing device clearly responds to weight. The former would give us the same result wherever we used it. The latter would give slightly different readings at the bottom of a coal mine or at the top of Mount Everest (due to a slight variation in the value of *g* as the distance from the centre of the earth changes), and a significantly different reading on the moon. In practice, of course, we will not often take our kitchen or bathroom scales to the moon.

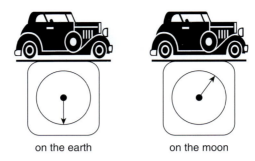

on the earth   on the moon

Figure 8.3   *Change in weight indicated on spring-type weighing device*

So the scales can safely be graduated in grams and kilograms, or pounds and ounces, and you can be confident that when you weigh something on the earth's surface and the arrow on the dial points to one kilogram then you do actually have a mass of about one kilogram.

Teachers may, therefore, be perplexed to be told that it is actually incorrect from a scientific point of view to say that the object weighs one kilogram or that the weight of the object is one kilogram. Strictly speaking, it is the mass of the object that is one kilogram. Unfortunately, from the point of view of the children's conceptual understanding, nearly everyone says that the weight of the object is one kilogram; and the idea of measuring weight in newtons will be introduced to children only in the later primary years.

Later on in secondary school students will need in their science lessons to distinguish between weight and mass, and the majority will find this very difficult. No doubt part of the difficulty will be unlearning the erroneous language of primary school and the marketplace. We offer some suggestions that might help with this problem. These are scientifically correct, mathematically sound and reasonably straightforward. First, be consistent in referring to those things you use to counterbalance the objects being weighed as masses, not weights. In the classroom cupboard you will have boxes of 1-gram masses, 10-gram masses, 100-gram masses, and so on. It seems a bit strange at first, but you soon get used to it! The word 'mass' is thus encountered when you shift from weighing with non-standard units to weighing with standard units.

Second, we suggest that young children's experience of weighing should be primarily with balance-type weighing devices. Third, when we have weighed something we say something along the lines of: 'The book weighs the same as twenty marbles' or 'The book weighs the same as a mass of 200 grams' or, simply, 'The book weighs the same as 200 grams'. The key phrase is 'weighs the same as', emphasizing the equivalence that has emerged. Finally, if an object weighs the same as, say, a mass of two hundred grams then we can also say that this object has a mass of two hundred grams.

Measurement in general

In this section we will consider what might be some of the fundamental mathematical ideas involved in the process of measuring. These ideas include the notion of comparison and ordering, the principles of transitivity and conservation, the idea of a unit, the use of non-standard and standard units, the importance of approximation and accuracy, and estimation.

Comparison

The primary purpose of making a measurement is to make a *comparison* between two items according to the magnitude of some attribute, such as length, weight, capacity, age, value, and so on, and thereby to put them in order.

> Even the youngest children in my nursery class are able to make comparisons. The other day a 3-year-old said, 'My piece of cheese is the smallest, so I should get another piece!'

Associated with this idea is the extensive set of language of comparison given in Table 3.6 and discussed in Chapter 3: longer, shorter, heavier, lighter, younger, older, and so on.

We should note that, particularly in early experiences of measuring, comparisons of this sort are often made directly without the use of any measuring units. So two children can stand next to each other and determine who is the taller and who is the shorter. Two objects can be put on either end of a simple see-saw balance and a deduction made about which is the heavier and which is the lighter. It is helpful at this stage of the child's development of understanding of the particular measuring concept that they experience objects that exaggerate the attribute in question. A large, light object can be balanced against a small, heavy object to focus the attention on the weight rather than the size. Water can be poured from a tall jar with a small capacity into a short, squat jar with a large capacity. Comparing by weight pairs of identical-looking sealed yoghurt cartons filled with materials of different density – sand, sawdust, ball bearings – again focuses the attention on the one way in which they are different, namely, in terms of their heaviness. Amy, for example, in the anecdote at the head of this chapter, would benefit from discovering and talking about the fact that two boxes might be as big as each other, but that one can be too heavy to lift and the other can be lifted easily: because one is heavier – not bigger – than the other.

Incidentally, it is often surprisingly difficult to compare by hand the weights of two objects and decide which is the heavier and which the lighter. This is probably because the pressure on your hand is dependent on the shape of the object and the area in contact with your hand. For example, put this book in one hand and a 500-gram mass in the other and try to decide which is the heavier. However, if you put the two objects into plastic carrier-bags and hold the bags rather than the objects you will find that it is markedly easier to make the comparison. This is a good tip for teachers wanting to give children practical experience of comparing weights by hand.

We should remind ourselves of the fundamental idea that every comparison statement has an alternative equivalent form (see Table 3.6 in Chapter 3), and that children should be encouraged always to make both statements. This is such a key aspect of language and mathematical development that it cannot be overemphasized. Table 8.1 provides some examples of pairs of such equivalent statements, demonstrating that this is a key principle that pervades all areas of measurement.

Table 8.1   *Equivalent statements of comparison*

The table is higher than the desk.	The desk is lower than the table.
Breakfast is earlier than dinner.	Dinner is later than breakfast.
The book is heavier than the pencil.	The pencil is lighter than the book.
John is older than Meg.	Meg is younger than John.
London is bigger than Norwich.	Norwich is smaller than London.
A motorway is wider than my street.	My street is narrower than a motorway.
Your car is faster than my car.	My car is slower than your car.
My teddy is taller than yours.	Your teddy is shorter than mine.

In making comparisons of this sort we are attending to what is different about two objects, in other words to a transformation that occurs when we shift our attention from some attribute of one to the same attribute of the other, such as height, weight, and so on. As in the example of the identical yoghurt cartons, the two objects may in all other outward respects be the same.

But there is, of course, another possibility when two objects are compared for some particular attribute: we may decide that they are equal. So two objects, such as a book and a box, may be very different in a number of respects, such as their size or their shape, but be equivalent in another. For example, they may weigh the same. So we see that what have been referred to in Chapter 1 as the concepts of transformation and equivalence are here associated with the most fundamental idea of measuring. These two ideas appear to permeate all mathematical thinking. The equivalence notion, 'is the same as', will turn up frequently in measuring experiences, in such language forms as 'is the same length as', 'weighs the same as', 'happens at the same time as', and so on. The photograph shows a child in a nursery class with balance scales trying to make the two sides weigh the same – which she achieved successfully and described with appropriate language. What she did not yet get was that when the two piles of bricks did not balance it was the one that went down that was the heavier!

Ordering and transitivity

An important principle common to any ordering relationship is that of *transitivity*. This principle is evident when three or more objects are being ordered according to a particular attribute, such as their length, their weight, their time of day, their capacity, and so on. In Figure 8.4(a) the arrow could represent any one of our comparison statements, such as 'is longer than', 'is lighter than', 'is earlier than', 'holds more than', and so on. The objects A, B and C have been ordered using such a relationship, by comparing A with B and then B with C. The principle of transitivity allows us to make the logical deduction about the relationship between A and C, shown in Figure 8.4(b): A is longer than C, or A is lighter than C, and so on. The relation is said to be transitive when the following is necessarily the case: if it occurs between A and B and between B and C, then it can be 'carried across' directly from A to C.

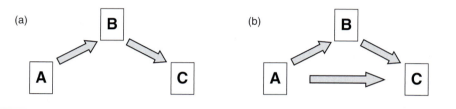

Figure 8.4   *The principle of transitivity*

Formally, this principle is expressed in one of two ways, as follows:

a using the symbol > to stand for any 'greater than' relationship
   if A > B and B > C then A > C
   (If A is greater than B and B is greater than C then A is greater than C.)

b using the symbol < to stand for any 'less than' relationship
   if A < B and B < C then A < C
   (If A is less than B and B is less than C then A is less than C.)

All the different ways in which we measure things satisfy these properties – because putting things in order is a fundamental property of any form of measurement. In addition to the 'greater than' and 'less than' transitivity properties, there is a third form of transitivity in the context of measurement. Clearly the arrows in Figure 8.4 could also represent *equivalence*. For example, they could stand for statements about *equal* length or *equal* weight, such as 'is the same length as', 'weighs the same as', and so on. It is not a difficult logical deduction that, if A is equal to B and B is equal to C, then A is equal to C. So, we should note therefore that equivalence also satisfies transitivity. This example of transitivity is expressed in symbols as follows: if A = B and B = C then A = C. Although this might appear to be a rather obvious statement, in the context of measurement it is actually very significant. It is this property that allows us to make repeated copies of standard measurements, such as the kilogram or the metre, without always going back to the originals! In the context of the classroom children will experience this, for example, by making their own 100-gram mass, by balancing play-dough against a standard 100-gram mass, and then using their play-dough version to generate further copies.

To understand the concept of transitivity it might be helpful for the reader to experience some non-exemplars as well as exemplars. We have seen how the arrows in Figure 8.4 might represent any relationship of the form 'is greater than', 'is less than', or 'is the same as'. But not all mathematical relationships are transitive. In fact, part of our understanding of any relationship must be an implicit awareness of whether it is or is not transitive. To demonstrate this, readers may care to assess their understanding of the concept of 'factor' by asking this question: if the arrows in Figure 8.4(a) represent the relationship 'is a factor of', where A, B and C are three natural numbers (positive whole numbers), does the relationship between A and C shown in Figure 8.4(b) necessarily follow? We posed this question to some of the teachers we worked with:

> S. *Remind me again – what's a factor?*
> D. *A number that divides exactly into another number. For example, four is a factor of twelve, because four divides into twelve exactly.*
> E. *So, if A is a factor of B and B is a factor of C we want to know if A is a factor of C.*
> S. *I haven't the foggiest idea. It might be, I suppose.*
> E. *Four is a factor of twelve and twelve is a factor of 24. That works. Four is a factor of 24.*
> D. *Will it always work?*

Try the same exercise with other mathematical relationships, such as 'is one more than', 'is half of', 'is a multiple of'. The facility with which you make the deduction about whether or not the fact that A is related to B and B is related to C necessarily implies that A must be related to C is a good indicator of your understanding of the mathematical relationship. If you do not find it immediately obvious then you are in a similar situation to young children learning about measurement. Having compared A with B and B with C they will not automatically make the deduction about the relationship between A and C.

Transitivity is one of the logical principles that Piaget identified as a key indicator of children's development in their understanding of measurement. Whether the difficulty for children who appear not to grasp the principle is a failure in logic or simply an inability to recall and process at the same time all the details in the situation is a matter of some debate. But, whatever the correct interpretation of children's responses to tasks assessing their grasp of this principle, it would seem to us to be self-evident that – since transitivity is such a fundamental property of measurement – children learning about measuring should simply have a considerable amount of experience of putting three (or more) objects in order according to their length, their weight, their capacity, and so on. It would appear likely that through practical experience of this kind of ordering activity – supported by well-focused questions and discussion with their teachers – they will be helped to get this mathematical structure into their thinking about measurement in general.

Conservation

Another fundamental and crucial principle that applies to many aspects of measurement is that known as *conservation*. This refers, for example, to the fact that a ball of play-dough will still weigh the same when it has been squashed into a sausage shape or broken up into a number of smaller pieces; that the volume of water in a tall, thin flask does not change when it is poured into a short, squat flask; that the length of a pencil remains the same when it is displaced a little to the right. We have already noted in Chapter 2 that grasping the conservation of number is a key component of learning to count: children have to learn that changing the arrangement of the objects being counted does not change the number. Figure 8.5 provides some examples of tasks that have sometimes been used to assess children's grasp of this principle in various measuring contexts. (See also the Research Focus in Chapter 2.)

Demonstrating a grasp of this principle of conservation, first of all with number, then with length, weight and volume, has also been identified by Piaget as one of the key indicators of a child's intellectual development. However, many of the tasks used to assess the child's grasp of conservation, such as those in Figure 8.5, have been justifiably criticized as not being embedded in a context that has any meaning or

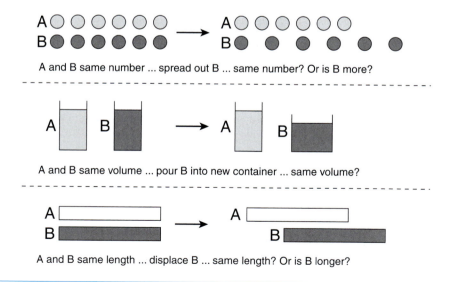

Figure 8.5   *Assessing understanding of conservation*

purpose for a child. It appears to us to be the case that quite young children seem to use the principle of conservation of measurement quite happily when engaged in a purposeful task in a meaningful context. When, for example, they are cooking, they will measure out quantities of water and flour, and then they will proceed to transfer these from one container to another without any apparent concern that these activities might alter the quantities they measured out in the first place!

In spite of such reservations as these about some of the methods used to assess children's understanding of conservation, we should stress that this is nevertheless a key component of understanding measurement. Children will certainly benefit from activities and discussion designed to focus their attention upon this principle. In fact, we would argue that the thinking process involved is an instance of fundamental mathematical reasoning, because the principle of conservation provides yet another experience of the concepts of transformation and equivalence that we are highlighting throughout this book. What the child has to grasp, for example, is that if you take a quantity of water in a container and apply to it certain transformations, such as pouring it into a different shaped container, the volume of water stays the same. In other words, there is an equivalence, something the same about the two situations, in spite of the transformation that has occurred to, say, the height of the water level, or the shape of the water. In fact, we could say that what the child has to learn is which of the transformations that can be applied in a range of measurement contexts preserve which equivalences and which transformations destroy which equivalences. If you take a square piece of paper and transform it by moving it to a different position or by cutting it up into two triangles, the area is preserved: it will still cover the same amount of the table surface. If, on the other hand, you screw the paper up into a tight little ball, or set light to it, these are transformations that destroy this equivalence. The reader may find it a challenging, but useful exercise to analyse, in terms of which equivalences are preserved or destroyed, transformations such as rearranging some building blocks, boiling some water, rolling up a tape measure, taking an object to the moon, or putting the clocks forward for summer time.

Units

Common to all aspects of measurement is the idea of a *unit*. Instead of using measurement concepts just to order two or more objects, we now move to comparing some attribute of a single object with a number of equal units. So a child might use, for example, a set of unused pencils as units for measuring. They would already be confident with statements such as 'the book is longer than a pencil'. But now they would move on, for example, to laying out a line of pencils along the edge of the table and saying 'the table is about ten pencils long'.

It is conventional to introduce children to the idea of a unit through the use of non-standard units – for example, measuring lengths in pencils, as above, or weighing objects with marbles – before moving on to standard units such as centimetres and grams. Some of the teachers we talked to were very uncertain about the point of getting children to use non-standard units for measuring, especially since children will often have met the standard units from shopping. We outline below a number of reasons that can be put forward for the value of incorporating experience of non-standard units.

First, by using non-standard units in the early stages, children are introduced to the idea of measuring in units through familiar objects – such as pencils, marbles, hand spans, feet, and so on – rather than going straight into those mysterious things called centimetres and grams. In this way they are not required to handle a new piece of vocabulary for the unit at the same time as meeting a new measuring experience. As far as the mathematical ideas involved are concerned, there is no essential difference between measuring a table in pencils and measuring it in centimetres, so if children find a familiar non-standard unit less threatening then all well and good.

Second, it is suggested that the non-standard unit can be a more appropriate size of unit for the first practical measuring tasks that young children will undertake. Centimetres may be too small and therefore too numerous for your first experience of measuring the length of the desk top, or the height of a friend – and metres are clearly too large a unit for this purpose. Grams are very small units for weighing most of the objects around the classroom, such as books, scissors, shoes, and so on, and a kilogram of iron will put the child in hospital if dropped on their foot. Something like a Lego brick is likely to be a more appropriate unit to begin with, because it will result in measurements of just a handful of units, rather than hundreds of them.

Third, we should note that adults do not always use standard units when engaged in practical measuring tasks. Whether or not they do might depend on the accuracy required by the task. For example, most of us are happy to measure out fertilizer for our lawns by the handful, and we will often use spans and paces for certain stages of practical jobs around the home.

Finally, it is argued that through using non-standard units children will become aware of the need for a standard unit – for example, when they discover that the classroom is twenty paces wide when they do the measuring, but only eleven paces wide when the teacher does it.

- When my 6-year-olds were measuring lengths in spans and feet they made me do them all as well. They seemed fascinated by the idea that my span or my feet always gave a smaller number.
- I find that a lot of useful mathematical talk takes place when a group of children are deciding what to use to measure something – like whether to use spans or cubits to measure the length of their table.
- A favourite activity in my nursery class is to count how many bricks tall they are.
- When you talk to them about measuring with non-standard units they do seem to pick up the idea of the need for a standard unit quite quickly.

- My 3- and 4-year-olds enjoy measuring their heights in centimetres using the height chart on the wall. They get very excited when they are more than 100! They seem to get the idea that the taller you are the bigger the number is.

One teacher had serious doubts about using units like spans and paces with young children:

I always find an element of competition creeps in when they start measuring in hand spans or paces, and the maths goes out of the window. One girl refused to admit that her span was shorter than someone else's and got quite upset. Then when they were pacing out the length of the corridor all the boys started taking enormous leaps, rather than strides, to see who could do it in the smallest number!

We take this teacher's point, and it may be that there are occasions when impersonal spoons and sticks might be preferable as units to individuals' spans and strides. But we wonder whether it is really the case that the mathematics has gone 'out of the window' in these examples. These children seem very aware of the significance of the size of the units being used, and the experience has clearly provoked a competition and discussion based on mathematical criteria!

SI base units and other metric units

Teachers may come across references to the SI (International System/Système International) version of metric units. This is an internationally accepted convention used in trade and industry, and in technological and scientific work. The main feature of this system is that each aspect of measurement should have just one base unit. Some of these are shown in Table 8.2 for aspects of measurement likely to concern teachers, together with the appropriate symbol. It is an accident of history that the base unit for mass is the kilogram (kg) not the gram (g).

Table 8.2   *Some SI units*

Measure	SI Unit	Symbol
length	metre	m
mass	kilogram	kg
time	second	s
volume	cubic metre	m^3

According to the SI convention, all lengths, for example, would be measured in metres. This would mean that the width of a piece of A4 paper (about 21 cm) would be given as about 0.21 m. If other units are to be used, by the use of various prefixes, then there is a further convention that as far as possible only those representing powers of a thousand should be employed. Some of these 'preferred prefixes' are shown in Table 8.3.

Table 8.3   *Preferred prefixes*

Prefix	Meaning	Symbol	Example
mega	a million	M	1 Mg = one million grams
kilo	a thousand	k	1 km = one thousand metres
milli	a thousandth	m	1 mm = one thousandth of a metre
micro	a millionth	µ	1µg = one millionth of a gram

Using a preferred prefix (milli) the width of the piece of A4 paper would then be given as about 210 millimetres (210 mm). However, for practical purposes other prefixes are required because the base unit and the base unit with a preferred prefix turn out to be inappropriate sizes of unit for the task in hand. For example, for many tasks that involve measuring length the millimetre is too small and the metre too large. This is why the *centimetre* is used so frequently, even though 'centi' is not a preferred prefix. So, for example, it is much more convenient to give the width of a piece of A4 paper as about 21 cm. Some of these other prefixes are shown in Table 8.4. Of those shown here the two we are most likely to meet are *centi* and *deci*.

Table 8.4   *Some other prefixes*

Prefix	Meaning	Symbol	Example
centi	a hundredth	c	1 cm = one hundredth of a metre
deci	a tenth	d	1 dm = one tenth of a metre
deca	ten	da	1 dag = ten grams
hecto	a hundred	h	1hg = one hundred grams

There are some other metric units that are derived from SI units. The commonest of these, encountered in everyday experience, is the litre (l), used for measuring liquid volume or capacity. A litre is the same volume as one thousand cubic centimetres of solid volume. Based on the litre are the millilitre (1 ml = one thousandth of a litre), the centilitre (1 cl = one hundredth of a litre) and the decilitre (1 dl = one tenth of a litre). We have noticed that bottles of wine are variously labelled as 0.75 litre, 7.5 dl, 75 cl and 750 ml. Those who purchase solid fuel, for example, may also encounter the tonne, referred to in speech as 'the metric tonne'. This is a thousand kilograms (1000 kg) or a million grams (that is, one megagram, 1 Mg).

We conclude this section with an assortment of facts and conventions about metric units that teachers will find helpful.

- One litre is the same volume as 1000 cm³.
- 1 ml is the same volume as 1 cm³.
- A medicine spoon holds 5 ml.
- Base-ten materials for number work are often based on centimetres; if the unit is a centimetre cube then the 'ten' is a decimetre long, the 'hundred' is a decimetre square, and the 'thousand' is a decimetre cube.
- A decimetre cube is 1000 cm³, the same volume as a litre.
- A litre of water has a mass of 1 kg.
- Hence 1 ml of water has a mass of 1 g.
- A cubic metre of water has a mass of one tonne (1000 kg).
- The distance from the North Pole to the Equator is approximately ten thousand kilometres (10 000 km).
- A simple pendulum of length 1 m ticks once approximately every second.
- The symbol for litre is l (el), but because this can be confused with 1 (one) we recommend writing the word 'litre' in full.
- Note the correct spelling of 'gram'.
- The symbol for gram is not gm but g.
- Symbols for units do not have plural forms, so do not write, for example, 5 cms, but 5 cm.
- The symbol for kilo is a lower case k, not a capital K; so we write km, not Km.
- English readers should note that the stress in the word 'kilometre' should be on the first syllable, not the second!
- No full stops should be used after a symbol for a unit, such as 5 cm or 10 kg, except at the end of a sentence.

Approximation and accuracy

An interesting feature of measurement is that nearly all measurement is *approximate*. Except when the measurement is simply a form of counting, such as when 'measuring' the value of the coins in my pocket, we always measure to the nearest something. It is not possible, for example, to make an exact measurement of the length of anything. All we can do is to measure the length of the table to the nearest centimetre, or nearest millimetre, and so on. Even with the most refined measuring device in the world we would still be making an approximate measurement. This is a difficult idea for us to incorporate into our thinking about measurement, because we tend to think of mathematics as providing exact results.

Even in the early stages of measuring in non-standard units, young children will encounter this problem and have to find a way of expressing their observations. So they might be helped to formulate language patterns like:

- The book weighs more than 8 blocks but less than 9 blocks.
- The book weighs a bit more than 8 blocks.
- The book weighs between 8 and 9 blocks.

The limits of 8 blocks and 9 blocks here are examples of what are known technically as the lower and upper bounds of the measurement. If you have carried out a very careful measurement of the width of a piece of A4 paper to, say, the nearest millimetre, you will only be able to assert, for example, that the width of the paper lies between a lower bound of 210 mm and an upper bound of 211 mm.

We also have to learn the importance of measuring to an appropriate level of *accuracy.* In measuring a person's age, for example, it is often appropriate to do this to the year below or the year above. So a child might say 'I'm seven' or 'I'm eight next birthday'. For many purposes we measure time of day to the nearest five minutes, so that we would be amused by someone who said, 'I'll meet you at 4:23 this afternoon' – because they appear to be employing an inappropriate level of accuracy. But we would not be amused if a train timetable advertised a departure time of 16:25 and we missed the train because it had left at nearer 16:23.

Consequently, all that we have said earlier about equivalence should be understood in these terms. Phrases such as 'is the same length as' and 'weighs the same as' must be interpreted as implying that the comparison has been made to an appropriate level of accuracy. We might actually mean something like 'is the same length to the nearest millimetre' or 'weighs the same as far as we can judge using this balance'. There is no way in which we can assert that two lines are *exactly* the same length or that two objects have exactly the same mass.

To sum up, the notions of approximation, upper and lower bounds, and the appropriate level of accuracy are important ideas that are fundamental to most aspects of measurement. Experience and discussion of all these aspects of measurement are often insufficiently emphasized in work with children.

Estimation

Children's understanding of measurement is developed significantly through experience of making estimates. When children estimate which is longer or shorter, which holds more or holds less, which weighs more or weighs less, whether they have enough of some materials, and so on, they are engaging with the attribute of the measurement in a way that makes sense to them and which uses the key principles of comparison, ordering and approximation. Even in the earliest stages of their developing awareness of the size of things or the amount of something, young children will make estimates. This became clear when we asked some pre-school teachers about 3-year-olds' early experiences of informal measurement.

- Some of the children were playing in a tent. One of the girls said to one of the boys, 'You can't fit in, because you're too big!'
- Emily looked at a large area she wanted to paint green and her supply of green paint and told me there wasn't enough paint to do it.
- The children like guessing where someone will come to before we mark their height on the wall; they do this by comparing different children's heights.
- Harry wanted some water to put in a bowl to float a plastic boat. When the class assistant gave him a bottle of water to use he looked at it and said, 'I need more than that!'

PAUSE TO REFLECT   Reasonable estimates

It will help enormously to develop your confidence with units of measurement if you get into the habit of making estimations of length, mass, time and capacity, using standard metric units. To do this you need to have at your finger tips some reference items. A good start is to memorize your own measurements, such as: height, waist and pace measured in centimetres; weight (mass) in kilograms.

Here are some questions we think it would be useful if you were able to answer without much thought. How many kilometres is it approximately from where you live to where you work? About how many seconds would it take you to walk 100 metres? How many litres of water does your watering can hold? About how many millilitres are there in a small glass of wine? What would be an average birth weight in kilograms for a baby? About how many grams would you expect to be the mass of this book?

Do you have your own favourite reference items that you use for comparison when making measurements? Share your ideas with a colleague. You might have a competition to see who is better at estimating time intervals in seconds.

Types of measuring scales

In the final section of this chapter we discuss from a mathematical perspective three different kinds of measuring scales. We do this to raise the awareness of teachers of young children to some fundamental mathematical principles of measurement, examples of all of which are encountered in the earliest experiences of measurement in the classroom. The easiest kind of measuring scale is what is called an *ordinal scale*. More sophisticated is an *interval scale* and the most sophisticated is a *ratio scale*. For ease of explanation it is best to consider these in reverse order. We aim to show how these different kinds of measurement scales provide contexts for the different aspects of number and number operations outlined in Chapters 2, 3 and 4.

Ratio scales

Length, mass, capacity, time interval, and so on, are examples of what is called a *ratio scale*. They are called ratio scales because the ratio of two measurements has a real meaning. So, for example, we can compare a length of 90 cm with one of 30 cm, not just by the difference (60 cm), but also by the ratio (3). Hence, using the ratio comparison, we would observe that a length of 90 cm is three times as long as a length of 30 cm; or that 90 cm can be made up by combining three lengths of 30 cm. Similarly, with measurements of mass, we can observe that a mass of 100 g is ten times as heavy as a mass of 10 g; or that a mass of 100 g is equivalent to ten masses of 10 g. Likewise, with measurements of time, we can assert that a time interval of 240 minutes is 6 times longer than a time interval of 40 minutes; or that a period of 240 minutes can be made up of 6 periods of 40 minutes. Notice that the two central ideas in these comparisons are ratio and scaling – two ideas that are central in division and multiplication, as explained in Chapter 4.

In fact, this basic property of ratio scales implies that these are the only kind of measurements on which it is usually legitimate to perform many aspects of arithmetic involving multiplication or division. Some of the structures of multiplication and division discussed in Chapter 4 have meaning only in those measurement contexts that are ratio scales, such as measurements of length, mass, volume and capacity, and time intervals – especially the scaling structure of multiplication and the ratio structure of division.

Hence, it is legitimate and meaningful to make statements such as these, only because in each case the measurements involved are taken from a ratio scale:

- Three 25-kg sacks of potatoes have a total mass of 75 kg. (The repeated addition structure of multiplication.)
- The walk to school takes 15 minutes. There and back will be double this, that is, 30 minutes. (The scaling structure of multiplication.)

- A length of 30 m of ribbon shared between three people gives a length of 10 m each. (The equal sharing structure of division.)
- From a jug of 250-ml capacity we can fill five containers of 50-ml capacity. (The inverse of multiplication structure of division.)
- This stick of length 80 cm is four times the length of that stick of 20 cm. (The ratio structure of division.)

We should note that 'monetary value' is also essentially a ratio scale, because we can compare two amounts of money or prices by ratio. We can, for example, make meaningful statements about how many times more expensive or less expensive one thing is than another, by what scale factor a salary might be increased or decreased, rates of inflation, percentage rises in the cost of living, and so on. These are all employing the ideas of scaling and ratio that are central to the notion of a ratio scale.

Interval scales

Ratio scales can be contrasted first with what are called *interval scales*. In an interval scale two measurements can be compared only by their difference, not by their ratio. The two most familiar examples of interval scales are (a) measurements of tempera-ture in degrees Celsius, and (b) the time of day. They are called interval scales because the steps from one mark on the measurement scale to the next are equal intervals. This means that the interval between 1 and 2 is the same as that between 2 and 3, and between 3 and 4, and so on. For example, it takes the same amount of time to move from 2 p.m. to 3 p.m. as it does to move from 3 p.m. to 4 p.m. It takes the same amount of heat energy to raise the temperature of something from 2 °C to 3 °C as it does to raise it from 3 °C to 4 °C. Of course, what is true about interval scales is also true of ratio scales. But there are more restrictions on what can be said and done meaningfully with measurements on an interval scale.

For example, to compare a temperature of 30 °C with one of 10 °C you can use only the difference (20 °C), observing that one temperature is 20 °C hotter or colder than the other. It makes no sense at all to talk about one temperature being 'three times hotter' than the other. You cannot make up a temperature of 30 °C from three temperatures of 10 °C! Similarly, 6 p.m. is not in any sense three times 2 p.m. To compare 6 p.m. with 2 p.m. we can make use only of the idea of difference (it is four hours later), not the idea of ratio.

This marked contrast between the two types of measuring scale is related to the fact that in a ratio scale the 'zero' is actually 'nothing' or 'an absence of something' (see the discussion of zero in Chapter 2). So, a length of 0 cm or a mass of 0 kg really is nothing. But in an interval scale the zero is arbitrary. For example, it is quite arbitrary that in the celsius temperature scale the freezing point of water should be taken as

0 °C. Similarly, it is clearly an arbitrary decision that 'zero hours' (midnight) comes when it does – otherwise we would not be able to put the clocks forward and back for summer time, or to have different time zones for various sectors of the globe. So, when the temperature falls to zero it is not the case that there is now no temperature or that the temperature has become 'nothing' – there is a very definite temperature and we can certainly feel it! And time does not disappear at midnight when your watch indicates zero hours (00:00).

The nature of interval scales means that – in contrast to ratio scales – we cannot meaningfully do any arithmetic involving many aspects of multiplication and division, particularly those related to the ideas of ratio and scaling. There are no meaningful statements in the contexts of time of day or temperature that have the same structure as the examples of multiplication and division statements given in the previous section for ratio scales. For example, three people would not share a temperature of 30 °C and have 10 °C each! The addition and subtraction structures discussed in Chapter 3 that have most application in these contexts are those of increasing, comparison and difference, and reduction. These allow us to make statements in the contexts of measurement of temperature and time of day such as these:

- Her temperature was 38 °C yesterday, but it rose 2 °C during the night and is now 40 °C. (The increasing structure of addition.)
- The train arriving at 16:30 gets to London 2 hours later than the one arriving at 14:30. (The comparison structure of subtraction.)
- The temperature was 30 °C at midday, but it has fallen by 10 °C, so it is now 20 °C. (The reduction structure of subtraction.)

Of course, statements with the same structures as these could also be made in the context of ratio scales, such as measurements of length and mass. We should also emphasize the distinction made earlier in this chapter between the two aspects of time: time intervals and recorded time. We now see that the essential difference in the way we handle these two concepts is that the first is a ratio scale and the second is an interval scale.

We will mention one further legitimate and meaningful arithmetic process that can be applied to measurements on interval scales and ratio scales. This is the process of finding an average (strictly called an arithmetic mean). So, for example, given three lengths of 30 cm, 20 cm and 16 cm (a ratio scale), we can legitimately add them up and divide by 3 and assert that the average length is 22 cm. Similarly, given maximum temperatures on three consecutive days of 30 °C, 20 °C and 16 °C (an interval scale), we can add these up and divide by 3 and make the meaningful statement that the average maximum temperature was 22 °C. This is permissible only because the steps between measurements on an interval scale are equal intervals. Without this property the process of finding an average (arithmetic mean) would be entirely bogus.

Ordinal scales

Finally, there is what is called an *ordinal scale*. This is a measuring scale that makes use of no more than the basic ordinal aspect of number. We show in Chapter 2 that sometimes numbers used in an ordinal sense label things and put them in order. It is in this way that numbers are used in ordinal scales – for labelling and putting in order. For example, we are using an ordinal scale when measuring how good a hotel is by a system of star ratings; or when determining children's achievement using, say, levels 1, 2, 3, 4, 5 or 6. Sometimes letters rather than numbers are used for an ordinal scale – for example, performance in a public examination is often measured by a system of grades, such as A, B, C, D, E, F, making use of the alphabetical ordering associated with letters. These are all ordinal measuring scales – because they do no more than put things in order according to specified criteria. No one could ever assert that the steps between the measurements are equal intervals, so they do not qualify as interval scales. We can assume only that a four-star hotel – according to some stated criteria – is better than a three-star hotel, that a grade B result is better than a grade C, that a child at level 3 has attained more in mathematics than a child at level 2, and so on.

Of course, ratio scales and interval scales also share the same properties as ordinal scales, in that they can also be used to put things in order. But, in an ordinal scale, the measurements can be used *only* for ranking and ordering and in no other way. It certainly makes no sense to use ratios for comparison of measurements of something that is only an ordinal scale, as we would with the numbers used for measurements in ratio scales. A four-star hotel is not twice as good as a two-star hotel. A level 4 child has not achieved twice as much as a level 2 child. It also makes no sense to talk about the intervals between various measurements, as we would with the numbers used for measurements in interval scales. Progression from level 2 to level 3 in a National Curriculum subject is in no sense equal to progression from level 3 to level 4 – although numbers are used for these levels we should not assume that there is an equal amount of learning involved! All we can deduce is that level 4 is a higher level of achievement than level 3, and so on.

The consequence of this analysis is that any attempt to do arithmetic with measurements on an ordinal scale is invalid and will lead to meaningless statements. For example, any aggregation of levels of achievement – such as calculations of averages – is invalid, simply because the intervals between different levels cannot be assumed to be equal steps. You cannot equate the achievement of three children gaining levels 1, 2 and 3 on an ordinal scale with three other children each gaining level 2, on the basis that the 'average' is the same for the two groups – because getting from level 1 to level 2 is not the same thing as getting from level 2 to level 3. This is the problem with using numbers for ordinal scales – as soon as people see numbers they start doing arithmetic with them, regardless of whether their conclusions have any mathematical validity or meaning.

In conclusion, we note, therefore, that we have different types of measuring scales, characterized by different mathematical properties, with different degrees of validity for the application of various arithmetic processes. But what remains throughout, even with ordinal scales, is the ever-present transitive property. We can still conclude that if A is better than B and B is better than C, then A is better than C. For without this property we could not put things in order, and without ordering there would be no measurement.

RESEARCH FOCUS   Time to understand

Teaching young children to tell the time can be a very frustrating business as, almost invariably, they find it harder than you might anticipate. Having said that, do you know any adults who *cannot* tell the time? We don't. Generally, people learn to tell the time in practical real-life contexts where they need to do this.

A quick on-line search of *Google Scholar* suggests that there has been little recent research on the subject of learning about time. But, if you delve more deeply, you will find there was quite a bit in the 30-year period, 1946–76. For example, in 1946 Ames reported on a large-scale study she undertook with American children between the ages of 18 months and 8 years who were deemed to be of higher than average intelligence. She noted that it was not until they were 6 years of age that these children showed an understanding of the four seasons. This is hardly surprising, given that, in their relatively short lives, they are unlikely to recall more than three or four winters or springs, and so on. What is even more relevant to this discussion, however, is that the majority of these able children were unable to tell the time (from an analogue clock) until they were 7 years old. Discussing Ames's work, Lovell (1966) pointed out that being able to tell the time does not necessarily mean that a child has a well-developed concept of time, for reading a clock only demonstrates that someone can read a dial.

Why might learning to tell the time be tricky? Hopkins, Pope and Pepperell (2004) point out that the face of an analogue clock is a linear scale presented as a circle, rather than as it usually appears as a horizontal number line. This in itself may perplex some children. But consider too, for example, the fact that '1' on an analogue clock can signify 1 o'clock but it can also represent 5 past the hour: in essence the same numeral has at least two meanings depending on which hand is pointing to it (and we haven't even touched on seconds). Added to that, unlike other measures children learn about, telling the time involves focusing on not one but two pieces of information – for example, the information provided by the two hands on a clock. Dudgeon and Hansen (in Hansen, 2011, p. 115) remind us that the same time of day can be described in a number of ways, making life even more confusing. They illustrate this idea with:

Twenty-five to nine

Eight thirty-five

Twenty-five to nine in the evening

Eight thirty-five in the evening

Eight thirty-five p.m.

Twenty thirty-five

Returning to the idea of understanding time as a concept, we note that Piaget (1969) concluded that it was necessary for children: (1) to appreciate that events occur in a temporal order; and (2) to have a sense of the duration of time between these events. The first of these is the ordering stage of the development of the concept of measuring time in the sense of 'the time at which something happens' that we have identified earlier in the chapter. The second is the idea of a time interval. Research by Kerslake (1975) suggests that – certainly in the past and we suspect this may still be the case in many classrooms – the idea of time intervals may be particularly difficult to acquire if, for example, lessons on telling the time involve a teacher setting the hands of a clock to one time, asking for the identification of the time depicted, and then swiftly moving the hands to another time, and then another.

Our own experience as practitioners suggests that more important than focusing on digital or analogue clocks at any early age is simply talking with young children about the order in which events occur. Shatz, Tare, Nguyen and Young (2010) investigated preschoolers' understanding of 'time-duration words', namely, minutes, hours, days and years, in relation to the duration of various events in the child's life. They concluded that, 'Like Piaget, we believe that children's early knowledge of time is very likely grounded in their personal experiences of activity and that it gradually becomes conventionalized through language' (p. 34). They then go on to recommend that, 'We situate time-word learning within the larger context of a general strategy for language learners to use conversations as an entrée into building a lexicon of abstract-word domains even before they know the meanings of individual abstract words' (p. 34). They also warn, as does Cockburn (1999), that adults have a tendency to use idioms such as 'just a minute' in a very loose sense. This may explain to some extent why, on coming to school, children's notion of time duration is weak. If you stop to think about it though, even in our more mature years, an hour doing something you enjoy can 'pass in a flash' whereas other, less enjoyable, activities of the same duration may feel as if they are lasting forever.

Long and Kamii (2001) have done some ingenious research into children's understanding of the principle of transitivity in the context of time, using extracts of music and various bits of equipment that the children could use to record informally how long these extracts lasted (water bottles and marker pens, and so on). They found that by the age of 7 years about half the children they studied could reason that, if extract A takes the same time as event X and extract B takes the same time as event Y, then they could compare the time taken for extracts A and B by comparing events X and Y. When you think about it, that's very sophisticated reasoning! But by the age of 9 years, 90% of children could reason in this way.

Some activities to use with children

Children will best develop their understanding of measurement concepts through a great deal of practical experience of measuring and talking with each other and with the teacher. The more purposeful this is – such as solving real problems, planning events, constructing timetables, cookery, shopping, science experiments, and so on – the better. Teachers in our group have noted that the automation of weighing, pricing and payment in supermarkets makes the need for practical experience in the classroom even greater. We provide here just a few examples of activities that might be used to focus on some of the central ideas in this chapter.

 ACTIVITY 8.1   Measurement Role Play

3–4	4–5	5–6	6–7	7–8
☐				

Objective

To develop young children's awareness that the process of measuring is part of real life.

Materials

Dressing-up clothes and imitation equipment such as watches, tape measures, thermometers, weighing scales.

Method

Encourage children to include in their role play various situations from real life that involve measuring. For example, the children driving round the playground on their toy cars have to stop at the garage every now and then to fill up with fuel. The child playing the part of a doctor or nurse pretends to take patients' temperatures. One child giving out dressing-up clothes has to measure the other children first to decide which clothes will fit. Children pretending to be bakers measure out their ingredients on a weighing scale. None of these are real measurements, of course. The children are simply beginning to learn that measuring is something people do.

 ACTIVITY 8.2   Children as Non-Standard Units

3–4	4–5	5–6	6–7	7–8
	☐	☐		

Objective

To give children experience of estimating and measuring lengths and distance using non-standard units, and to explore the effects of using different-sized units.

Method

A group of children stands shoulder to shoulder along one of the classroom walls, from one corner to the other, and another child counts how many children there are. The children are then asked how many would be needed to fill up the opposite wall. A group of children line up shoulder to shoulder to check this. Next they estimate how many children are needed for the length of the other two walls. This is then done and the results recorded. This is then repeated with the children standing with arms outstretched touching fingertips, and then again standing in a queue one behind the other as close as they can get. Each time the children are invited beforehand to guess how many will be required.

This experience is then extended to estimating distances (from one point to another). For example, they might estimate the number of children required to stretch diagonally across the room from one corner to the other, again using the three different units (shoulder to shoulder, fingertip to fingertip, and queuing). They might then go into the hall or into the playground and try this with the distances between two chairs placed in various positions. All this should be followed by discussion about what is discovered.

	3–4	4–5	5–6	6–7	7–8
ACTIVITY 8.3 Estimation Challenge				☐	☐

Objective

To familiarize children with the sizes of some standard units of measurement.

Materials

A 30-cm rule; scrap paper; something to act as a small screen (such as a large book).

Method

This is a simple but effective game for a small group of children. Players take turns to draw on a piece of scrap paper a line with a length of any number of centimetres they wish, using the ruler. They do this behind the screen, so that the others cannot see them doing it. The line is then shown and each of the other players estimates how long it is. One player should write down all the estimates. They then check the length of the line with the ruler. The player (or players) getting nearest wins a point. They win a bonus point if they get the length spot on.

Variations of this game can be devised using other aspects of measurement. For example, children could use a balance to weigh out quantities of sand into a yoghurt pot (using 10-g masses only), again behind a screen – the others then have to estimate the mass.

	3–4	4–5	5–6	6–7	7–8
ACTIVITY 8.4 Conservation Game (Volume and Mass)					
				□	□

Objective

To give children experience related to the concept of conservation of mass and volume.

Materials

A number of different-shaped clear plastic or glass containers and measuring jars; a small cup; a supply of water; three identical non-transparent containers with lids (such as yoghurt pots); a supply of sand; a balance; a ball bearing.

Method

This is a game for four players, in two teams of two. Team A measures out the same quantity of water into three clear containers, and then adds one extra cupful of water to one of them. While they are doing this, team B measures out the same mass of sand into the three pots, buries the ball bearing in one of them and replaces the lids. They then challenge each other to identify the odd one out. Team B is allowed only to look at the containers of water. Team A is allowed to pick up – but not to rattle vigorously – the pots of sand. After they have made their judgements each team can check to see if they are right, by pouring water or by balancing pots. They then swap over and repeat the experiment with team A doing mass and team B doing volume.

	3–4	4–5	5–6	6–7	7–8
ACTIVITY 8.5 Investigating Ordering					
				□	□

Objective

To give children experience of transitivity and ordering.

Materials

(1) A set of cards with events of the day written or depicted on them – alarm goes off, get up, have breakfast, and so on. (2) A collection of containers, such as bottles and jars. (3) A balance and a set of identical-looking sealed parcels, filled with a variety of materials, such as sand, sawdust, ball bearings. (4) A list of tasks taking various amounts of time (count to a hundred, tie up your shoe laces, do ten press-ups, and so on).

Method

These materials provide four different opportunities for children to develop a strategy for ordering three or more items (events, containers, parcels, tasks). In each case they should start with three items and order these. Then extend to four, five, six or more. The four activities are as follows:

1   The children have to put the events of the day in order from earliest to latest. To start with, any three cards can be used. A nice touch is to have letters written on the backs of the cards, so that when the whole set is finally ordered they can be turned over to reveal a message such as 'well done!'
2   By pouring water from one to another the children should order three containers by capacity. Gradually extend this by adding a fourth container, a fifth, and so on.
3   Using the balance and the parcels, the children explore the same problem with mass.
4   Two children perform two of the tasks starting at the same time, and discover which takes the longer and which takes the shorter time. Eventually they must order the whole list from the one taking the least amount of time to the one taking the greatest.

ACTIVITY 8.6 Talk about Time	3–4	4–5	5–6	6–7	7–8
				☐	☐

Objective

To develop children's understanding of the language of time.

Materials

The list of words and phrases associated with time given earlier in this chapter.

Method

Write on the board a small collection of words or phrases from the list of time language. Seat the class on the carpet and simply hold a discussion with them incorporating the words on the board. For example, you might ask the children to think of a sentence that includes one of the words or phrases. Here are two examples of suitable collections of words and phrases: (1) day, weekend, week, lifetime, long time, short time, brief, temporary, for the time being, non-stop, never-ending, permanent; (2) how old, age, age group, year group, teenager, young, old, elderly, middle-aged, underage, older, elder, oldest, younger, youngest.

ACTIVITY 8.7   Ordering Packets

3–4	4–5	5–6	6–7	7–8
			☐	☐

Objective

To provide more experience of ordering, and to heighten children's awareness of measurement in the world outside school.

Materials

Children are asked to bring in from home as many different empty packets as possible marked in grams or kilograms.

Method

Along the whole length of a wall, make a number-line frieze, marked from 0 to 2000 g. As packets are collected, children display them on the appropriate part of the number line. Write the number of grams in large numerals underneath. The children should be challenged to seek out at home packets with different numbers of grams from those already displayed.

ACTIVITY 8.8   Recording with Arrows

3–4	4–5	5–6	6–7	7–8
			☐	☐

Objective

To develop understanding of the principle of transitivity in measurement.

Materials

Three objects labelled A, B and C; three cards labelled A, B and C; three arrows cut from card, labelled 'is heavier than'; three further cards labelled 'is lighter than'; a balance for weighing.

Method

The layout of arrows shown earlier in the chapter in Figure 8.4 provides a useful way for a small group of children to record their comparisons of three objects. They are given the three objects, the three cards labelled A, B and C, and the three arrows with 'is heavier than' written on them. Their task is then to compare A with B, B with C, and A with C, using the balance, to construct an arrangement of the arrows and cards as shown in Figure 8.4, and then to discuss the ordering of the three objects that emerges. The same task with the same objects should then be undertaken with the arrows labelled 'is lighter than'.

Variations on this basic activity can be devised in any measuring context, using appropriate objects and labels, with the arrows indicating various aspects of the language of comparison.

Summary of key ideas

1 Measurements in units of length and distance might refer to a wide variety of situations, such as the straight or curved parts of objects, lines drawn on paper, imaginary lines drawn through the air or through objects, straight or curved paths.

2 Volume is the amount of three-dimensional space occupied by an object.

3 Only containers have capacity. The capacity of a container is the volume of liquid it can hold. In the metric system, capacity and liquid volume are often measured in litres.

4 Two meanings of time are: the time at which an event occurs (recorded time); and the time that something takes to happen (time interval).

5 Kilograms and grams are units of mass, not weight. A key phrase for describing the results of weighing is 'weighs the same as' (for example, the book weighs the same as 200 grams).

6 A basic purpose of measurement is for comparison and ordering.

7 The principle of transitivity is that if A is greater than (less than/equal to) B, and B is greater than (less than/equal to) C, then A must be greater than (less than/equal to) C.

8 Conservation of quantity involves recognizing which transformations (such as pouring a quantity of water into a different-shaped container) preserve which equivalences (e.g. the volume of water stays the same).

9 There are good arguments for introducing children to measuring in units by means of experience with non-standard units.

10 The metre, kilogram and second are examples of base units in the SI version of metric units.

11 Prefixes for deriving other units include: mega (million), kilo (thousand), hecto (hundred), deci (tenth), centi (hundredth), milli (thousandth) and micro (millionth).

12 Nearly all measurement is approximate – normally you can only ever measure to the nearest something.

13 Estimation is an important experience for developing understanding of measurement concepts.

14 Three different kinds of measuring scales are: ratio scales, such as length and mass, in which measurement can be compared by ratio as well as by difference; interval scales, such as temperature or time of day, in which measurements can be compared by their difference, but not by their ratio; and ordinal scales, such as examination grades and levels of achievement, in which measurements can only be compared by ordering.

15 Transitivity applies in all three types of measuring scale.

Suggestions for further reading

Fenna (2002) is an extensive dictionary of measurement that will provide authoritative answers to any questions about units, prefixes and styles for recording measurements, as well as some fascinating material about the historical and scientific background to the measurements we use.

Chapter 22 of Haylock (2010) provides further detailed coverage of the mathematics of measurement.

Chapter 4 on young children's responses to measurement systems in Nunes and Bryant (1996) is well worth reading.

Those who work with younger children should read Margaret Donaldson's classic book on children's learning (Donaldson, 1978), in which she examines critically some of Piaget's theories. In particular, she identifies the differences in children's performance when they are engaged in disembedded tasks and those that are embedded in contexts that have meaning for them.

Also highly recommended is section 2 of Dickson, Brown and Gibson (1984), which provides a thorough and fascinating survey of what research shows us about children's understanding of measurement concepts; this includes consideration of Piaget's work, fundamental ideas such as conservation and transitivity, and the difference between counting and measuring.

Some of the potential difficulties young children face with time concepts and when reading analogue and digital clocks are discussed in Chapters 7 and 8 of Cockburn (1999).

The entries on 'Conservation' and 'Transitivity' in Haylock with Thangata (2007) provide further discussion of these key concepts.

Leather (2000) is a very practical book full of activities and strategies for teaching measurement.

Finally, we would recommend Chapter 10 of Gifford (2005), which is entitled 'Measuring'.

CHAPTER 9

UNDERSTANDING SHAPE AND SPACE

In this chapter

In this chapter we endorse the validity and significance of this kind of experience for young children, as providing a foundation for the later development of geometric thinking. We explain how number work and geometric thinking are linked through the two fundamental processes of transformation and equivalence that are at the heart of thinking mathematically. We then provide an analysis of what children will learn about shape and space using these two key concepts: looking at all the different ways in which shapes can be transformed, and all the ways in which shapes can be recognized as being in some sense the same, or equivalent.

Number and shape: two branches of mathematics

In our view, the two boys on their tricycles described above were undoubtedly engaging in mathematics. Life in a well-equipped nursery is full of such crucial experience of shape and space: building models; playing with construction materials; packing away the toys; putting things in the right place where they fit the available spaces on shelves or in boxes; creating patterns with shapes; rearranging the furniture; moving some objects by pushing and others by rolling; and so on. This kind of informal, intuitive experience of shape and space is the kind of foundation on which geometric concepts are built. It is essential that teachers of young children recognize the value and validity of such experience. Mathematics in the nursery is much more than just numbers and counting.

Number work and the study of shape and space have always appeared side by side in curriculum statements for mathematics. But both teachers and children may regard them as very different kinds of activity, as illustrated by these comments by some of the teachers we worked with:

- When the parents of one of the children in my class asked her what she did in maths yesterday she said, 'We didn't do maths – we did some stuff with shapes instead.'
- Number work and shape are quite distinct as far as I'm concerned. I never think of them as being the same subject.
- My class does shape for one session a week and number work for the rest of the time. They don't think of the shape work as real maths.
- It's something to do with pattern, isn't it? You get patterns in number and patterns in shape.

It is at first sight a little surprising that two activities apparently as different as arithmetic (number) and geometry (shape and space) should form two prongs of a single subject called mathematics. We may well wonder what is the connection between the two aspects of learning, one of which includes activities like place-value notation and calculations with whole numbers, fractions, decimals and percentages, and the other of which is concerned with things like putting shapes into sets, exploring symmetries and making Christmas decorations.

One of the recurring themes in this book is that we understand mathematics by making connections. In the early chapters we talk extensively about the importance of connecting symbols with pictures, such as number lines and set diagrams. So, in fact, we are already making a link between numerical and spatial thinking. This link is made stronger in Chapter 6 where we explore the ways in which geometric patterns and images can support our understanding of number relationships. The teacher's comment above about patterns in both number and shape is pertinent to our argument here. But we would suggest that the connection is even more fundamental than that. As with our analysis of number, we show below that the two basic processes for understanding shape and spatial concepts are – yet again – equivalence and transformation.

Guess my rule

A simple game, called 'Guess my rule', that can be played with either numbers or shapes, demonstrates how the same underlying processes are shared by these two aspects of mathematics. In this game one person has a rule in their mind that they use to sort numbers or shapes and challenges the other players to guess the rule. In the number version, to work out the rule the players suggest various numbers to which the challenger responds 'yes' or 'no', depending on whether or not the rule is satisfied. For example, if the rule is 'odd numbers', then 7 would be a 'yes' and 8 would be a 'no'. As they are called out the numbers are written in either the 'yes' set or the 'no' set. Figure 9.1 shows what has been written on the board for one particular rule after several suggestions have been made. By this stage someone may be able to articulate the rule being used, namely, 'less than eleven'.

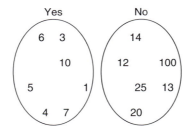

Figure 9.1   *Guess my rule: numbers*

The situation we have here can be analysed using the notions of equivalence and transformation. The numbers in the 'yes' set in Figure 9.1 are different, but there is something that is the same about them, something that for the purpose of this game makes them equivalent: they are all less than eleven. You could focus on various attributes of the numbers in this set, such as noticing that six is bigger than five, or that six is twice three, and so on. But you have to ignore all such observations of how the numbers are different from one another in favour of the one thing that they have in common.

   A game with exactly the same mathematical structure can then be played with a set of shapes, either three-dimensional solid shapes or two-dimensional plane shapes. The set of shapes is set out on a table and once again the challenger uses a rule to sort them into a 'yes' set and a 'no' set. After a while, in a game using a set of plastic

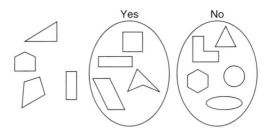

Figure 9.2   *Guess my rule: shapes*

shapes, the situation shown in Figure 9.2 might have arisen. In identifying the rule as 'four-sided', precisely the same kind of fundamental cognitive processing is involved here as with the number game. The shapes in the 'yes' set are all different from one another, but we are recognizing them as being in some sense the same. As our eye sweeps from one shape to the other, we ignore all the transformations taking place and seek to identify the equivalence.

Equivalence and transformation again

It is our contention then that the fundamental mathematical notions of transformation and equivalence are common to understanding both number and shape, and it is this that makes these two areas into a unified subject. The two basic types of learning involved in understanding concepts of shape and space are *classifying* shapes and changing shapes. First, we put shapes into sets according to 'samenesses'. Then we look at various ways of making shapes change, discussing what is different. In other words, we recognize equivalences and we apply transformations. We have seen right from our earliest discussions in this book that these two ideas are at the heart of mathematical thinking. In Chapter 1 we show that a statement such as 3 + 5 = 8 can be viewed as a statement both about a transformation being applied to the 3 and the 5, and to an equivalence that emerges. In Chapter 2 we show that the concept of a cardinal number can be analysed in terms of recognizing what is the same about a number of sets of different objects; in other words, recognizing an equivalence. In Chapter 8, we show that these ideas of transformation and equivalence are the basis of the notion of conservation in measurement.

Three-dimensional or two-dimensional shapes

Later in this chapter, as we use these two concepts of transformation and equivalence to analyse geometrical experiences, we will focus particularly on two-dimensional shapes. However, many of the ideas that we discuss in the subsequent material can be applied equally well to three-dimensional shapes – but the analysis becomes more complex. We are aware from our discussions with teachers that some put more emphasis in the early stages on activities with solid shapes:

- A lot of the schemes seem to start with three-dimensional shapes, cubes and cuboids and things like that.
- I find that the children come to school already knowing a lot of the words for flat shapes, like square and circle – but not the words for solid shapes.
- What's the argument for starting with three-dimensional? Wouldn't it be simpler to start with two-dimensional and build up?
- But they live in a three-dimensional world and are used to handling three-dimensional objects, like boxes and tins and toys. You should start with three-dimensional things you can pick up and handle, and move down to the two-dimensional shapes.
- A lot of my children call a cuboid an oblong anyway.

It seems clear to us that two-dimensional and three-dimensional experiences – flat shapes and solid shapes – need to go hand in hand. Of course, children do live in a three-dimensional world of solid shapes, but in order to describe, identify and classify these shapes, we have to focus on the shapes of their *surfaces*. Hence the confusion mentioned above between a cuboid and an oblong.

The photograph shows a three-year-old girl matching blocks with different shapes with spaces on a board; understandably, she describes the block she has just placed as a green *triangle* and has correctly matched it with a green triangle on the board. But 'triangle' is the name of one of the surfaces on this block: it does not describe the shape of the block (which is, strictly, a triangular prism). So, as teachers, without perhaps realizing it, we often encourage children to look at a solid shape, ignore the fact that it is solid and just focus on one of the surfaces. One nursery teacher described the way she helped the children to relate a surface shape and a solid shape.

> I hide a solid shape, such as a cuboid, inside a piece of cloth, so all they can see is one face. We talk about the shape they can see. It might be a square, for example. Then I tell them I am going to 'stretch the shape', and I gradually push the shape out from the cloth until the cuboid is exposed. This way they see the cuboid as growing out of the square.

We should also bear in mind that, even before they come to school, children will have spent a lot of time looking at pictures in books and at screens, so that much of their experience of shape is in fact two-dimensional. Also, an important way in which young children develop mastery of mathematical concepts is by making marks on paper to go with their words; they can make simple drawings of squares and circles, but they cannot do this with cubes and cylinders.

A mathematical analysis of shape and space

In this analysis of geometric thinking we shall compare sets of two-dimensional shapes, each time asking in what sense are the shapes in the set the same, and in what ways are they different. In other words, we shall be identifying what transformations have been applied and which equivalences are preserved. The analysis is structured according to a mathematical progression, using a way of classifying geometric experiences originally proposed by a German mathematician, Felix Klein, in 1872. In our analysis we shall use one geometric shape, that shown in Figure 9.3,

Figure 9.3   *Shape used for analysis of transformations*

to generate further sets of shapes, in which the original shape is distorted more and more, until the final set of shapes considered have very little in common. But we shall see that – in spite of the extensive transformations that have taken place – they are still in some sense equivalent.

This analysis helps us to see that sometimes we as teachers expect children to focus on the ways in which things are different, and at other times to focus on the ways in which they are the same. It seems as though learning geometry for the child is a matter of picking up clues as to what the teacher expects you to ignore or to take into account on any particular occasion!

In the course of our analysis we shall identify some of the mathematical concepts needed to discuss the samenesses and differences involved. In this way we hope teachers will see (1) how the fundamental ideas of transformation and equivalence underpin almost all geometric experiences, and (2) how the various concepts that children encounter in classifying and changing shapes fit into a coherent mathematical system. Thus, we hope that by making such connections you will feel that your own understanding of the significance of the kinds of geometric experiences that are presented to young children has been enhanced. In order to do this analysis comprehensively it will be necessary in the material that follows to discuss occasionally some ideas that may not be usually associated with the mathematics curriculum for children in the age range 3–8 years. But this is material that it is important to understand if you are to recognize the significance of even the earliest, informal and intuitive experiences of shape and space in contributing to the construction of a coherent framework of geometric concepts.

Translation

Consider the set of shapes shown in Figure 9.4. Are they the same shape?

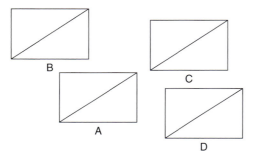

Figure 9.4   *A set of shapes produced by translations*

In one of our groups some of the responses of teachers to this question were:

- They look identical to me.
- But they're not actually the same, are they? They're like identical twins. They look alike in every respect but they're different people.
- They've got different names as well. This one's called A and that one's called B.
- They're drawn in different places on the page.

We should start by noting that when we draw, for example, a 'rectangle' on a piece of paper or on a page of a book, then we are drawing only an approximate representation of an abstract mathematical idea. This abstract idea is a four-sided figure, consisting of lines of no thickness, meeting at right angles at points of no area! So in our discussion about sameness and difference we are not concerned with the actual molecules of ink constituting the drawing on the paper, but with the abstraction that this represents. We will disregard questions such as whether the thicknesses of the lines in the various shapes are exactly the same, and questions relating to the approximate nature of all measurement. With these provisos we could then conclude that the shapes in this set are the same in every respect – except one. They are all rectangles with a diagonal drawn from the bottom left- to top right-hand corner, they have the same dimensions, the angles are the same, corresponding sides point in the same direction, and so on. But they differ in that each one is drawn in a different *position*. Position is a fundamental concept in any study of shape and space, which is why the experience of the boys on the tricycles quoted earlier in this chapter is significant. Basic language required to talk about position would include: *here, there, nearer, further, closer, higher, lower, above, below, in front of, behind,* and much more.

The transformation that changes one of these shapes into any other one in the set is called a *translation*. This is a sliding, without turning, from one position to another. To describe such translations we need concepts of *direction*, such as *up, down, left, right, forwards* and *backwards*. So, the geometry of translations requires the experience and development of all the basic vocabulary of position and direction. An interaction with a boy in a nursery class shows that there are some quite subtle things to be learnt here.

David had drawn two rockets on a large piece of paper (see Figure 9.5(a)). I asked him whether the rockets were going up or down and which rocket was higher. He told me they were going up and that the one on the right was the higher. I then turned the picture upside down (see Figure 9.5(b)). He told me they were now coming down. But when I asked him which one was higher now, he told me it was the one on the left!

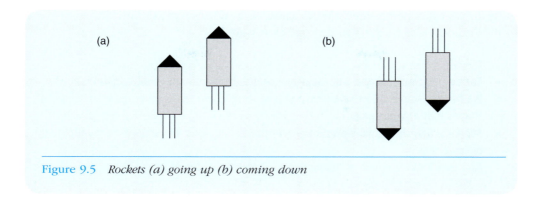

Figure 9.5   *Rockets (a) going up (b) coming down*

However, we do not often consider solid and plane shapes to be different if they differ only in position. When we do, we require some form of *co-ordinate* system to pinpoint position. An example would be in locating a seat in a room where seats are arranged in rows as, say, 'the fourth seat from the left in the third row'.

If we tell the children to sit at the same tables as yesterday, then we would be asking them to take position into account then, wouldn't we? The tables might be the same shape and same size, but when we say 'the same table' we mean the same position as well.

Rotation

Having discussed and identified translations, from now on in our analysis of whether shapes are the same or different we ignore them. In other words, we do not take position into account, so that two shapes are regarded as the same if one is produced merely by translating the other. Now consider the set of shapes shown in Figure 9.6.

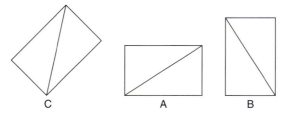

Figure 9.6   *A set of shapes produced by rotations*

Again we ask whether they are the same, or in what ways are they different? Some of the responses of teachers to this question were:

- They are the same shape, but they have been turned through various angles.
- We have examples like this in our maths scheme where the children have to colour in shapes that are the same.
- Some children find it very hard to realize that a cuboid is the same if it's standing up or on its side.
- And they'll call a square a diamond if it's standing on one of its corners.

Again we see that in many contexts we would regard the shapes in Figure 9.6 as being the same shape. The difference now is that they are oriented in space differently. Corresponding lines in the shapes point in different directions. To get from one shape to another the transformation that is applied is called a *rotation*. In order to take into account this particular transformation, the geometric concept required is that of *angle*. There are basically two ways of thinking about the concept of angle, one dynamic and the other static. The static aspect of angle is discussed later (see Figure 9.12). But here we are using the *dynamic* aspect: an angle as a measure of the amount of turn or rotation that has occurred. For example, the transformation from A to B in Figure 9.6 is a rotation through a quarter-turn. A quarter-turn is also called a *right angle*: this is shorthand for upright angle. This is the angle that a stick turns through when you move it from flat on the ground to an upright position. To be more precise about a rotation, we might also need to specify whether it is *clockwise* or *anticlockwise*. The rotation from A to C in Figure 9.6 is half a right angle anticlockwise.

Sometimes a shape does not change when it is rotated through certain angles. For example, the diagram in Figure 9.7 can be rotated through a half-turn (two right angles) and it would look the same. To convince yourself of this just turn the book upside down. While you've got the book upside down you might decide whether some letters of the alphabet, such as S, A, C or N, have this same geometric property.

This property is called *rotational symmetry*. In their practical explorations with two-dimensional shapes, young children can experience this property by drawing a box round a shape and then seeing how many different ways the shape will fit into its

Figure 9.7   *A shape with rotational symmetry*

box, without picking it up and turning it over. Young children experience the same idea when posting shapes through holes in the lid of a box. Some shapes can be rotated into a number of different positions in which they fit into their holes. A shape without rotational symmetry is the hardest to do, because it will fit through its hole in only one way. We should make clear that we are not suggesting that young children should necessarily be taught to analyse shapes in terms of this concept of rotational symmetry. But we hope that their teachers' awareness of this concept might help them to identify the relevance of some of the informal, practical explorations in which young children might engage – moving shapes around, drawing round them, fitting them into boxes, posting them through holes, matching them with shapes on a board as shown earlier in the photograph – as foundational experience for more formal analysis at a later stage.

PAUSE TO REFLECT   On rotation

To introduce children to the concept of rotation it is helpful to talk explicitly about experiences in their lives where they physically rotate something. For example, to open a screw-top bottle or a jar they could hold the bottle in one hand and rotate the cap (or lid) anticlockwise. Or they could hold the cap (or lid) and rotate the bottle clockwise. How many complete turns would be needed to get the cap (or lid) off? Try this out next time you are doing this. What about opening a door by pushing on a handle? If the handle is on the left of the door do you rotate it clockwise or anticlockwise? And on the right? What fraction of a turn is involved? About a quarter of a turn? Is it the same for a door-knob?

What other situations can you think of that involve the child physically in rotating something? How could you exploit these in teaching this concept? Then the thing being rotated could be the child's own body. Discuss with a colleague how physical movements of children in the playground could be used to develop the language and concept of rotation.

Reflection

From now on in our analysis of whether shapes are the same or different, we shall ignore rotations as well as translations. In other words, we do not take into account changes in position or changes in orientation. The result of translating or rotating a shape is regarded as the same shape. We turn our attention to the two shapes shown in Figure 9.8, and again ask in what sense they are the same shape, and in what ways they are different.

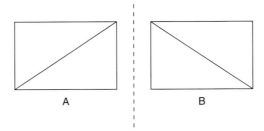

Figure 9.8   *Mirror images*

Some of the responses of teachers to this question were:

- They're different because they're mirror images of each other.
- It's like a pair of shoes. They're the same in one sense, but they're different because one's for the left foot and the other for the right foot.
- They're the same, but one's been flipped over.
- It's as though you have to learn the conventions. Sometimes in maths lessons we ask children to pick out the same shape, and expect them to regard mirror images as the same, but then we correct them when they don't distinguish between the letter d and the letter b!

Again we have a situation where for many purposes we would regard shapes as being the same, yet on other occasions we would focus on the differences. If you look in a mirror and comb your hair you are making use of the equivalence between yourself and your mirror image. When a child picks out a pair of shoes from the heap in their bedroom they look for two that are the same as each other; but then when they have to decide which shoe goes on which foot they focus on the difference between them. So, again, both equivalence and transformation are involved in the classification and manipulation of the shapes involved.

The transformation that would change one of the shapes in Figure 9.8 into the other is called a *reflection*. Associated with each reflection is a *mirror line*. The dotted line shows where a mirror could be placed in Figure 9.8, so that one of the shapes becomes the mirror image of the other.

To take into account the changes produced by reflections, the concepts of *left* and *right* are particularly important. Thus when you look into the mirror and raise your right arm, the person in the mirror raises their left arm. It is important to note that 'left and right' are different kinds of ideas from 'up and down', which is why children find them trickier to master. Up is the same direction for all of us, all the time – at least as we move around locally on the earth's surface. But left for one person might be right for another, and what is on your left now will be on your right when you turn round.

Sometimes a shape does not change when it is reflected. This property is called *line symmetry*. For example, the mirror image of the diagram in Figure 9.9 would look the same as the original. To convince yourself of this, look at the diagram in a mirror, or hold the book up to the light and look through the other side of the page. While you're doing one of these you might investigate whether any capital letters of the alphabet, such as **S, A, C** or **N**, have this geometric property. Remember that we are disregarding changes produced by translating or rotating the book, so when you are looking at the mirror image you are allowed, for example, to turn it upside down.

Figure 9.9   *A shape with line symmetry*

In their practical explorations with two-dimensional shapes young children can experience line symmetry in a number of different ways. They can draw a box round a shape and then investigate whether the shape will fit into its box when it is picked up and turned over. Shapes that do fit into their mirror image in this way have line symmetry. Or they can cut out a shape and discover whether it can be folded along a line so that one half matches the other half. Such a fold line is called a *line of symmetry*. The two halves are mirror images of each other, with the line of symmetry as a mirror line. Children can experiment with looking at shapes in mirrors and seeing what happens when a mirror is placed along a line of symmetry. Another useful experience is to copy shapes on to a transparent sheet and then to compare the original with the shape that appears on the reverse side of the sheet.

PAUSE TO REFLECT   On reflection

Why is it that your image in a mirror is reversed left to right but not reversed up and down? For example, if you raise your left arm, the person you can see in the mirror raises their right arm. But when you point up, the person in the mirror does not point down! Now test your understanding of reflection by imagining a few other scenarios.

(Continued)

(Continued)

- What would you see in the mirror if you stood on your head in front of a mirror with a paper bag over your left foot?
- What would you see if you lay on your right side facing the mirror and pointed upwards with your left arm?
- What do you see when you are driving on the left in a right-hand drive car and you look in the rear-view mirror at the car behind. Do you see someone driving on the right in a left-hand drive car?
- Now imagine going up a hill and looking down at a lake surrounded by trees. What would you notice about the reflections of the trees in the lake?

So, what do you think? Is it true to say that mirrors reverse images left to right but not up and down?

Similarity

If we now decide to disregard translations, rotations and reflections, when comparing shapes, then we would consider all the shapes in Figure 9.10 to be the same. Mathematicians would say that these shapes are *congruent*.

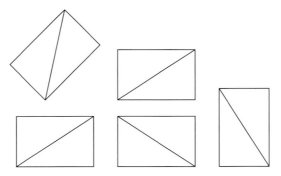

Figure 9.10   *A set of congruent shapes*

Figure 9.11 introduces a further way in which shapes may change, while still in some senses staying the same. Now the sizes of the shapes are different, but we would still in many contexts regard them as the same shape. This is what happens when children are putting plastic shapes into sets. Sometimes they put, say, the large triangles and small triangles into the same set (the set of triangles), regarding them as the same. But

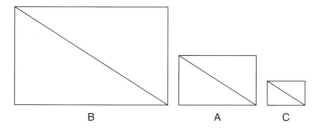

Figure 9.11   *A set of shapes produced by scaling*

sometimes they put them into different sets (the set of large shapes or the set of small shapes), regarding them as different. Whether they regard them as the same or different depends therefore on which attributes they are using to sort the shapes.

The transformation being applied as we move from one shape to another in Figure 9.11 is technically called a *similarity*. The shapes are said to be *similar*. This is, of course, using the word 'similar' in a precise technical sense, not in the colloquial sense where you might say that your sister or brother and yourself have similar looks. We can think of a similarity as being either a scaling up or a scaling down. We are talking about what happens, for example, when we use a photocopier to enlarge or reduce something. The key concept required to specify a scaling is that of *scale factor*. In Figure 9.11, for example, B is the result of scaling A by a scale factor of 2. The effect of this is to multiply the lengths of all the sides by 2. Likewise, C is the result of scaling A by a scale factor of ½. These are instances of the scaling structure of multiplication discussed in Chapter 4. Since all the lengths are scaled by the same factor, the ratio of any two lengths in the shape remains the same. Young children experience scaling in model cars, dolls and dolls' houses, maps and plans, scale drawings, play houses, photographs, and so on, all of which provide excellent starting points for informal discussion of these ideas.

- One of my boys measured the playground to make a plan, then said he couldn't do it. He said the paper wasn't big enough, because it was only about one metre long, but the playground was thirty metres!
- We were reading a book about a monster and there was this picture of a huge foot next to a small man. None of my children got it. They didn't seem to appreciate the significance of scale at all.
- I get my class to make a larger version of a small picture, by drawing a grid over it and copying it onto a larger grid.
- I showed some of my Year 3 children how to enlarge and reduce on the photocopier. They were fascinated by it and quickly picked up which numbers you use to make things bigger or smaller, like 141 and 71.

Once again we note that there are times when we focus on the transformation, and expect children to take differences in size into account, and times when we focus on the equivalence, disregarding the difference in scale. Consider what happens when a teacher draws a large square on the board and asks the children to copy it. Without questioning the instruction, the children will all quite happily choose to ignore the size of the square and make a smaller (scaled-down) drawing on their own piece of paper. And this is probably what the teacher intends them to do. Somehow, even though the size of a shape is one of its most significant attributes, children pick up the idea that there are times when the teacher wants you to ignore it.

Under scaling, the angles in a shape remain unchanged. We are using the word angle here in its *static* sense. This is a measure of the *difference in direction* between two lines. So the angle X in Figure 9.12 is smaller than the angle Y, because the difference in the direction of the two lines meeting at X is smaller than that of the two lines meeting at Y. Notice how the two diagrams used for comparison here have been chosen to exaggerate the attribute in question, with the longer lines (X) enclosing the smaller angle – see the discussion of comparison in measurement in Chapter 7.

Figure 9.12   *Which angle is smaller?*

Family likeness

From now on in our analysis of geometric thinking, we regard similar shapes, such as the set shown in Figure 9.13, as equivalent. We are now disregarding differences resulting from translations, rotations, reflections, and scalings. As far as we are concerned, from this point on, all the shapes in Figure 9.13 are the same shape.

Now consider the set of shapes shown in Figure 9.14. Although our original shape has changed quite considerably, we might still recognize that there is something the same about all the shapes in this set. Even though the shapes are not geometrically similar, there is still a *family likeness*, some shared properties that lead us on some occasions to ignore the differences between the members of the family. We might select them from a collection of shapes, recognizing an equivalence and distinguishing them from other shapes that do not share the family likeness.

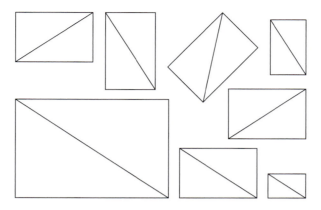

Figure 9.13   *A set of similar shapes*

One teacher described an instance of a child recognizing this kind of equivalence:

My children were doing an exercise in the maths scheme where they had to colour in the cuboids on a shelf. One of them coloured in the shelf, because she said that was a cuboid as well! I thought that was very clever.

Figure 9.15 provides another example of a set of shapes, including our original shape, all of which share one of these family likenesses. The technical word for the transformation that changes our original shape into one of the others in either the set shown in Figure 9.14 or that shown in Figure 9.15 is an *affinity*. The precise analysis of this kind of transformation is fairly involved and not particularly helpful for a teacher of young children. But we may notice that the shapes in Figures 9.14 and 9.15 have been produced by stretching or shearing the original. In order to recognize and to discuss equivalences of this sort, we would need particularly the concept of *parallel*. Two lines are parallel if they are pointing in

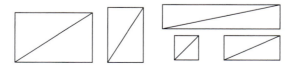

Figure 9.14   *A set of shapes with a family likeness*

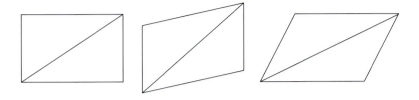

Figure 9.15   *Another example of a family likeness*

the same direction. One condition of an affinity is that parallel lines must stay parallel.

When young children are sorting a collection of shapes into sets using various criteria, often what they are doing is identifying shapes that share various family likenesses. For example, within the set of *polygons* (two-dimensional shapes with straight edges), they can identify sets of shapes such as *triangles* (three sided), *quadrilaterals* (four sided), *pentagons* (five sided), *hexagons* (six sided), and so on. Then they discover that the set of quadrilaterals contains some particularly interesting examples of family likenesses. For example, there is the family known as *rectangles*, some of which are shown in Figure 9.16. These share the property that all four angles are right angles.

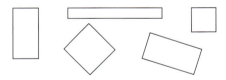

Figure 9.16   *A family of rectangles*

Some teachers raised some questions about this family of shapes:

- Aren't some of those squares not rectangles?
- Is a square a rectangle then?
- Why has the word oblong gone out of fashion?

There is a small confusion here that often arises. A square is definitely a member of the set of rectangles, since it shares the family likeness, having all four angles as right angles. It is, in fact, a special sort of rectangle, since all the sides are equal. If we want to distinguish between squares and other rectangles then we can refer to square rectangles and oblong rectangles. This confusion is reinforced if, when children are sorting shapes, we refer to squares and rectangles as though they are separate sets of shapes. We can, however, correctly sort the rectangles into those that are squares and those that are not squares.

A second important family of quadrilaterals is the set of *parallelograms*, some examples of which are shown in Figure 9.17. The family likeness here is that they all have two pairs of opposite sides that are parallel.

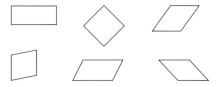

Figure 9.17   *A family of parallelograms*

More questions are raised in response to this family of special quadrilaterals:

- So a rectangle is a parallelogram?
- And since a square is a rectangle, is it a parallelogram as well?
- What's a rhombus?

The answer to each of the first two of these questions is 'yes'. All rectangles, including squares, are parallelograms – they share the family likeness, having two pairs of opposite sides parallel. The third question leads to one last example of a family of shapes. The set of *rhombuses*, some examples of which are shown in Figure 9.18, are parallelograms with all four sides equal in length. We can imagine the transformation involved here as taking a square of any size, hinged at the corners, and changing it by tilting it to one side or the other.

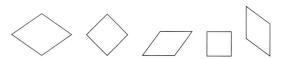

Figure 9.18   *A family of rhombuses*

5-year-old Jack was looking at a picture of a square drawn at 45 degrees to the edge of the paper. I asked him what shape it was. He said it was a diamond. I said, 'No, it's not, it's a square. Look!' and I rotated the paper through 45 degrees. 'Now it's a square,' he said, and then, rotating it back to where it was, 'Now it's a diamond again!' I drew him a diamond shape, and said, 'Now, that's a diamond.' 'No, it's not,' he replied, 'that's a rhombus!' I gave up and decided we would return to this later.

Finally, in this section, we ask the reader to note that there is a square in each of the families shown in Figures 9.16, 9.17 and 9.18. A square is a special kind of rectangle, one with equal sides. A square is a special kind of rhombus, one with equal angles. A square is therefore a very special kind of parallelogram. To transform any old parallelogram into a square there are two ways you can do it: (1) first make the angles equal, so the parallelogram becomes a rectangle, and then make the sides equal, so the rectangle becomes a square; (2) first make the sides equal, so the parallelogram becomes a rhombus, and then make the angles equal, so the rhombus becomes a square.

Perspectivity

In the previous section we have identified some examples of families of shapes, such as rectangles, parallelograms and rhombuses, which can be considered as equivalent because they share some particular property. But would we ever recognize the shapes shown in Figure 9.19 as being the same?

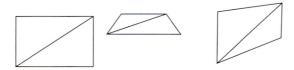

Figure 9.19   *Are these all the 'same' shape?*

In fact, we apparently recognize sets of shapes like those in Figure 9.19 as being the same all the time as we move around our three-dimensional world, since these are merely *perspective* drawings of the same shape. If we imagine our original shape drawn on the side of a box, then the other shapes in Figure 9.19 are simply representations of how the shape might appear to us as we turn the box round and view it from different angles, as illustrated in Figure 9.20.

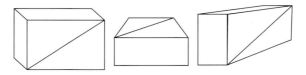

Figure 9.20   *Perspective drawings of the same shape*

The analysis of perspectivity is difficult mathematics and should not detain us now. But it is interesting for us to observe that when young children learn to recognize shapes viewed from different perspectives in our three-dimensional world, they are actually learning to ignore the changes in the shapes associated with perspective transformations.

One teacher asked her 4- and 5-year-olds to draw a table. Figure 9.21 provides some typical examples of their drawings. About half of the children drew a side view of the table, like the drawings done by Peter and Laura. But the other half drew what was

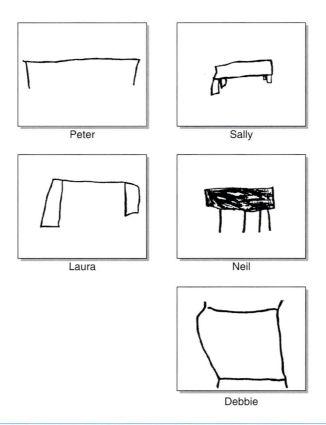

Figure 9.21   *Four- and five-year-olds draw tables*

basically a rectangle, with some legs attached somewhere, like the drawings of Sally, Neil and Debbie. It is fascinating to note that even such young children have already learnt to recognize a rectangle, apparently ignoring the perspective changes, even when looked at from the very low angle at which they presumably view tables!

This suggestion is confirmed by what happened when the children were asked to draw the tables in the school dining hall. These tables were semi-hexagonal. The examples of the children's drawings in Figure 9.22 show that they realize that they are not looking at rectangles, even though most of them clearly have some difficulty in representing the actual shape.

Figure 9.22   *The tables in the dining room*

It could be because we learn to ignore perspective transformations at such an early age that it is actually very difficult to make ourselves consciously aware of them. So, when we look at a rectangular window as we walk past a house, even though the image on the retina of our eye must change, most of the time we are not consciously aware of the shape of the window changing. As far as we are concerned it stays a rectangle.

Topological transformation

In the course of our analysis of geometric thinking we have gradually distorted our original shape more and more, by applying various transformations to it. As we have done this we have noticed that there are still situations in which we regard the various shapes produced as being equivalent, in which we concentrate on what is the same about the shapes, rather than on what changes from one to another – even though the changes have been quite drastic. The final step in this analysis is to transform our shape to generate a set of shapes like those shown in Figure 9.23. Although in most situations we would regard these as being different shapes, we may still recognize something about them that makes them equivalent. For example, if these diagrams were represent-ing pieces of wire constituting electrical circuits then they would all be the same circuit.

To generate each of the shapes in Figure 9.23 we have applied what is called a *topological transformation* to the original shape. In a transformation of this sort, the shape can be pulled, stretched or distorted in any way you like, provided that no lines are broken or joined in the process. Clearly none of our usual geometric properties – such as length, angle, parallelism, ratio of lengths, the number of sides, or even the

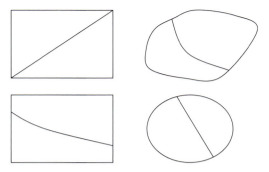

Figure 9.23 *Are these in any sense the 'same' shape?*

straightness of sides – is preserved under such transformations. But if we think of a two-dimensional shape as no more than a network of *paths*, enclosing *regions*, meeting at *junctions*, then we can see that all the shapes in Figure 9.23 are the same. Each is a network of three paths from one junction to another, enclosing two regions. This indicates that it is often essentially topological thinking that is involved in giving directions for a route. For example, we can describe a route like this: 'Go out of the drive, turn left, then the second on the right, just past the postbox, carry on until you come to a roundabout, take the second exit, …'. These instructions are useful even though they contain no reference to distance, scale or direction, but simply refer to a network of paths and junctions, to what is passed on a particular path, and whether you turn left or right at any particular junction. A useful topological exercise for children is to articulate their route from home to school.

Some of the most fundamental geometric ideas are those that are preserved under a topological transformation: ideas such as *between*, *next*, *meet*, *inside* and *outside*. So, if one junction lies between two other junctions in a network, it will still lie between them after a topological transformation. The next junction along a path will still be the next junction; two paths that meet will still meet; a point inside a region will still be inside the region, and so on. We hope that this analysis helps to make clear to teachers of even the youngest children the significance in mathematical terms of such basic spatial language as this.

We conclude this section with one final observation, which demonstrates the importance of topological thinking. An interesting phenomenon is that young children are able to recognize all the shapes in Figure 9.24 as being the same letter. But in what geometric sense are they the same? They are certainly not congruent, or even similar. They are not a family of shapes, in the sense of sharing an affinity, nor are they just one shape seen from different perspectives. They are, of course, topologically equivalent. It is really quite amazing that the young human brain is capable of categorizing all these shapes on the basis of what is the same about them while ignoring the many ways in which they are different.

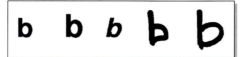

Figure 9.24   *A set of topologically equivalent shapes*

A nursery teacher told us that some of her class who were children of European migrant workers got really confused because the way their parents wrote a seven had an extra line in it (7̶). They could cope with variations in size, serif, angle and proportion, in the way this symbol is written, but not with a symbol that is *topologically* different. It was the same with the symbol 4, if someone wrote it without joining the vertical line to the diagonal line. This suggests that topological equivalence may be the most basic concept of sameness and that it forms a starting point for geometric thinking. From this basis we have to provide a range of practical experiences of shapes – picking them up and looking at them from different angles, drawing round them, cutting them out, moving them round, fitting them in boxes, matching them, comparing them, contrasting them, scaling them, looking at them in mirrors, turning them over, folding them, rotating them, fitting them together, sorting them into families, and so on – in order to equip the children with the language, skills and concepts needed to recognize the full range of equivalences outlined in this chapter. For it is this recognition of what stays the same when things change that is the basis of the understanding of shape and space.

RESEARCH FOCUS   Two- and three-dimensional shapes

In the 1970s there was much discussion as to whether teachers of young children should focus on two- or three-dimensional shapes first. Weinzweig (1978, as reported by Dickson, Brown and Gibson, 1984) suggested that, because a child's first experiences are with solid objects, they should begin to develop an awareness of two-dimensional shapes from experience with solid shapes; for example, by making prints with the flat surface of a cube or a prism. Egsgard (1970, also in Dickson et al., 1984) stressed the importance of spending time working with three-dimensional solids *before* considering two-dimensional surfaces – but then relating the two, for example, through wall-building, specifying the need for at least one of the surfaces to be flat. As we have said earlier in the chapter such arguments overlook how large a part two-dimensional shapes play in the young child's experience. More recently two research groups in Germany have been working on introducing children to relationships between two- and three-dimensional shapes.

The first is based on the ancient art of paper folding – origami – and is discussed by Brigitte Spindeler and Bernd Wollring (2007). In this chapter they explain how you might present a child with a three-dimensional house made out of paper. Their task is to build a similar house by studying – and deconstructing as necessary – the model they have been given. Once successful they are encouraged to explain to others how they completed the task by designing a poster of the steps they took. Such exercises provide considerable discussion of all manner of shapes! By way of example, consider Figure 9.25. What famous 3-D landmark could you make from this 2-D shape? Discussion of how the two-dimensional shape is used to make the three-dimensional shape contributes to the child's understanding of both.

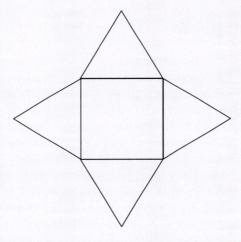

Figure 9.25   *What famous 3-D landmark can you construct from this 2-D shape?*

The second research work we would draw your attention to might appear very different at first sight, as it is far more up-to-date technologically. It does, however, serve many of the same purposes and it too has proved highly motivating and successful. This research makes use of the *BlockCAD* computer program which was designed by Anders Issakson in Sweden and which can be downloaded free. At the time of writing more details were available at http://blockcad.net. Should this prove unsuccessful, a search engine should quickly locate it. Using *BlockCAD*, Diana Hunscheidt and Andrea Peter-Koop (2007) worked with young children and student teachers building real Lego models from virtual ones and vice versa. As participants quickly discovered, the program is highly versatile and the range of model-making experiences extremely motivating. One of the teachers exclaimed, 'Oh this is cool. I loved playing with Lego when I was a kid.' (p. 57). We would urge you to try *BlockCAD* – even if you do not have any Lego to hand – as we are sure you will see why Diana and Andrea's research has proved successful in developing a range of

(Continued)

(Continued)

spatial and communication skills, and, perhaps more importantly, a desire and confidence to play and experiment with what are essentially mathematical concepts. In doing this you will have to engage with the relationship between the two-dimensional virtual Lego world and the three-dimensional real Lego construction.

Some activities to use with children

The starting point for teaching shape and space is to provide masses of informal, unstructured opportunities to experience geometric concepts through playing and talking. In addition, the main text of this chapter contains a number of suggestions of the sorts of practical activities in which children might engage. The game, 'Guess my rule' is a good starting point for any series of lessons on shape, whether with two- or three-dimensional shapes. All experiences of classification of shapes provide children with opportunities to develop the language of shape and space and to focus on equivalences. Teachers might also, for example, get children to explore rotational and line symmetry by cutting out shapes, drawing round them, looking at them in mirrors, and so on. Additionally, they might experiment with making photocopy enlargements and reductions of children's drawings and get the children to cut them out and investigate the spatial relationships. All this can be supported by discussion of what is the same and what is different. We conclude with a few further suggestions for more structured, practical activities.

ACTIVITY 9.1 Stolen Shape	3–4	4–5	5–6	6–7	7–8
	☐	☐			

Objective

To develop young children's ability to sort shapes according to various attributes.

Materials

A set of 12 plastic shapes: all combinations of large and small, red and blue, triangles, squares and circles.

Method

First, two or three children work together to sort the shapes into different categories, to become familiar with their attributes. Then they close their eyes while the teacher jumbles up the shapes and 'steals' one. The children have to work out which shape has been stolen and describe it to the teacher; for example, 'a large red circle'. When the children have mastered this game the number of pieces can be gradually increased.

ACTIVITY 9.2   Shapes in the Environment

3–4	4–5	5–6	6–7	7–8
	☐	☐	☐	☐

Objective

To heighten children's awareness of shapes used in the world around them.

Materials

A sheet for each child with drawings of shapes. An example is shown in Figure 9.26. This can be simplified for younger children.

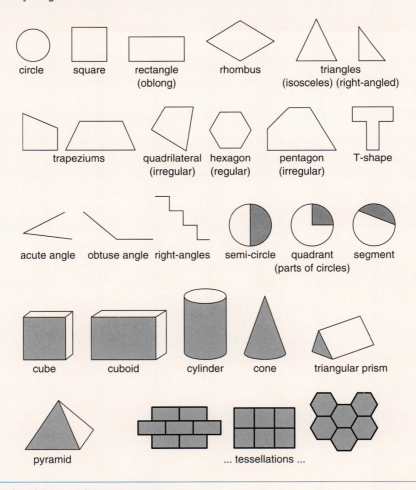

Figure 9.26   *Shapes in the environment*

(Continued)

(Continued)

Method

The children explore an area outside looking for examples of the shapes illustrated. When they find them they tick them off on their sheets. (The sheet illustrated in Figure 9.26 has been used by hundreds of children on a mathematics trail around the University of East Anglia in Norwich.)

	3–4	4–5	5–6	6–7	7–8
ACTIVITY 9.3 **Guess my Two Rules**				☐	☐

Objective

To give children structured experience of sorting shapes according to their properties.

Materials

A set of two- or three-dimensional shapes; a network diagram as illustrated in Figure 9.27.

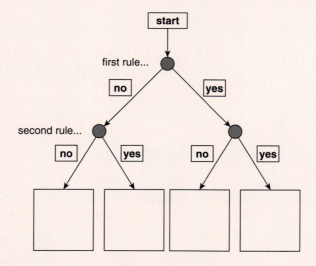

Figure 9.27   *Network diagram for 'Guess my two rules'*

Method

This is played like 'Guess my rule' but this time the challenger has two rules. The shapes are taken along the network and sorted into four sets, according to two rules, turning left at a junction if the shape satisfies the rule, and right if it does not. Once some shapes have been sorted the other children have to predict which way a given shape will go at each junction. Eventually the rules should be articulated and checked.

		3–4	4–5	5–6	6–7	7–8
ACTIVITY 9.4	Dismantling Boxes			□	□	□

Objective

To help children to identify the plane shapes forming the constituent parts of solid shapes.

Materials

Ask children to bring in from home two each of any interestingly-shaped boxes from their family shopping – pyramids, cylinders, tetrahedra (a tetrahedron is a solid with four faces), cubes, cuboids, prisms are all quite common. If necessary, supplement these with your own examples.

Method

The children should go round the edges of one of the boxes in each pair with a thick, black marker-pen. Then they dismantle this box and cut out and identify the shapes that have been marked out, discarding the flaps. The other box in the pair and the cut-out shapes are then mounted in a display, to highlight the various flat surfaces used to make the solid shape, as illustrated in Figure 9.28.

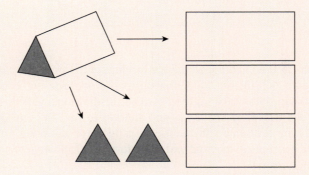

Figure 9.28   *Identifying the flat surfaces in solid shapes*

3–4	4–5	5–6	6–7	7–8
		☐	☐	☐

ACTIVITY 9.5   Odd One Out

Objective

To provide experience of transformation and equivalence in shape and space.

Materials

The teacher prepares several examples of strips of sets of shapes, as shown in Figure 9.29. Also needed are blank strips for children to use.

Figure 9.29   *Which shape is the odd one out in each row?*

Method

The strips are shown to the children, who have to identify the odd one out and explain why. For example, in Figure 9.29(b) the third drawing is the odd one out because it is a mirror image. The children can then make up their own set of drawings with three the same and a fourth as the odd one out. They challenge one another to find the odd one out. Discussion about why the three are the same and the fourth is different will bring out many of the fundamental geometric concepts associated with transformation and equivalence that have been the theme of this chapter.

Summary of key ideas

1   Teachers in the Foundation Stage especially should recognize the significance and value of informal and intuitive experience of shape and spatial concepts through play and other activities in and out of the classroom.

2   Geometrical thinking is mainly about classifying shapes and changing shapes. This involves recognizing both equivalences and transformations: ways in which shapes can be regarded as being the same and ways in which shapes differ or change.

3   The fact that these concepts of equivalence and transformation are fundamental to understanding both number and shape is one of the reasons why these two aspects of learning are considered to be two branches of one subject.

4   Transformations that might be applied to a shape, in order of increasing distortion of the original shape, are translation, rotation, reflection, similarity, affinity (family likeness), perspectivity and topological transformation.

5   Geometric concepts and language needed to identify and discuss transformations and equivalences in shape and space include: position, here, there, nearer, further, closer, higher, lower, above, below, in front of, behind, direction, up, down, left, right, forwards, backwards, co-ordinates, clockwise, anticlockwise, angle (dynamic and static), right angle, rotational symmetry, mirror line, line symmetry, congruent, similar, scale factor, scaling up, scaling down, family likeness, parallel, polygon, side, triangle, quadrilateral, pentagon, hexagon, square rectangles and oblong rectangles, parallelogram, rhombus, perspective drawing, path, region, junction, between, next, meet, inside, outside.

Suggestions for further reading

Chapters 23, 24 and 25 of Haylock (2010) explain in more detail the mathematics of angle, transformations, symmetry and the classification of shapes.

Section 1 of Dickson, Brown and Gibson (1984) deals with spatial thinking – fascinating and thorough, with plenty of references for further consideration.

A chapter by Hejný and Slezáková entitled 'Investigating mathematical reasoning and decision making' in Cockburn (2007) provides an interesting range of activities to encourage classification, including that of shapes.

Blinko (2000) provides a clearly presented selection of activities on shape and space for young children, including ideas for extension and differentiation and involving parents.

Linfield and Coltman (2008) is a very structured but nonetheless useful collection of ideas for introducing shape in the Foundation Stage.

Also for this age range, we recommend Chapter 4 of Montague-Smith and Price (2012), which includes practical suggestions and interesting conversations with children about shape.

Chapter 9 of Gifford (2005) is on shape and space, and provides interesting insights into children's experience and learning in the Foundation Stage.

In a chapter entitled 'Making space for geometry in primary mathematics' in Thompson (2003), Jones and Moody argue the case for provision of plenty of practical experience of shape and space, as a foundation for later learning of formal geometry.

Finally, Martin Gardner's wonderful book, *Mathematical Puzzles and Diversions* (written in 1959, but latest edition, 1991), has a highly amusing addendum on reflections in mirrors in the chapter entitled 'Left or Right?'.

CHAPTER 10

UNDERSTANDING DATA HANDLING

A CONFUSING CATEGORIZATION

I put the children in my class into groups at the beginning of the year – green apples, yellow bananas, and so on – they work in these groups for everything. Jamie never cottoned on to the fact that he was a yellow banana. He was always wandering around lost. Then when we were getting ready for the Christmas play I told all the shepherds to go to one side. Jamie didn't move. 'Go on, Jamie,' I said, 'over there – you're a shepherd'. 'No, I'm not', he said, 'I'm a yellow banana!' (Reception class teacher).

- Think of some other examples of situations when Jamie is likely to get labelled and put into various sets, groups or categories.
- Jamie's problem seems to be the idea of being in two categories simultaneously: being both a shepherd and a yellow banana. What diagram could be connected with this overlapping of categories?

In this chapter

In this chapter we look at some of the basic mathematical ideas involved in the early stages of learning to handle simple statistical data. We start with the process of classification, which is fundamental to all aspects of mathematics – from the first stages of counting and cardinal numbers onwards, and, as we saw in Chapter 9, in making sense of shape. In the lower primary years children will often engage in sorting and classifying objects (including, especially, themselves) according to various criteria. They will learn to record these experiences using a range of pictures and diagrams. From classification into various sets they will move on to considering how many there are in each set. This numerical data can then be organized into frequency tables and presented in simple graphical forms, such as pictograms, block graphs and bar charts.

Meaningful, purposeful and cross-curricular

The work here has the advantage that it is likely to score highly in terms of meaningfulness, purposefulness and cross-curricular links.

Meaningfulness

By 'meaningfulness' we mean that the children are familiar with the context of the tasks in which they are engaged. From their own direct experience they are aware of what is significant, they recognize what is a problem and appreciate what counts as a solution. Clearly, in teaching data-handling there is great scope for the teacher to exploit the child's own direct experience in the questions posed and the data collected – and thereby to make the work meaningful.

Purposefulness

By 'purposefulness' we mean that the tasks have some purpose from the child's perspective. So much of what children do in school has very little genuine and immediate purpose other than to satisfy the demands of the teacher. With this area of mathematics the tasks can have a real purpose, such as: to answer a question; to solve a problem; or to gather, organize and communicate information within an area of enquiry. All our experience suggests that motivation for learning is directly proportional to the degree of purposefulness in the learning tasks.

> [When] surveys are related to issues which affect them, they are more interested. Children in one nursery were engaged by the question, 'Do the boys hog the trikes?' and so collected data to investigate this, by tallying boys and girls. (Gifford, 2005, p. 98)

Cross-curricular

Of all the different strands in the mathematics curriculum, handling data is the strand with the greatest potential for linking mathematics with other areas of the curriculum. Science experiments, geography and history topics, performance in physical education, for example, are all sources of data that can be collected and processed in order to address questions, to solve problems and to provide insights. In doing this, the teacher will plan for the children to be involved in all the stages of handling data – being involved in determining what data should be collected; then collecting it and recording it; then organizing it; then representing it in some kind of a graph, and, finally, interpreting it.

An example

For example, as part of a topic on food, one group of 7- and 8-year-olds was involved in all these stages when investigating some of the less familiar fruits available in the supermarket – where they came from, how they got here, what they cost, and so on. They decided to find out which of four exotic fruits were most popular with the children in their class. The children organized a tasting session and recorded in a table each child's favourite fruit from the four options. Next, they produced a tally chart showing how many chose each fruit, converted this into a frequency table and then a block graph (see page 272). Finally they wrote a paragraph summarizing their findings:

> The children in our class tasted 4 fruits. These were mango, papaya, star fruit and tamarillo. Most children liked the mango best. We liked the papaya and tamarillo the same. Only one boy chose the star fruit. The mango had 4 more than the tamarillo and the papaya. The star fruit had 6 less than the tamarillo and the papaya. We should tell the supermarket to sell more mangoes and if they keep the star fruit longer it might get sweeter.

Pictorial representation

Making connections

It is not difficult to recognize the significance of this kind of activity in terms of understanding mathematics, using the underlying idea of making connections that has been one of the themes of this book. The mathematics here starts with a real-life situation – in the example above this was the children's tasting of four exotic fruits. The observations are recorded in symbols, in a frequency table, connecting numbers with the real-life situation. This is then transformed into a graph, connecting the symbols with a picture. And the whole activity promotes mathematical language, starting with the articulation of a question to be investigated and concluding with the implications drawn from the data and the graph. The strong connections between concrete situations, symbols, pictures and language involved here imply that this is a very significant area of activity for developing children's understanding and confidence with number and number relationships. For example, the representation of the data in pictorial form gives a visual image to support such concepts as 'more than', 'less than', 'greatest' and 'least'.

Differences between numerical and pictorial representations

We asked some of the teachers we worked with what they saw as the main differences between presenting some data in purely numerical form and presenting the same data in pictorial form, as shown in Figure 10.1.

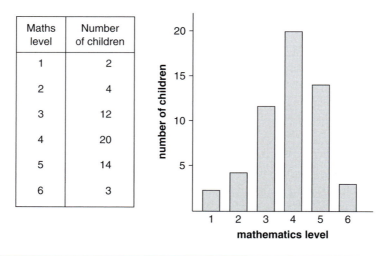

Figure 10.1 *Comparing numerical and graphical representation of data*

In what ways did they consider one or other format more useful or more helpful? Their responses bring out clearly the significant principles here:

- In the pictorial form the same information is more accessible visually and comparisons like 'bigger than' and 'smaller than' can be made more immediately.
- The bar chart is a more interesting way of presenting the information; it can be understood at a glance.

- You get an instant impression with the graph. It's easier to take in the important facts.
- Level 4 obviously stands out above the others in the bar chart – and it's immediately apparent that there are few children at levels 1 and 6.
- The pictorial representation is better where the trend over the level range is more important than the exact numbers involved.
- It might be difficult to read across if you wanted the exact numbers, so the table would be more accurate.
- The table of numbers is easier to use if you're doing calculations that need specific values – the graph would have to be translated back.

Data in numerical form lends itself to sequential analysis, as you examine the detail of the data bit by bit. You can manipulate numbers, add them up, calculate differences and ratios, find averages and so on. By contrast, the pictorial representation provides an overall, at-a-glance picture of the situation and the relationships involved. The graph provides a global synthesis of all the data, so that you can take it all in – in one go. Some of the detail is harder to get hold of in the picture, but you get an immediate impression of the differences and ratios involved, for example, without any manipulation or calculation.

Both kinds of thinking and representation are significant in doing mathematics. Often, a picture enables us to conceptualize and get an overall view of a problem or a mathematical situation. This gives us some idea of what it's all about and may suggest a strategy for proceeding. Then, actually to solve the problem we usually find ourselves representing it in mathematical symbols (numbers or algebra) that are amenable to manipulation. In the course of problem solving, mathematicians will often move backwards and forwards between pictorial and numerical or algebraic representations – and will be very likely to use pictorial representations to communicate their thinking and conclusions to others. The work that young children do in school in collecting numerical data and representing it in pictorial form is, therefore, an early experience of this moving between two kinds of representation that are central to thinking and working mathematically.

Ways of representing data

In this section we discuss the different forms of representation of data – the different kinds of pictures – that children should learn to use. The examples we use will refer to data collected by a class of 26 children. These examples illustrate the wide range and different types of information that can be collected by children about themselves as the basis for meaningful learning in this area of mathematics.

Representing discrete sets

The first kind of representation we will consider are *set diagrams* – sometimes called *Venn diagrams*. For our purposes in this section we will represent the 26 children in the class by the 26 letters of the alphabet. The most natural way in which we classify children in a class is by putting them into two quite separate sets: boys and girls. Sets that have no members in common like these are called *discrete* sets. They can be represented in a simple set diagram by two enclosed regions that do not overlap, as shown for our 26 children in Figure 10.2(a).

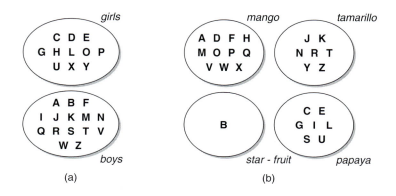

Figure 10.2   *Set diagrams showing (a) boys and girls; (b) choice of fruit*

This kind of set diagram is the most basic form of pictorial representation of data, showing a simple classification into two sets. The sex of the child is an example of what is called a *discrete variable* – because it is a variable (that is, something that can vary from one member of the class to another) and it separates the class of children into discrete, non-overlapping sets. In Chapter 3 we explain how the union of two discrete sets – putting the two sets together to form one set – is the basis of one structure for addition (see Figure 3.1). So Figure 10.2(a) provides a picture that connects the question 'How many children altogether?' with the addition 11 + 15.

Often a discrete variable will separate the items available into more than two sets. The children's choice of favourite fruit, for example, separates them into four discrete sets, as shown in Figure 10.2(b). One teacher gave us one of her favourite examples of children collecting discrete data:

I get my Year 2 class to collect the number of letters in the first name of each child. They always enjoy investigating and representing this data. We usually get something like seven discrete sets, ranging from three-letter names to nine-letter names.

Figure 10.3 shows an alternative way of representing data by focusing on just one particular value of the variable in question. To sort the children in Figure 10.3(a) the question asked is, 'Are you a girl? Yes or no?' So the children are categorized as 'girls' (inside the circle) and 'not girls' (outside the circle). In Figure 10.3(b) the question asked is, 'Did you choose mango? Yes or no?' The children are then categorized as 'mango' (inside the circle) and 'not mango' (outside the circle).

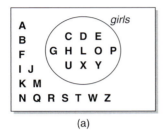 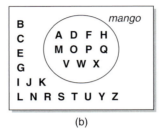

(a)   (b)

Figure 10.3   *Sorting by one value of a variable: (a) girls, (b) choosing mango*

The rectangle drawn around the outside in Figure 10.3(a) and (b) represents what is called the *universal set* – this is a mathematical term meaning 'all the things we are considering'. In this case the universal set is the 26 children in the class, all of whom are within the rectangle somewhere. The set of children who are 'not girls' is called the *complement* of the set of girls. In Chapter 3 (see Figure 3.6) we discuss how the complement of a set is one example of a structure represented by subtraction. So, for example, Figure 10.3(a) connects the question 'How many are not girls?' with the subtraction 26 – 11.

Intersecting sets

Sometimes, of course, sets will overlap, because they have members in common. This is a sophisticated idea that children come to grasp gradually – as is illustrated by the anecdote at the head of the chapter, where Jamie had problems with being both a yellow banana and a shepherd. However, as their experience of classification increases, children will be able to engage in sorting objects (and themselves) according to two variables at a time. For example, they might be interested to show how the split between boys and girls within their class is related to their age in years. Two sets such as 'girls' and '7-year-olds' will intersect, because some girls may be 7-year-olds and some not – and some 7-year-olds may be girls and some not.

A set diagram like that shown in Figure 10.4 provides one way of representing the classification of children by two variables such as those involved here, namely, sex and age in years. One region encloses the set of girls, the other the set of 7-year-olds.

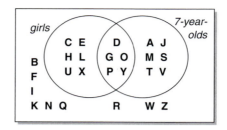

Figure 10.4   *Two intersecting sets*

The set of children in the overlapping region (the 7-year-old girls) is called the *intersection* of the two sets. Notice that there is a place for every child. The diagram in Figure 10.4 divides the set of 26 children into four subsets:

- those who are girls and 7 years old (the intersection)
- those who are 7 years old but not girls
- those who are girls but not 7 years old
- those who are not girls and not 7 years old.

We should also note that, because the two sets (girls and 7-year-olds) are not discrete, the union of the two sets (all those who are girls or 7 or both) does not correspond to addition: there are eleven girls and eleven 7-year-olds, but there are only 17 in the two sets put together (not 22). So, when we make the connection between addition and the union of two sets we must add the rider that the two sets are discrete, that they do not intersect.

Databases and spreadsheets

In today's technological world all the processing of data can be done quickly and efficiently by a computer. Many examples of simple database and spreadsheet software are now available for children in their earliest years of schooling. In the simplest versions of a database, children enter their answers to various questions and the computer then organizes the data and displays it in an appropriate tabular or visual form. The value of this kind of activity is that the child can focus on the two stages of collecting and interpreting the data, while the computer does the more technical stages of organizing it and representing it. In interpreting the data, children can interrogate the database. For example, having entered the information about sex and age, in some versions of a database children could ask to have listed 'girls and 7' which would produce the intersection of the two sets. Similarly, a request for 'girls or 7' would produce the union of the two sets.

The language of logic

The potential in this kind of classification activity for the development of the basic language of logic is considerable – not just the specific vocabulary of logic (not, all, some, none, or, and, both) but also the characteristic language patterns of logical arguments. For example, in Figure 10.5, one of the subsets from Figure 10.4 has been removed (the girls who are not 7). Once this is done we can make at least these two statements that are true about the children who remain on the diagram:

1 All the girls are 7 years old.
2 All those who are not 7 are not girls.

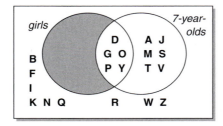

Figure 10.5   *Two intersecting sets with one subset removed*

You should now pause and convince yourself that these two statements are logically equivalent – they use different words to say the same thing! Similar logical challenges can be posed by removing any one of the subsets in Figure 10.4.

Other ways of representing classifications

There are many other diagrammatic representations of these kinds of classification. Any Foundation Stage or Key Stage 1 classroom is likely to have examples on display. In one classroom we see the names of children displayed in three columns labelled 'school dinner', 'packed lunch' and 'home'. This is a simple – but nevertheless significant – form of pictorial representation of a classification into three sets. In another classroom we see sets of words beginning with the same letter written inside spaces in the shape of that letter. Another teacher has on the wall an arrow-diagram, with the names of the children listed in a column down the left-hand side, with arrows matching the children to their teams.

I got the children in my nursery class to help me find out how many tomatoes, satsumas, bananas, or carrots we needed to provide each morning for snacks. They each chose a picture of their favourite, we put their names on these and assembled them in a pictogram. We counted how many there were in each column and decided which snacks were most popular and least popular. I was surprised at how much children as young as this seemed to understand what was quite a sophisticated mathematical picture. And how much they engaged with it.

As children get older, the kind of network diagram for sorting shown in Figure 9.27 (see Activity 9.3 in Chapter 9) can be used for classification of two intersecting sets. For example, asking the two questions 'Is the child a girl?' and 'Is the child 7 years old?' at the two stages of the sorting process generates the same four subsets as in the set diagram shown in Figure 10.4. Another diagrammatic representation of this kind of classification is what is called a *Carroll diagram,* as shown in Figure 10.6 (named after Lewis Carroll, 1832–98, who was not just the author of the *Alice* books, but also a mathematician and logician). This format has the advantage of making the identification of the four separate subsets clearer and the logic of the word 'not' more explicit. It also introduces the important procedure of two-way reference, which is the basis of the co-ordinate system. In placing

	girls	not girls
7-year-olds	D G O P Y	A J M S T V
not 7-year-olds	C E H L U X	B F I K N Q R W Z

Figure 10.6   *Carroll diagram for two intersecting sets*

an object or a name in one of the four cells in the Carroll diagram the child must refer simultaneously to both the vertical label and the horizontal label.

Representing frequency

Frequency tables

From just classifying objects and children into various sets and subsets we then move on to pictorial representations of data that show how many there are in each subset. Using the data about choice of fruit, for example, the children counted how many chose each fruit. The number in each of these subsets is called the *frequency*. An important skill in computing the frequency, particularly with a large amount of data, is *tallying* (see Figure 6.7 in Chapter 6) – with one child calling out the values and another doing the tallying. This can then be converted into a *frequency table*, a simple tabulation of results as shown in Table 10.1. Tabulation, because it encourages systematic processing and careful organization of information, is an important mathematical skill that children should be encouraged to develop and use as often as possible. Now we are moving into the realms of statistical data we can refer to the universal set (in this case, all 26 children) as the *population*.

Table 10.1   *Frequency table for choice of fruit*

Choice of fruit	Number of children (frequency)
Mango	11
Papaya	7
Star fruit	1
Tamarillo	7
Total	26

Moving towards a bar chart

Figure 10.7 shows four possible stages in the development of pictorial representation of data such as that shown in Table 10.1. Prior to this, of course, the data can be shown using the actual objects (or children) themselves. For example, the children making the various choices of fruit can line up in the hall according to their choice, ensuring that the lines are straight and the children equally spaced in each line – like soldiers on parade. Comparisons of the numbers in each subset can be made with the children looking across the rows to answer questions such as 'How many more chose mango than chose papaya?'

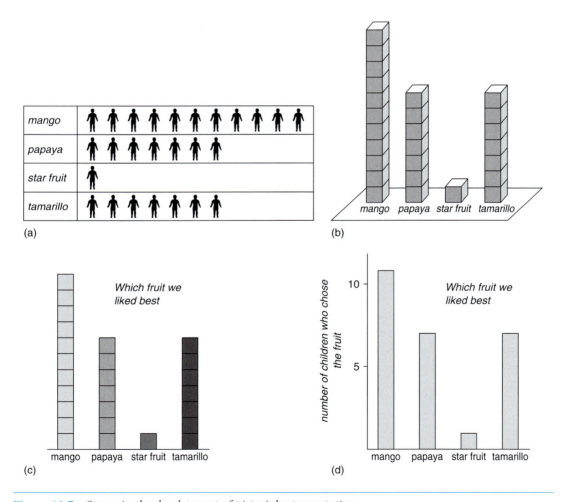

Figure 10.7   *Stages in the development of pictorial representation*

From using the actual objects or children themselves we move on to using a picture to represent the object or child, as shown in Figure 10.7(a). This kind of representation is called a *pictogram*. The rows of pictures can be horizontal or vertical – but what is important is that they are orderly, with the pictures equally spaced. This can be achieved by children drawing pictures on equal-sized squares of paper. Later on, with a larger population, children will learn to use one picture in a pictogram to represent, say, 10 objects – and then an appropriate part of the picture to represent less than 10. From using a picture to represent each item children can move on to using something more abstract, such as a cube – thus producing a three-dimensional *block graph* as shown in Figure 10.7(b). An alternative to this would be to represent the data with beads on wires or strings. Again, these arrangements could be either horizontal or vertical, although the teacher may wish to start establishing the convention of vertical columns, which is usually associated with block graphs and bar charts.

From these three-dimensional arrangements of solid objects we can move to what is possibly a slightly more abstract representation – colouring individual squares on squared paper, as shown in Figure 10.7(c), producing a two-dimensional block graph. Each square, coloured separately, corresponds to one object or one child in the population in question. At this stage the individual contribution of each child is identifiable – and the number in each subset can be found simply by counting the number of squares.

A significant step is moving from columns of individually coloured squares to the representation in Figure 10.7(d) – the conventional *bar chart*. Now the individual contributions are no longer identifiable and the frequency in each subset is repre-sented by the *heights* of the columns. In order to determine the height of the column a scale must be provided along the vertical *axis*. The following observations from teachers raise an important point:

- I'm never sure whether the labels on the axis should go on the lines or in the spaces.
- Sometimes you see it done one way and sometimes another. Is there any reason for this?
- Sometimes the children label the spaces and then read off the wrong value because they don't know whether it's the number above the line or below the line that they should use.
- They find it tricky learning to label the lines – especially when they're used to labelling the squares.

Note that the labels on the vertical axis in Figure 10.7(d) are correctly located on what would be the lines on the paper – if we were using squared paper – not in the spaces between these lines. This is because we are measuring the heights of the columns, not counting the number of squares in each column. Because of this it is unnecessary and actually unhelpful to get children to draw and label a vertical axis showing the frequency when they are doing diagrams of the form shown in Figure 10.7(c). Because they are counting the squares here they would tend (rightly) to label the spaces along the axis (that is, the spaces between the lines on their squared paper). This then becomes something they have to unlearn when they move on to representations based on the height of the column rather than the number of squares, when the labels on the axis have to line up with the tops of the columns.

Finally, in this section, we should note again that the actual organization of the data and production of the graphs could nowadays be handed over to a computer, by using an appropriate database or spreadsheet application designed for primary schools. For example, a number of sets of data about the children in the class (age, sex, choice of fruit, number of letters in first name, and so on) could be entered on one database. The information about each child constitutes one *record* and each set of data is called a *field*. The computer can be instructed to display the records for any given field – and appropriate frequency charts and bar charts appear like magic. This allows children to focus on the interpretation of the data rather than on the mechanics of producing the graphs – which can be a very time-consuming process. Having said this, we do think there is considerable value in children having opportunities to draw their own graphs in various ways, in order to develop their understanding of how they work before handing over the job to the technology.

PAUSE TO REFLECT   Some chance!

Imagine trying to draw a bar chart to show the frequency of tickets winning various prizes in the National Lottery. In a typical week one ticket might win the top prize of around £2 million. Say this one ticket was represented by a column 1 cm high. The number of tickets that win the next size of prize would be represented by a column about 6 cm high. But how high would you expect the column to be that represents the number of tickets (over thirteen and a half million) that do not win a prize at all? What do you reckon? Higher than the tallest building in the world? (The answer is at the end of the chapter.)

Different kinds of variable

Unordered and ordered discrete data

We explain above that, because they separate the population into discrete sets, variables such as the choice of fruit and the number of letters in the first name are called *discrete variables*. There is, however, a difference between these two examples of discrete variables. In the case of the choice of fruit the order in which the data is displayed in the frequency table is arbitrary. We might decide to arrange them in alphabetical order, as shown in Figure 10.7, but this is not necessary – we could equally decide to arrange them from smallest frequency to largest frequency, once we had counted up how many in each set, or in some other order. The variable here is non-numerical: it does no more than assign a label (mango, papaya, star fruit or tamarillo) to each individual member of the population. But in the case of the number of letters in the child's name the variable is numerical: each child is associated with a number. So, because of the ordinal aspect of number, it would be perverse – or at least unusual – to display the data with the subsets appearing in anything other than their numerical order, starting with 3-letter names, then 4-letter names, and so on, as shown in Figure 10.8.

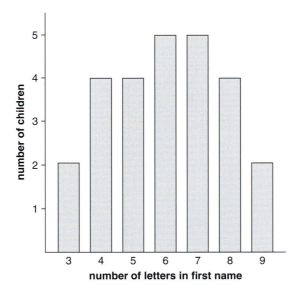

Figure 10.8   *Bar chart for ordered discrete data*

So, we may sometimes classify by using an unordered, non-numerical, discrete variable, such as your sex, your favourite television programme chosen from a list of six possibilities, your method of transport to school, or the kind of shoes you are wearing. And, at other times, we may classify using an ordered, numerical, discrete variable, such as how many children in your family, how many pets you have, or the size of the shoes you are wearing. (In a few cases of non-numerical data – such as the month of birth – there is also a specific order that would normally be used.)

Grouped discrete data

In one investigation a class collected data about how many pages there were in each child's library book. This data also arises from a discrete, numerical variable. The problem here is that it separates the children's books into too many subsets. The smallest number of pages was 16 and the largest was 87. If we had one subset for each possible value of the variable, from the smallest number of pages in their reading books to the largest we would have 72 subsets, many of which would be empty! This is an example where the data is best *grouped*, so that it can be represented pictorially in a way that makes an appropriate visual impact. We recommend that, normally, grouping should be used when there are potentially more than twelve values of the variable and that it should group the population into between five and twelve subsets. Any less than five subsets and too much information will be lost. Any more than twelve subsets and the graph will contain too much detail to be of any use – you might just as well present the original data. Figure 10.9 shows a bar chart for the data about library books. The data has been grouped in intervals of 10 pages, since this produces eight subsets in total. One principle to be remembered when grouping data is that the intervals used must be equal. We would give a very distorted picture of the distribution in this example if we chose to put, say, children in the range 10–29 in one group and those in the range 30–34 in another.

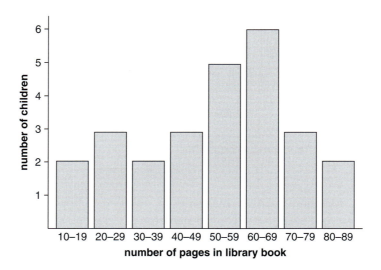

Figure 10.9   *Bar chart for grouped discrete data*

Continuous data

As part of their work on measurement of length a class of children may collect data about their heights. The height of a child, like any measurement of length, is an example of what is called a *continuous variable*. This differs from a discrete variable in that it is possible for the variable to take any value on a continuum within some range. So, for example, a person's height during their lifetime passes through every real number from their height at birth to the tallest height that they achieve. It does not jump suddenly from 125 cm to 126 cm, for example, but moves continuously through all the heights in between, including 125.1 cm, 125.367 cm, and so on. This kind of variable contrasts with a discrete variable, which can only take particular, separate values and which goes from one value to another in jumps. So, for example, a child might have 7 letters in his or her name or 8 letters, but cannot have 7.456 letters! Most measurements – such as length, mass, capacity, time – are continuous variables. Now, in practice, we always make these measurements 'to the nearest something'. For example, children might measure their heights to the nearest centimetre. This effectively changes the variable to a discrete variable, because now we are only allowing whole numbers of centimetres! So, in practice, the processing of continuous data rounded to the nearest something is no different to that of grouped discrete data. This means that – with an appropriate structure provided by the teacher – the collection, organization, representation and interpretation of continuous data, such as heights and masses, are well within the competence of some children in the age range we are considering in this book. Figure

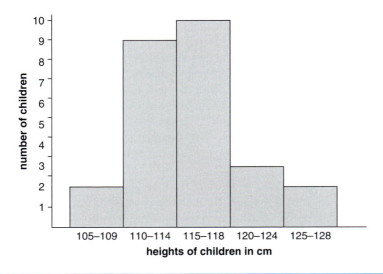

Figure 10.10   *Bar chart for data from a continuous variable*

10.10 shows an appropriate way of grouping and representing some data about children's heights. This uses 5-cm intervals to produce five subsets.

Notice that in Figure 10.10 we have drawn the columns touching each other, whereas in the previous graphs we have left gaps between them. This is to emphasize that the original variable in Figure 10.10 is a continuous one that moves without gaps from one value to another. When the variable is discrete – that is, when it divides the population into distinct, separate subsets – it is more appropriate to represent the data with a graph that shows the subsets as separated columns with gaps between them.

RESEARCH FOCUS   Mark-making and graphicacy

The subject of this chapter has been the ways in which we use pictures in mathematics to represent data. To balance this emphasis on children learning to use pictures in the ways that the curriculum prescribes, we thought it would be useful to reflect a little on the significance of children's own idiosyncratic pictures and scribbles in their early years of engaging with mathematical ideas. This is often referred to as mark-making: a term that has been used to describe the ways in which young children create and use their own marks and pictures to represent and aid their thinking.

In his Foreword to the second edition of Elizabeth Carruthers and Maulfry Worthington's (2006) *Children's Mathematics: Making Marks, Making Meaning* John Matthews writes:

> This is one of the most important books on emergent mathematical thought in infancy and early childhood ever written. Those of us who have devoted our lifetimes attempting to understand the origin and development of expressive, representational and symbolic thought in infancy and childhood, and how best to support it, quickly came to realise that the beginnings of linguistic and mathematical thought are embedded in rather commonplace actions and drawings made by the infant and young child. Developmentally, these beginnings are of the most profound importance. They form the child's introduction to semiotic systems without which her life in the symbol-rich society of humans will be dangerous if not impossible. Tragically, these crucial beginnings of expressive, representational and symbolic thought are often discounted completely and receive little or no support from the pedagogical environment. (p. xiii)

This extract is so passionate and, in our view, sadly, accurate, that we thought it important to include it. If you refer back to Figure 1.1 in Chapter 1 you will note that we think pictures are a crucial component to a sound understanding of mathematical concepts, and, indeed, this has been a theme of our book. In Chapter 9, in discussing 2- and 3-dimensional shapes, for example, we made the point that making marks to go with their words is a key way in which young children develop mastery of a concept. And yet, as Matthews so eloquently puts it, this key component of learning mathematics is all too often neglected as children become increasingly absorbed into formal schooling.

Carruthers and Worthington (2006) build on the work of others – most notably Martin Hughes (1986) – to present a wealth of research-based material including insights from their own extensive observations of young children of children's mark-making. Their book goes beyond this, however, to demonstrate – using examples from their own early years' classrooms – how adults can engage with children and encourage them to use both their natural mark-making and the mathematical symbols and pictures they have been taught, such as the number line. Thus, for example, using a combination of her own drawings, numerical jottings and a number line, 7-year-old Ann worked out how many packets of nectarines (3 per pack) would be required for 26 children to have one each.

In their later work, (see, for example: www.Childrens-Mathematics.net/graphicacy.htm) Carruthers and Worthington have suggested that the term 'mark-making' fails to do justice to young children's use of graphics in all forms to record and aid their thinking. They have therefore found that the term *graphicacy* encompasses better all the aspects of visual representations that children use. Aldrich and Sheppard (2000) define graphicacy as:

> The ability to understand and present information in the form of sketches, photographs, diagrams, maps, plans, charts, graphics and other non-textual two-dimensional formats... The information can be directly representative of what we see (as in photographs or drawings), or more abstract – for example, information which is spatial (as in maps, plans and diagrams) or numerical (as in tables and graphs). (p. 8)

A useful summary of Carruthers and Worthington's research is provided in their chapter entitled 'Children's mathematical graphics' in Thompson (2008). One of their key points is that

> ... all young children's mathematical marks and representations are significant: their scribble-marks and early drawings, for example, have as important a role in children's development as later personal strategies they use in their calculations. (p. 147)

A prominent theme in their work is that the child's representation of the *process* of their thinking is more significant in terms of quality and depth of learning than making a record of the *product* of their thinking.

For further research in this area we would refer you to the work of van Oers (2010) in the Netherlands (mentioned in the Research Focus in Chapter 3) and that of Jaslow and Jacobs (2009) in the US.

Some activities to use with children

Children will benefit from plenty of practical experience of posing a question, deciding what data to collect, collecting that data, organizing it, representing it and interpreting it. We repeat here that the best opportunities for developing the skills in handling data are those where the context is meaningful, the task is purposeful and the data is drawn from other areas of the curriculum. Below we give just three examples of this kind (Activities 10.3, 10.4 and 10.5). The actual activities that a teacher might use may be similar in structure to these, but should be determined by the interests and topics being studied by their class. We also provide two examples of activities (10.1 and 10.2) focused on sorting and logical thinking.

		3–4	4–5	5–6	6–7	7–8
ACTIVITY 10.1 Sorting the Children				□	□	□	

Objective

To develop the language and visual imagery of sorting into sets according to one or more criteria.

Materials

A large area, such as the playground or the school hall, with some means of marking out regions in which the children can stand.

Method

Draw large regions on the playground or lay out ropes on the floor of the hall to produce large-scale versions of set diagrams like those shown in Figures 10.2, 10.3 and 10.4. Then get the class to sort themselves according to various criteria, such as age in years, boy or girl, which village they live in, how they travel to school, whether they stay for school lunch, month of birthday. The best way to do this is to ask a question related to each set to which the answer is clearly yes or no for each child. For example: 'Did you walk to school today?'; 'Is your birthday in a month beginning with a J?'

The most interesting classifications will be those where there are two overlapping sets (as in Figure 10.4) with some children in each of the four regions. For example, there may be some children who walked to school who have a birthday in a J-month, some who walked to school whose birthday is not in a J-month, some who did not walk to school who have a birthday in a J-month, and some who did not walk to school and whose birthday is not in a J-month. With the children sorted in this way, ask each subset in turn to describe themselves and then to sit down.

Repeat all this, sorting the children by using large-scale Carroll diagrams (Figure 10.6).

		3–4	4–5	5–6	6–7	7–8
ACTIVITY 10.2 Negating						□	□

Objective

To develop logical thinking and the language of logic associated with classification.

Materials

A set of logic blocks (48 blocks, covering every combination of: red, blue, yellow; triangles, oblongs, squares, circles; large, small; thick, thin).

Method

A group of four children sits around a table with the logic blocks shared equally between them. Each child places one block at random in the centre of the table. The children first agree on a statement that is true about this set of four shapes of the form 'All the … shapes are …' For example, if the set consists of the red large thick triangle, the red small thick hexagon, the blue large thin square and the yellow large thin square, they might say, 'All the red shapes are thick.' One child must then select a shape from his or her collection to add to this set to make the statement no longer true. For example, he or she could put down the red large thin triangle. The children must now agree on another statement that is true about the set of five shapes – for example, 'All the square shapes are large' – and then negate this by adding a sixth shape. The activity continues in this way until they are no longer able to make a statement of the required form. The activity is not a competition between the four children. They should co-operate with one another, with the aim being to keep going as long as possible.

ACTIVITY 10.3 Voting	3–4	4–5	5–6	6–7	7–8
				□	□

Objective

To provide purposeful experience of all the stages of handling discrete data in a meaningful context, by collecting data to answer a question.

Materials

Whatever is necessary for producing a good-sized graph (pictogram, block graph, bar chart), appropriate to the skills of the children.

Method

The teacher looks for an opportunity for the class to make a democratic decision on an issue of some concern to the children. For example: 'What shall we sing in the class assembly?' or 'Where shall we go for our class outing?' The question is posed and the children discuss how it might be decided fairly. This could lead to the preparation of a simple voting sheet that is duplicated for completion by each child. This activity works best if the teacher manages the process in some way to ensure that only about six options are available to be voted on. One group of children can then organize and present the data in an appropriate graphical form. The class discusses and interprets the graph, and the decision is made. In some cases it may be possible and appropriate for the children to enter the data on to a computer database and to process it that way.

		3–4	4–5	5–6	6–7	7–8
ACTIVITY 10.4	Litter Survey				☐	☐

Objective

To provide purposeful experience of all the stages of handling discrete data in a meaningful context, including tallying, by collecting data to provide information related to a cross-curriculum study.

Materials

Whatever is necessary for producing a good-sized bar chart or pictogram, appropriate to the skills of the children.

Method

As part of their study of the quality of the local environment children might carry out a survey on litter in various roads near the school. Discussion might lead to the question, 'What kinds of things cause the most litter?' A group of children, escorted by an adult, could undertake a preliminary survey to determine the various categories of litter, such as empty drink cans, snack packets, cigarette packets, and so on. We suggest that no more than ten categories should be used, otherwise the data collection will become too cumbersome. The teacher may have to guide the children here and lead them to design an appropriate record form for their survey and explain to them how to fill it in, using tallying. Escorted groups of children would survey their chosen road, recording (but not collecting!) the litter observed. This can then be organized, presented in graphical form and interpreted. In some cases this might even lead to positive action, such as the children writing politely to a local shopkeeper suggesting a litter-bin outside the shop. The completed graphs could form part of a display of work related to the topic. As with the previous activity, a computer database may also be used to organize and process the data.

		3–4	4–5	5–6	6–7	7–8
ACTIVITY 10.5	Pulse Rates					☐

Objective

To provide experience of all the stages of data-handling in a meaningful context, by collecting and presenting grouped discrete data arising from a science investigation.

Materials

A seconds-timer; appropriate materials for the production of good-sized bar charts.

Method

Much of the investigative work that young children carry out in science inquiries will generate data that can be organized, presented and interpreted purposefully. For example, in their study of the human body and the importance of exercise, a standard investigation is to measure and record pulse rates before and after exercise. This generates discrete data from a class of children that is ideal for experience of grouping into appropriately sized intervals. The 'before' and 'after' data should be processed and represented in graphs separately. In each case show the numbers of children with pulse rates in various ranges, such as 50–59, 60–69, 70–79 ... beats per minute. The two graphs can then be presented side by side for comparison, discussion and interpretation. Once again, a computer application might be used to process this data.

Summary of key ideas

1 Mathematical activities are meaningful for children if they are familiar with the context and aware of what is significant.

2 Activities are purposeful if they have some purpose from the child's perspective.

3 Activities related to handling data have the potential for high levels of meaningfulness, purposefulness and for cross-curricular links – particularly if the data is collected to answer a question or to provide information related to an area of interest.

4 Stages in handling data include: posing the question, determining what data should be collected, collecting it, organizing it, representing it, interpreting it.

5 Mathematical problem-solving often involves moving backwards and forwards between numerical/algebraic representations and pictorial representations of the problem.

6 The purpose of pictorial representation of data is to provide an at-a-glance, overall impression of the distribution and the relationships within the data.

7 The universal set is the set of all the things being considered (in the contexts of surveys also called the population).

8 Discrete sets are those that have no members in common.

9 A discrete variable is one that divides the universal set into a number of discrete subsets.

10 The union of two sets A and B consists of all those elements that are in A or B (including those that are in both A and B).

11 The intersection of two sets A and B consists of those elements that are in both A and B.

12 The complement of a set A is the set of all those elements not in the set A.

13 The basic language of logic includes: *not, all, some, none, or, and, both*. This is developed by discussion of various diagrams showing the classification of different elements into sets.

14 Diagrams to represent classification into two intersecting sets include: set diagrams with two overlapping regions; network diagrams; Carroll diagrams.

(Continued)

(Continued)

15 Examples of ways to display pictorially the number of items in each subset (the frequency) are: an orderly arrangement of the objects (or children) themselves; a pictogram; a three-dimensional block graph with one cube representing each object (or child); a two-dimensional block graph, colouring in one square for each object (or child); a bar chart where the heights of the columns represent the numbers in the subsets.

16 Computer databases and spreadsheets allow children to focus on the collection and interpretation stages in handling data. Key notions in using databases are records and fields.

17 Some discrete variables (such as choice of fruit) are non-numerical and the order in which the subsets are arranged is arbitrary. Others (such as age in years) are numerical and ordered.

18 Data arising from numerical, discrete variables with, say, more than twelve possible values should normally be grouped into equal-sized intervals, to produce between five and twelve groups before being represented in pictorial form.

19 A continuous variable is one, such as height, which can take all possible values on a continuum over an appropriate range, not just specific values going up in jumps. Since measurements are made to the nearest something (for example, heights to the nearest centimetre), in practice, such data is usually processed in the same way as discrete data.

 ## Suggestions for further reading

Three of Derek's books provide further information on the material discussed in this chapter: Chapter 27 of Haylock (2010) deals with data-handling techniques in more detail; many of the check-ups in Haylock (2001) will help teachers who want to improve their own skills in handling and interpreting data presented in official documents such as government education and Ofsted reports; Haylock with Thangata (2007) has entries on 'Meaningful Learning', 'Purposeful Activity' and 'Cross-Curricular Mathematics'.

Section 4 of Pepperell et al. (2009) provides some good examples of purposeful activities for teaching data-handling in primary classrooms.

For those working with younger children, a chapter entitled, 'What is your favourite colour?' by Jared and Thwaites in Anghileri (1995) is a thoughtful discussion of the early stages of sorting and pictorial representation.

Note: See Pause to Reflect earlier in this chapter.

The column would have to be about 84 miles high, which is about the distance from London to Southampton! The tallest building in the world (at the time of writing), the Burj Khalifa in Dubai, is not much taller than half a mile.

CHAPTER 11

UNDERSTANDING PROBLEM SOLVING AND REASONING IN MATHEMATICS

A CHALLENGING SUBJECT

Seven-year-old Cathy had spent almost an hour working on problem solving with structural apparatus and coins when she suddenly swept everything off the table and announced, 'I'm fed up with this, I want to do some maths!' What she meant, of course, was that she wanted to sit down and complete a page of sums or some such activity where she knew she would not have to do so much hard thinking.

- Cathy's reactions and her comment raise the question: what kinds of activities do we see as being the essence of mathematics?
- How prominent in our perception of this subject are such things as problem solving, enquiry and distinctive ways of mathematical reasoning and explanation?

In this chapter

In this chapter our aim is to help teachers of young children to be more aware of what is important in mathematical work, other than just the body of knowledge and skills; to be open to the range of activities that might form part of a balanced mathematics curriculum for children in the age range 3 to 8 years; and to recognize the significance of some of the kinds of reasoning that their children might demonstrate when they are using and applying mathematics.

The nature of mathematics

Content and cognitive processes

It is important that those who teach young children are clear in their minds that mathematics is more than just a collection of skills, concepts and principles. It is also a collection of ways of thinking and reasoning: ways of organizing and internalizing the information we receive from the external world; and ways of using and applying that information both in the real world and within mathematics itself. Most people probably conceptualize mathematics in terms of its content: number, calculations, measurement, shape, equations and formulas, and so on. Of course, content of this kind is important and central to the nature of the subject. In this book we have given much of our attention to the development of understanding of central concepts in mathematics: cardinal and ordinal number, place value, addition, subtraction, multiplication, division, length, mass, time, liquid volume and capacity, and the classification of shapes. Every significant field of human knowledge has its own central concepts such as these. But, equally important, each discipline also has its own characteristic ways of making and justifying its assertions, its own distinctive ways of thinking and reasoning. This is certainly the case with mathematics.

Using and applying

The importance of developing the characteristic ways of thinking mathematically in teaching mathematics is reflected, for example, in the emphasis on using and applying mathematics that has been a feature of the National Curriculum in the various countries of the United Kingdom since its inception. Key experiences such as problem solving, enquiring and investigating, representing, thinking creatively, generalizing and communicating can be present in all levels of mathematics, from children's first experiences in nursery and reception classes onwards. Even in the earliest years of schooling there has been an expectation that mathematics is to be learnt not just in activities focusing on the development of specific mathematical knowledge and skills, but also in other activities where children engage with numbers, shapes and patterns in the environment and in their daily routines. Mathematics provides us with knowledge and skills that are valuable not just for their own sake but because we can apply them to situations in real life and across the curriculum.

Key processes

So far, in the earlier chapters, we have identified a number of the most significant ways of thinking mathematically that are characteristic of learning this subject. These are the key cognitive processes that are distinctively mathematical in the way in which learners organize and internalize the information they receive from the external world. In summary, we have discussed the importance in learning mathematics of the following processes:

- recognizing and applying equivalences (classification, discussing samenesses);
- recognizing and applying transformations (changing, discussing differences);
- making connections – particularly between symbols, pictures, concrete situations and language;
- using a symbol to represent a network of connections;
- moving between symbolic representations (numerical/algebraic) and pictorial or visual representations.

In the rest of this chapter we make explicit some other processes that are fundamental aspects of thinking and reasoning that are relevant to young children using and applying their mathematics.

Two dimensions in using and applying mathematics

Figure 11.1 shows how we can describe activities in using and applying mathematics by reference to two dimensions: the abstract/real-life dimension; and the open/closed dimension.

Abstract or real life

Along one dimension in Figure 11.1 we can consider the extent to which the context of the task is abstract or real life. At one extreme of this dimension would be a task

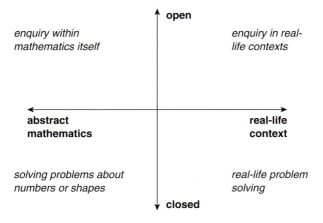

Figure 11.1   *Two dimensions in using and applying mathematics*

that is purely abstract mathematics (that is to say, just about numbers, mathematical symbols and shapes), in which the outcome is of little apparent practical significance. At the other extreme would be a task that is a genuine, real-life situation, in which the outcome is of immediate, practical use or relevance.

At the 'abstract' extreme of this dimension, we might see some 6-year-old children engaged in finding as many ways as possible of putting numbers into a 3 × 3 grid so that all the rows and columns add up to 5. At the 'real-life' extreme the same children might be running the tuck shop at playtime, involved in pricing drinks and biscuits, giving change, and so on.

Closed or open

Along the other dimension in Figure 11.1 we can consider the extent to which the nature of the task is either closed or open. By a closed task we mean one in which the goal is clearly prescribed. There is just one goal that is provided for the children and the activity is complete when that goal is achieved. In an open task, however, there may be several possible goals. The children may have opportunities to think more creatively and to participate in determining the goal; and when one goal is achieved there may be further goals that come to light.

For example, some 4-year-olds might be given the task of fitting a set of shapes into their fixed places in a box. This is a closed activity with one prescribed goal – when the shapes are in the box in their right places the task is completed. On another occasion, they may be given the set of shapes and allowed to experiment with them, to explore different ways of fitting them together, to find out what other shapes they can make, and so on. This is an open activity, more creative, without a clearly prescribed goal, giving the children some opportunity to determine their own goals.

The range of activities for children

In planning opportunities for children to use and apply mathematics, we suggest, therefore, that teachers should aim to cover the whole range of these two dimensions. We would advocate this for two reasons. First, this represents the true nature of mathematics from pure to applied, and from problem solving to open-ended enquiry. Second, different children will be most motivated by different categories of activity. For some children it is often a matter of searching for just the right kind of activity that will stimulate them to engage with mathematics. One teacher had given three of her 6-year-olds a set of tangram shapes, demonstrated how they could be used to make a boat and then suggested that the children might like to see what pictures they could make. The teacher told us how this open-ended task with a set of mathematical shapes was just the thing that caught one child's attention:

Emma and Rachel lost interest after about ten minutes and asked to do something else. Cassandra – who in most mathematical tasks is noted for her limited concentration span – concentrated for over half an hour on this task and produced 20 pictures. Next to her work she wrote: 'I did these all by myself and no one helped me'!

Solving problems

What is a problem?

We shall use the word 'problem' to refer to a mathematical activity towards the closed end of the open–closed dimension, involving the application of mathematics to a situation where there is a clearly defined goal. We should mention here that some mathematics educators – with some justification – argue that rather than problems we should talk about challenges, which would promote a more positive image of mathematical activity. We would encourage teachers to take this idea on board in the language they use to present activities to children, although we do not do this ourselves in the discussion below – mainly because problem solving is such an established area for study and research in the field of mathematics education.

The context of a mathematical problem can occur anywhere along the abstract/real-life dimension. For example, the following two mathematical tasks would probably count as problems for most children around 7 to 8 years; but in Problem 1 the context is abstract, purely mathematical, whereas in Problem 2 the context is very definitely real life:

Problem 1 Find how many squares there are on a 3 × 3 square grid. (The answer is more than 9!) See Figure 11.2.

Figure 11.2   *How many squares (Problem 1)*

Problem 2 Arrange eight A4 pages for photocopying back-to-back on two sheets of A3 paper to produce an eight-page booklet, with the pages in the right order. See Figure 11.3.

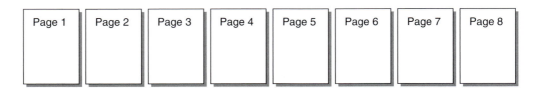

Figure 11.3   *Arrange these eight pages for photocopying (Problem 2)*

We suggest that these would probably prove to be problems for the children, rather than mere mathematical exercises, because there is not a routine process available for the children, which they have learnt and which can be used to answer the question. This is the key characteristic of problem solving. There is a gap between what is given and the goal.

Givens, goal and gap

The givens, the goal and the gap are what we call the three Gs of problem solving. Using these components a problem can be represented by the diagram in Figure 11.4. A problem starts with a given situation and a specified goal. For example, in Problem 1 above, the givens are the 3 × 3 grid in Figure 11.2 and what we understand to be a square. The goal is clearly to identify and count all the squares on the grid. This constitutes a problem for us if there is a gap between the givens and the goal – in other words, if we do not have immediately available a procedure, a formula or a routine that takes us more or less straight from the givens to the goal. The problem will be solved when we have closed the gap, when we have found a route from the givens to the goal.

Figure 11.4   *The three Gs of problem solving*

The first steps in problem solving of this kind are often to clarify the givens and to clarify the goal. These are the kinds of question that teachers might ask to help children to clarify the givens and the goal:

- What do you know about this?
- What else do you need to know to get started?
- What are you trying to find out?

- What do you need to be able to say at the end of this?
- Have you considered all the possibilities?

For example, in Problem 1, clarifying the givens and the goal might lead to a realization that squares can be different sizes, that squares can overlap and that the problem requires us to find all the squares in the grid, not just the nine small ones.

We do not want to give the impression that problem solving in mathematics is a routine process, involving a number of clearly defined steps from the givens to the goal that are followed one by one until the solution is obtained. It is rarely like that. Often, in getting from the givens to the goal we find that we have to specify and reach *subgoals*. For example, to solve the problem of how many apples you would need for each child in a class to have a piece, a subgoal would be for the children to find out by experiment how many pieces can be obtained from one apple. Getting this information first is a necessary step toward the goal.

Sometimes in solving problems you start at the givens and work forward; sometimes you start at the goal and work backwards, identifying subgoals; and sometimes you work backwards and forwards between the two until the two directions of reasoning meet in the middle. But in the end you have to link together the various bits of the solution into the appropriate, logical sequence. Often, the constraints of the actual problem will be taken into account at an early stage of the process, not just at the end.

Some children in Year 1 were working out how best to organize the class library on the bookshelves. They had decided on putting the books into various sets and determined that a subgoal was to find out how much shelf-space would be needed for each set. Trying to do this practically, using the actual books, led them to take into account a constraint of the actual situation in which the problem was posed – that books over a certain size would fit only on the bottom shelf.

Real-life constraints

This last example highlights an important distinction between real-life problems and abstract mathematical problems. This is that the real world imposes various practical constraints on the solutions we come up with. So, for example, the solution to the abstract question $33 \div 6$ is precisely $5\frac{1}{2}$. But consider the real-life problem, 'How many tables seating 6 children each do we need for a class of 33 children?' This is represented mathematically by $33 \div 6$, but has the solution 6 – because you cannot have half a table and all the children have to have a table to sit at. Giving children the opportunity and freedom to discuss the constraints and realities of an actual problem like this is an important part of their learning to use and apply mathematics. It is interesting to consider who is thinking mathematically in the quotation below – the teacher or the children?

> Some children in my class were working out how many boxes were needed to hold 73 calculators, if each box could hold 12 calculators. Because this gave 6 remainder 1, I wanted them to decide that the answer was 7 boxes. But they were insistent that 6 boxes would be enough – because you could always squeeze the extra calculator into one of the boxes, or keep it in the drawer!

Too often the kinds of problem-solving tasks children are given do in mathematics are sanitized, so that they do not have to face such constraints. The numbers are carefully chosen, division problems have nice answers, things work out neatly – and it all looks nothing like reality, thus perpetuating the perception that mathematics has little to do with the real world.

Enquiring and investigating

We would use the phrases 'mathematical enquiry' or 'mathematical investigation' to refer to an activity involving the application of mathematics that is towards the open end of the open/closed dimension in Figure 11.1. So this would be a task in which the goal is not too tightly prescribed. Here are some examples of possible mathematical enquiries, characteristically open in terms of the goals specified, but varying in terms of the abstract/real-life dimension:

- The model animals on the farm are all jumbled up. Sort them out for us, please. Then tell us how you have done it. (Reception class)
- Here are some items from my week's shopping bag and a balance for weighing them. Put any of the items you like into the balance pans and see what interesting or surprising things you notice. (Year 1)
- As part of our transport project, what can you find out about the journeys to school of the children in our class? (Year 2)
- What patterns can you discover in the way the numbers are arranged on the calendar for this month? (Year 3)

The essential quality of these tasks is that the children to some degree have the opportunity to determine or shape the goal. They will then be able to choose their own approaches, to make their own selection of data, and to decide how they will organize the resources and information. They have the opportunity to determine which attributes and what information might be significant or relevant. The tasks contain phrases like: What can you find out?' What can you discover? What do you notice? So an enquiry or an investigation provides a context for thinking more creatively in mathematics. And, as we illustrate later in this chapter, some investigations undertaken by children will be especially valuable in developing some key aspects of reasoning in mathematics, in particular the forming of generalizations.

Representing

The power of mathematics is derived from the fact that we can represent real-life or concrete situations in mathematical language, pictures and symbols. The development of understanding in mathematics through connecting concrete situations, language, pictures and symbols has been a key theme of this book. With this kind of understanding children are then in a position to use the language, pictures and symbols of mathematics to represent real-life situations, and thereby to use mathematics to solve real-life problems. We can see the beginning of this process when young children first use simple mathematical ideas to represent aspects of their world and to solve elementary problems.

> In a Reception Class a boy was asked by the teacher to find out how many children would choose each of four activities for the afternoon session. She gave him a sheet with four large circles drawn on it, one for each activity. He then went round the class and put a sticker for each child in the circle representing their choice of activity. When he had finished he counted up how many there were for each activity and presented his findings to the teacher.

Children will often use simple pictures like this to make a representation of a mathematical problem. Two 5-year-old boys were playing with toy cars and one of them complained that the other had more than him. The teacher helped them to count how many cars they each had: Ben had 12 and Carl had 16. The teacher asked them to work out how many Carl had to give to Ben to make the numbers the same. This proved to be a genuine mathematical problem for the two boys, as the teacher explained.

> Ben worked out that Carl had 4 more cars than him and said, 'So, he's got to give me 4 of his cars.' Carl did this and then they realized that now Ben had 16 and Carl had 12! They couldn't work out what they had to do with the numbers 16 and 12 to solve the problem. So Ben drew a picture of a line of 16 circles representing the 16 cars and a line of 12 circles underneath representing the 12 cars. He then crossed off one circle on the top row and added it to the bottom row, and then did this again. The problem was solved!

Notice how Ben used representation to enable him to manipulate the components of his problem. Eventually children will get to a stage where they can represent some real-life problems entirely in symbols and solve the problem by manipulating the symbols. For example, an 8-year-old working out how much it would cost for 4 children to pay £3 each to get in to a theme park and then spend £10 each on rides represented the problem by two multiplications and an addition: $4 \times 3 = 12$; $4 \times 10 = 40$; and then $12 + 40 = 52$.

Creativity in mathematics

The word 'creativity' is not one that we might normally associate with mathematics. We tend to think of the creative subjects in the curriculum as being art, music, dance and drama; and we talk about creative writing. But what might it mean for a child to think creatively in mathematics? What kind of experiences might we give to children to foster creativity in mathematics? And why might we want to do this?

We would characterize creativity in mathematics by distinctive kinds of thinking: thinking flexibly, rather than rigidly, divergently rather than convergently, showing originality and inventiveness, and being prepared to take risks. This kind of thinking is important in being a good problem solver. A common reason why someone may fail to solve a problem in mathematics is that they restrict their thinking in some way: they do not consider all the possibilities; they have one idea about how to approach the problem and then when they get stuck they fail to consider other approaches. Children can be encouraged to think flexibly and divergently by being given open-ended tasks with many possible responses. We like to include from time to time the challenge to try to come up with an idea that no one else in the group comes up with. Here is an example of such a task that we have used with children within a wide range of ages:

1 Draw a rectangle.
2 Now draw another rectangle that's different in some way from your first one.
3 Now try to draw one that you think will not be like any of the rectangles that other children in the class have drawn.

Problems with many solutions

One kind of open-ended task is a question or a problem that has many solutions. For example, in Figure 11.5 children are challenged to draw as many different rectangles as they can on the grids, by joining up dots with straight lines. (In this case rectangles do not count as different if they are the same sizes but drawn in different positions on the grid.) There are many solutions to this problem. We challenge the reader to find nine! To do this you will have to think creatively.

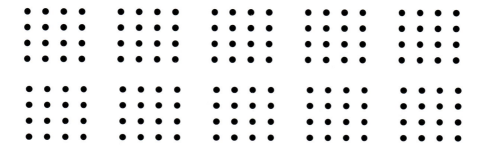

Figure 11.5 *Draw different rectangles on these grids by joining dots*

Other questions have many solutions in the sense that there are many different ways of doing them. Teachers, in encouraging children to use mental strategies for calculations, can at the same time encourage creative thinking by giving small groups of children calculation tasks framed like these:

- Find as many different ways as you can for working out 42 – 19.
- What is the cost of 12 things priced at 25p each? Find several different ways of working this out.

Question posing

Another kind of open-ended task is to ask the children to make up as many mathematical questions as they can think of about a particular situation. This gives children the opportunity to think divergently and inventively:

- *Look around the classroom. In your groups write down as many different maths questions as you can think of that you could ask about this room. See if you can come up with some ideas that no other groups think of.*
- *Make up as many questions and answers as you can that have just the numbers 3, 4 and 7 in them. (Example: what is 3 + 4? Answer: 7.) Try to think of some unusual questions.*

One group of bright 8-year-olds, working with one of the authors on developing creative thinking in mathematics, responded to the second of these tasks with some very imaginative questions, including:

- What number is 3 greater than 4? Answer: 7.
- How much more than 7p is 4p? Answer: 3p.
- I had 7 apples and I ate 3, so how many are left? Answer: 4 apples.

- What is $7 - 4 + 4 - 4 + 4 - 4$? Answer: 3.
- What is the difference between 3 and 7? Answer: 4.
- Find a number that lies between 3 and 7. Answer: 4.
- What does 3 times by 4 not equal? Answer: 7.

We suspect that most of us would agree that the quality of thinking involved here justifies the term 'creative'.

Teachers can also encourage children to pose their own questions when they have collected data and represented it in any kind of graph. For example, in Chapter 10, when children have produced any one of the graphs in Figure 10.7 they could be given the opportunity to make up six questions that could be answered from the graph.

Redefinition

A third kind of open-ended task engages the children in redefining various mathematical objects. Two simple examples of this would be:

- Tell me all the different things you can think of about the number 5.
- Tell me all the different things you can think of about this shape (using any 2- or 3-dimensional shape.)

These open-ended questions encourage children to look at a number or a shape in many different ways. So, the number 5 might be seen as the next number after 4, an odd number, a number between 1 and 10, half of 10, two 2s plus 1, the value of a coin (in pence), somebody's age, and so on. To start with, children may not know how to respond to questions like this if they are used to teachers asking them questions with only one right answer. But once they get into the swing of it they will surprise you with their creativity!

Here are two more examples of tasks that involve what we call redefinition:

- Look at these two shapes (for example, an oblong rectangle and a parallelogram with the same height and length). They are different shapes, of course. But what is the same about them? They both have four sides, for example. What else could you say starting with the words, 'They both …'?
- Here are two numbers (for example, 8 and 12). They are different numbers, of course. But what is the same about them? They are both less than 100, for example. What else could you say starting with the words, 'They are both …'?

The game, 'Guess my Rule?', described in Chapter 9, is another example of an activity where children can be creative using redefinition. In this game they are given a set of numbers or a set of shapes and make up lots of different rules for sorting the sets into two subsets. In this way they are continually redefining the numbers or the shapes according to a variety of properties. In one game, for example, the number 10 will go into the 'Yes' category because it is an even number; in another round because it is a two-digit number; in another round because it is in the 5-times table; and so on.

Generalizing

Our purpose in writing this chapter is to help teachers in primary schools to be more aware of the nature of genuine mathematical reasoning. So in this section we make explicit some important aspects of mathematical thinking – in particular, the reasoning and language associated with making generalizations. We also believe that, even in the first years of schooling, teachers can begin to develop in their children the kinds of mathematical thinking that emerge in this discussion. Here are some examples of the kinds of observations that might be made by young children that we would rec- ognize as generalizations:

- If you add 6 to a number and then subtract 6 from the answer you always get back to the number you started with.
- The odd-numbered pages in a book are always on the right.
- All triangles have three sides and three corners.
- The diagonal line in a rectangle is always longer than each of the sides.
- Every whole number ending in 5 is divisible by 5.
- If a number is in the 4-times table then it is in the 2-times table.

These are generalizations because they are statements in which there is a reference to something that is *always* the case. As soon as children begin to put words such as *each*, *every*, *any*, *all*, *always*, *whenever* and *if … then* into their observations they are generalizing – and, therefore, they are reasoning in a way that is characteristic of thinking mathematically.

An investigation with newspapers

To illustrate how children can be encouraged to formulate generalizations we describe some of the mathematics that might come out of an investigation with newspapers that one of the authors has used with various groups of children from about 7 years of age. In this investigation a group of children is given a newspaper and invited to find out what they can about the way the page numbers are arranged on the separate sheets of paper. (We use only newspapers that have four numbered pages on each sheet, with no inserts to upset the numbering system!) The teacher ensures that the children understand the way in which the words 'page' and 'sheet' are being used. In

our example the newspaper happens to have 40 pages and 10 sheets. After dismantling the paper and writing down some of the things they have noticed – with a little
nudging from the teacher to find a way of recording their observations – some children decide to tabulate the page numbers for the front and back pages on each of the
10 sheets, as shown in Figure 11.6. The children have experience of investigations that
generate sequences of numbers and tabulation is a familiar process that they turn to
fairly readily. This systematic way of setting out numerical information enables them
to notice and to articulate patterns in the sequences of numbers.

Front	1	3	5	7	9	11	13	15	17	19
Back	40	38	36	34	32	30	28	26	24	22

Figure 11.6   *Front and back pages on the 10 sheets of a newspaper*

The language of generalizations

Many of the observations that children make about the patterns in the page numbers
given in Figure 11.6 are examples of *generalizations*. They are not just observations
about a specific case – as would be, for example, the statement: pages 1 and 40 are
on the same sheet. In articulating a generalization, the children are making one statement that is true about a number of specific cases. Even observations as simple as
'there are 4 pages on each sheet' or 'the numbers in the top row get bigger every time
and the numbers in the bottom row get smaller' demonstrate this fundamental mathematical process of making a generalization.

Often, in articulating a pattern, the child will focus on what changes each time in
a sequence of numbers (or shapes). For example, in relation to Figure 11.6:

- The numbers in the top row go up by 2 each time.
- The numbers in the bottom row go down by 2 each time.

In this kind of generalization the child is focusing on the changes that takes place as
you move from one number to the next. This is essentially another instance of recognizing and articulating a *transformation* in mathematics. The statement tells us how
to get from one item in the sequence to the next. If the sequence were to continue,
this generalization is a pattern that would enable you to predict the next item, and the
next, and so on, by using the same transformation each time. So, for example, when
recording these results, we find that some children stop using the actual sheets of
newspaper after they have recorded the first five or six numbers in the rows in Figure 11.6.
They just fill in the rest by using the 'add 2' or 'subtract 2' pattern.

Instead of focusing on what changes from one sheet to the next in Figure 11.6, some
of the statements given by children are about what is the same each time. For example:

- All the front pages are odd numbers.
- All the back pages are even numbers.
- If you add the front and back page numbers the answer is always 41!

Statements such as these are further instances of recognizing and articulating *equivalences* in mathematics – because each of them is an observation about something that is the same, something that does not change.

To encourage children to make these kinds of observations and to use the language of generalization teachers might ask questions such as:

- What is the pattern you can see here?
- Is that always true?
- Does that happen every time?
- Does that work for all of them?
- What do you think will come next?
- Are you sure?
- What pattern are you using?
- How can you check that?

The newspaper investigation has terrific potential for developing this kind of mathematical reasoning. Here we have only looked at the generalizations that might be made about the front and back pages on each sheet, and only for a 40-page newspaper. There are two other numbered pages on each sheet – for example, one sheet contains pages numbered 13, 14, 27 and 28 – and these generate more patterns to be spotted and articulated. And children could explore how the generalizations apply to a newspaper with, say, 48 pages? Or any number of pages?

We asked some of the teachers we worked with for examples of when children might form and use generalizations:

- When my 3-year-olds are continuing a pattern of beads on a necklace, like blue, blue, red, yellow, blue, blue, red, yellow – they have to work out what the pattern is and then use it.
- One of the boys in my reception class worked out that when he builds a triangular tower of bricks he always uses one fewer brick for each row.
- When Year 1 children count up to a hundred they use the fact that there's a pattern that's the same every ten numbers. They know every time you get to 'something nine' you've got to move on to the next group of ten – that's a generalization, isn't it?
- My Year 2 children worked out that counting numbers always go odd, even, odd, even, and so on.
- One of my Year 3 children asked me the other day why numbers in the 5-times table always ended in 0 or 5. That was a generalization.

The reader should note that each one of these examples is making an observation about what is always the case, what happens every time. By encouraging children to think like this we encourage them to think like mathematicians.

Counterexamples

So far, all the examples of generalizations that we have used have been true. But, of course, we can make generalizations that are not true. In everyday life, people do this all the time: 'women can't read maps' and 'all politicians are corrupt' are familiar examples. We know statements like these are not true because we can usually think of a *counterexample*, an individual woman who can read a map (like Anne Cockburn, of course) or one politician who is clearly not corrupt. Here are two more generalizations:

- When you add 9 to a number the tens digit always goes up by 1 and the units digit goes down by 1.
- Boys always grow taller than their mothers.

Are these true or false? To test a generalization we go on the hunt for a counterexample. The first statement, for example, works in lots of cases: $25 + 9 = 34$, $42 + 9 = 51$, $347 + 9 = 356$. But it does not work, for example, for 30. So this one counterexample is sufficient to show that the generalization is false. Similarly, with the second statement, if you can identify one fully grown man who is shorter than his mother then the statement is shown to be a false generalization.

In our experience, children in the age range of this book can begin to learn to challenge generalizations with counterexamples, and thus start to engage with a sophisticated kind of mathematical reasoning. Here are some simple examples of generalizations that could be made by a teacher, who would then ask, is this true?

- Every child in our class is 4 years old.
- All the triangles in this box of shapes are green.
- All the green shapes in this box are triangles.
- All the books on the top shelf have more than 50 pages in them.
- All the items in this shopping bag weigh less than 100 grams.
- There are exactly four Saturdays in every month.
- If one number is 4 more than another number, then both numbers must be even.
- Any four-sided shape with all sides equal must be a square.

In each case, the teacher would encourage children to come up with one counterexample to show that the statement is not true.

PAUSE TO REFLECT   Where's the alien?

Figure 11.7 contains a challenging little problem for you to solve. It shows lines of squares. In the top line every second share is shaded. In the next row every third square is shaded; in the next, every fourth square; and then in the bottom row, every fifth square. The rows of shaded squares would continue like this up to 50 in each row. On the right of the diagram we show a section of these rows of squares. What is the number of the box to which the arrow is pointing?

Figure 11.7   *What is the number of the box to which the arrow is pointing?*

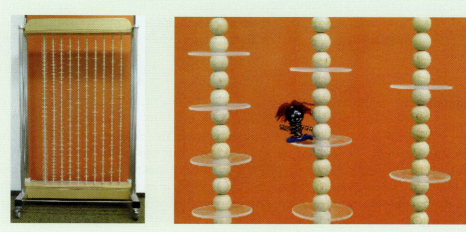

We have recently come across a delightful variation on this kind of problem, using a clever piece of equipment devised by Inge Schwank in Germany. As yet nothing is published about this in English but it would be worth looking out for. The equipment shown in the photograph on the left contains a number of strings

(Continued)

(Continued)

with 100 wooden beads threaded on them. In the first string of 100 beads plastic discs are placed between each bead and the next one. In the second the plastic discs are placed between every two discs; in the third between every three discs; and so on. On the extreme left there is an empty string, which represents groups of zero beads! We suggest you try to think of ways this equipment could be used with children.

As an example, here is one problem for you to solve. The photograph on the right shows an alien creature sitting on a plastic disc somewhere on the equipment. Whereabouts is this alien sitting? How many beads are beneath it?

(Solutions are given at the end of the chapter.)

Communicating

Throughout this book we have emphasized how understanding of many mathematical ideas involves making connections between language, pictures, symbols and concrete experiences. Now that we are focusing on using and applying mathematics, we look at the part that mathematical language, pictures and symbols play in communicating the outcomes of problem solving and enquiry.

Communicating results and findings

When a problem is solved or an enquiry completed, the challenge is then to communicate the results or findings to other people. This too is an important part of thinking mathematically. Solving a problem may be a somewhat chaotic, backwards and forwards, roundabout, hit-and-miss, trial-and-error process, but presenting the solution requires the problem solver to organize his or her ideas into a coherent, logical sequence. So communicating your mathematical thinking is an important aspect of using and applying mathematics.

Children need the opportunity to do this as part of their experience of solving problems or pursuing mathematical enquiries. They also need help from the teacher in organizing their ideas and conclusions. The children who had sorted out the class library, in the example described earlier in this chapter, then went on to explain to the other children how they had classified the books, how they had worked out how much space was needed for each group, what they had done about the taller books, and so on – with the teacher and the other children prompting them with appropriate questions. This was a significant part of their mathematical experience.

Explaining and proving

In the newspaper investigation described above, some children discovered the amazing result that the sum of the odd pages on any sheet of any newspaper gives the total number of pages. After we had checked a thousand examples of newspapers and found no counterexamples to this hypothesis, someone might justifiably point out that even a thousand specializations are not enough to prove a generalization. Of course, we would not do a thousand. Five or six would probably be enough to convince most people that the generalization would always work. But mathematicians are fussy people sometimes. They would say, 'But how can you be sure that it will always work? Can you prove it?'

The final stage in thinking mathematically would indeed be to produce a proof – a logical argument that is valid in all the cases being considered and that convinces a sceptic that the generalization really must be true in all cases. A discussion of the nature of mathematical proof and the different kinds of proof that can be employed is well beyond the scope of this book. Children in primary schools are not expected to prove their generalizations. But they can begin to experience this kind of mathematical reasoning by formulating simple *explanations*. They can be prompted to begin to think in these terms by looking for counterexamples and by the teachers asking questions such as:

- Does it work for …?
- Are you sure?
- What if …?
- Can you explain?
- Why does that happen?

For example, children may have formulated the fairly simple generalization that the number of pages in any newspaper is always four times the number of sheets. With appropriate prompting they could begin to explain why this must be the case – and to link the generalization with the 4-times table. Similarly, they may have discovered that it is always the case that the numbers on the inside pages of any newspaper get closer to each other as you work through the paper from the beginning. With prompting, they could then go on to explain *why* this must happen – for example, because the left pages are counting forwards and the right pages are counting backwards until they meet in the middle.

A final thought

So, here ends our discussion of understanding mathematics for young children. As we indicated at the start of the book, we hope that we will have helped the reader to be more aware of the significance of the mathematical ideas and experiences that are appropriate for the first few years of schooling and increased their own confidence in teaching them. If not, at least, after reading this chapter, you now have the option of dismantling this book and investigating the way the page numbers are arranged.

RESEARCH FOCUS   To generalize or not to generalize?

There is a well-established and famous phenomenon in the field of psychology called the *Einstellung effect*, first identified by Luchins (1942). This refers to a person's predisposition to solve a given problem in a specific manner even though there are better, more efficient or more appropriate methods of doing it. We see this behaviour in children (and adults, for that matter), who, when they get hold of a rule, will over-generalize and use the rule inappropriately. For example, children might be given a problem like this:

> *You have three jugs that will hold (A) 17 units, (B) 8 units and (C) 5 units of water and a bowl. How would you measure out 14 units of water into the bowl?*

The solution here is 'A + C − B': fill jugs A and C, pour them into the bowl to get 22 units, then use jug B to remove 8 units. The children are then given a series of problems like this, in which the solution every time is to add the capacities of two of the jugs and to subtract the other one. The final problem in the series is this:

> *You have three jugs that will hold (A) 32 units, (B) 20 units and (C) 8 units of water and a bowl. How would you measure out 20 units of water into the bowl?*

The majority of children (and adults!) give the solution, A + C − B, to this problem − even though they could have just used jug B to measure out the required 20 units! This is the Einstellung effect. It shows a tendency to rigidity in thinking which is the enemy of creative thinking. Children who do not show this kind of rigidity − who use rules but are always alert to the possibility that there may be a better, more elegant, more interesting, more efficient way of solving a problem − are those who are less reliant on stereotype responses and routines, more willing to take reasonable risks in mathematics and show higher levels of mathematical creativity (Haylock, 1997). So, generalizing in mathematics is important; but, if you want to be a good problem solver, so is creativity; and there are times when this is undermined by a tendency to over-generalize.

   At the time of writing, Anne has just returned from a conference focusing on generalization in the teaching and learning of mathematics. She ended her lecture with this statement: 'So, to return to my original question: to generalize or not to generalize? My answer is "yes", but only if you know what you are doing!' (Cockburn, 2012, p. 20). This might seem rather an odd conclusion given that so much of mathematics is built on generalization. Consider, for example, our system for counting numbers: 0, 1, 2 ... 10, 11, 12 ... 20, 21, 22 ... and so on. It is the generalization of the pattern in each group of ten and then in each group of a hundred, and so on, that enables us to go on counting for ever. In this chapter we have given many examples of mathematical generalization and stressed its importance in mathematical reasoning. So why was Anne's conclusion in her lecture a qualified one? There are several reasons, but here we will focus on two that relate to teachers themselves and our aims in writing this book.

   The first reason why teachers might make inappropriate generalizations is that sometimes they do not themselves have a thorough understanding of some fundamental mathematical concepts. We have in mind particularly the danger of some teachers suggesting to their children that certain things are always the case, when in fact they are not, and doing this because of their own shaky grasp of the mathematical ideas involved. We hope, of course, that the likelihood of your falling into this trap has been reduced by your reading and understanding of this book from cover to cover! But it is, nonetheless, a possibility that you should keep at the back of your mind.

Here are some examples of such inappropriate generalizations, arising from misunderstandings of fundamental concepts, which we have found to be common amongst early years' teachers:

a   Zero always stands for nothing.
b   Subtraction always makes things smaller.
c   Multiplication always makes things bigger.

Like all false generalizations these are undone by counterexamples. In statement (a) – which is a common misconception among some early years' teachers – we have seen, for example (see Chapter 7), that, when operating as a place holder in a number, the zero represents *the absence of something* (Cockburn and Parslow-Williams, 2008) rather than simply *nothing*; and when used on an interval scale (see Chapter 8), such as time or temperature, it represents a very real and important point on the scale, not nothing. In statement (b) we would point to subtracting zero, or subtracting a negative number, as counterexamples to show that the generalization is false. For example, $6 - (-3) = 9$, which is larger than 6. In statement (c), try multiplying by 1, or by 0, or by ½, or by 0.1. For example, $12 \times 0.1 = 1.2$, which is smaller than 12.

The second reason why teachers might make inappropriate generalizations is that teachers like to simplify things for the children they teach. So they give them a simple rule to memorize or a formulaic recipe that they can apply without understanding. This may be for a variety of reasons, including pressure to get through a syllabus or children finding it difficult to grasp a new concept or process. A classic case is where teachers tell children that to do a subtraction 'you always take the smaller number away from the bigger one' (Cockburn, 1999). Note the word 'always' here. This is a rule, a generalization. So, when children have to find $83 - 57$ (see Figure 7.19(g) in Chapter 7) is it surprising that many of them will start by taking the 3 away from the 7? This generalization is also going to have to be unlearnt when children do subtractions such as $3 - 7$ on a number line extending below zero.

Another example, which is extremely common, is the rule, 'when you multiply by 10 you add a zero'. Apart from the ambiguity of the phrase 'add a zero' (which could mean '+ 0'), the generalization applies only to whole numbers. Derek has recently completed a new book on mathematics for healthcare practitioners (Haylock and Warburton, 2013); he has been at great pains to ensure that his new readers recognize that 10 doses of 2.5 grams of a drug are equivalent to 25 g, not 2.50 g! This counterexample shows that you do not always 'add a zero' when you multiply by 10. This is a faulty generalization, one that will again have to be unlearnt if children are to progress in mathematics.

So, yes, generalizing should be a significant theme in your mathematics teaching, but please be aware of when it is appropriate to do so and when it is not!

Some activities to use with children

Throughout this chapter we have indicated the kinds of activities that teachers might use or adapt for their classes to promote problem solving and mathematical reasoning, and provided many examples. We conclude with a few further examples of problem solving, open-ended tasks and investigative activities that might be used.

	ACTIVITY 11.1 Building Bridges	3-4	4-5	5-6	6-7	7-8
				□	□	

Objective

To involve children in practical problem solving.

Materials

A supply of assorted building blocks; two toy cars.

Method

There are many construction challenges that involve children in problem solving in the context of play and that provide practical experience of handling three-dimensional shapes. Building bridges is a good example. Working individually or in pairs, children have to use the building blocks to construct a bridge so that one toy car can pass underneath. It must be secure enough to hold the other toy car on the top. This fits well with the problem-solving model in Figure 11.4. The child has a clear goal (to make the bridge with one car underneath and the other on top) and a clear set of givens (the building materials and the cars). But the child does not know immediately how to get from the givens to the goal. This will be a process of exploration, trial and error, trial and improvement, while using and learning about the properties of the various shapes and the relationships between them on the way.

Extension

In some cases teachers may judge it appropriate to challenge some children to find a 'better' solution than their first one (refining the goal) or they might disallow the use of certain blocks that make the task too easy (modifying the givens).

	ACTIVITY 11.2 Creative Shape-making	3-4	4-5	5-6	6-7	7-8
		□	□			

Objective

To provide opportunities for children to show creativity in constructing shapes.

Materials

Children in small groups are given, say, ten sets of three shapes: a square, an oblong rectangle, and a triangle.

Method

The children are challenged to find ten different ways of fitting the three shapes together to make a new shape. To add a bit of fun they might like to give each of the shapes they make a name! Figure 11.8 shows one example.

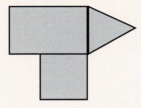

Figure 11.8   *A shape called 'Nosey'*

		3–4	4–5	5–6	6–7	7–8
	**ACTIVITY 11.3 Planning the Drinks**				☐	☐

Objective

To provide experience of using and applying mathematics in a real-life situation.

Materials

Squash; beakers; measuring jugs; or whatever else the children require.

Method

Many opportunities arise in the normal course of school life for children to use their mathematics to solve real problems. We would encourage teachers to look for occasional opportunities of this kind where mathematics can be used in a way that has immediate and genuine relevance to the children. Here is just one example. A group of children is given the task of planning how much squash should be bought for the class Christmas party and finding out how much it will cost. This will involve them in deciding what calculations are needed, doing the calculations, interpreting the answers, taking into account the constraints of the real world – with much practical mathematics involved, such as the measurement of liquid volume. With this kind of task, mathematics really can be seen to be something that can be used and applied in a meaningful context with a genuine purpose.

		3–4	4–5	5–6	6–7	7–8
ACTIVITY 11.4 Creative Weighing					□	□

Objective

To give children the opportunity to think divergently to solve problems in the context of weighing.

Materials

Four masses of 10 grams, 15 grams, 20 grams and 50 grams. If, for example, a 15-g mass is not available in the class weighing kit, then make one by taping together a 10-g mass and a 5-g mass and labelling it accordingly. Also required: a supply of sand and a weighing balance.

Method

The children are challenged to find out if it is possible to use this equipment to weigh out 5 g of sand, then 10 g, 20 g, 25g, 30 g, and so on, all the way up to 95 g. Some of these will require some particularly creative thinking! Encourage them to find some way of recording their solutions. (Hint: for some quantities of sand they have to put masses into both pans!)

Simpler versions of this activity suggest themselves: for example, using three masses of 10 g, 20 g and 50 g, to weigh out 10 g, 20 g, 30 g, 40 g, and so on, up to 80 g.

		3–4	4–5	5–6	6–7	7–8
ACTIVITY 11.5 Adding Odds and Evens					□	□

Objective

To give children the opportunity to formulate generalizations about adding odd and even numbers, to check this and to begin to articulate a simple explanation in terms of pattern.

Materials

A supply of plastic cubes that can be linked together to form towers, in two colours (say, red and white).

Method

A small group of children should use the coloured linking-cubes to construct two towers for each number from 1 to 10. Each tower should be made from alternating red and white cubes. For the odd numbers one of the two towers should have red cubes at both ends and the other should have white cubes at both ends. The children should sort the towers into two sets: odd and even.

They then investigate what happens when you combine an odd number with an odd number to form one tower. They must do this in a way that preserves the pattern of alternating red and white cubes (which is why they have the two different versions of each odd tower). Which set does the new tower go in? Does this always happen?

Discussion should lead to the formulation of a generalization: an odd number added to an odd number always gives an even number. The pattern of alternating colours may even enable the children to articulate some form of explanation as to why this is. The same procedure can then be followed for an even number added to an even number, and then for an odd number added to an even number.

		3–4	4–5	5–6	6–7	7–8
ACTIVITY 11.6 Sheep in a Field						☐

Objective

To provide experience of an investigation with potential for making and checking conjectures, formulating a generalization, considering special cases, and modifying the generalization accordingly.

Materials

A set of coloured rods representing the numbers from 1 to 10 (such as Cuisenaire or Colour Factor rods), with a good supply of ones (unit cubes).

Method

The children are given three 'kits' of rods, each kit consisting of two rods of one length and two rods that are 2 units longer. For example, they might be given three kits consisting of two 5-rods and two 7-rods. The story given to the children is that a farmer is to use these as fences around a field to keep the sheep in. The children have to arrange their kits of fences in the three different ways shown in Figure 11.9. Now they find out how many sheep they can squeeze into each field – the sheep are, of course, the unit cubes! It is to be hoped that they will discover that the three fields, although made with the same fences, can hold different numbers of sheep (21, 24, 25). Discussion of this might lead them to notice that the square field holds the most sheep.

They can then be given three kits of, say, 4-rods and 6-rods. They may conjecture that once again the square will hold the largest number of sheep – and then investigate whether this is the case. When they find that it is, they might now conjecture that the square will always hold the most sheep – and check this with other kits, such as 3-rods and 5-rods, 6-rods and 8-rods, and so on. A special case arises with kits comprising 2-rods and 4-rods, since one of the arrangements will not hold any sheep at all! But does the generalization still hold?

(Continued)

(Continued)

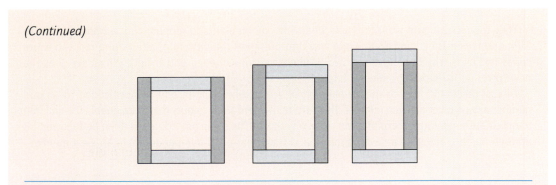

Figure 11.9   *Three fields made with the same 'fences'*

Extension

So far the kits have always had one size of rod 2 units longer than the other. What happens if we drop this restriction? For example, what happens with a kit of two 4-rods and two 7-rods?

		3–4	4–5	5–6	6–7	7–8
ACTIVITY 11.7	Triangles in Polygons				☐	☐

Objective

To develop skills in tabulation of numerical results derived from a geometric pattern, and formulating generalizations.

Materials

For each child a sheet containing drawings of a 3-sided, a 4-sided, a 5-sided, a 6-sided and a 7-sided polygon (see Figure 11.10).

Method

The children divide each polygon in turn into triangles, by drawing all the possible diagonal lines from one of the vertices (corners) of the polygon. They record in the table shown in Figure 11.10 the number of sides and the number of triangles in each polygon in turn. They can then predict what will happen with an 8-sided polygon, and so on, and check these out. They should articulate the pattern they find: the number of triangles is always 2 less than the number of sides. Teachers might challenge children to work out how many triangles there would be if they did this with a polygon with 100 sides.

In Figure 11.10 we have shown how the 7-sided polygon would be divided into 5 triangles and how this would be recorded in the table.

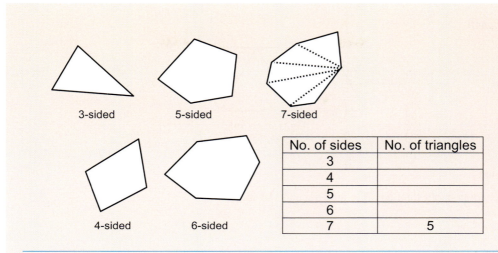

No. of sides	No. of triangles
3	
4	
5	
6	
7	5

Figure 11.10 *Polygons for Activity 11.7*

		3–4	4–5	5–6	6–7	7–8
ACTIVITY 11.8	**Triangle Chains**					☐

Objective

To provide another opportunity for tabulation of numerical results derived from a geometric pattern, and for formulation of generalizations.

Materials

A supply of dead matches – or something similar – for constructing polygons.

Method

Figure 11.11 shows the beginning of a chain of triangles made with matchsticks. The children investigate how many matches are needed to make 1 triangle, a chain of 2 triangles, 3 triangles, 4 triangles, and so on, arranged as shown. This can lead to tabulation of the results. Children can be led, through discussion, to formulate the generalization that the number of matches increases by 2 each time – and possibly to explain this with reference to how the next triangle in the chain is made by adding two further matches. More able children may even spot that the number of matches is two for each triangle, plus one more.

(Continued)

(Continued)

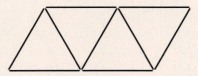

Figure 11.11   *A chain of 4 triangles needs 9 matches*

Extension

Some children might then go on to look at chains of squares.

Summary of key ideas

1 Learning mathematics includes not just a collection of skills, concepts and principles, but also the development of characteristic ways of thinking and reasoning in using and applying mathematics.

2 Two dimensions for identifying activities in using and applying mathematics are (1) the context, ranging from purely abstract mathematics (numbers or shapes) to practical, real-life situations, and (2) the nature of the task, ranging from closed problem solving to an open enquiry, determined by how tightly prescribed is the goal.

3 A problem-solving activity will have a clear goal, but can be located anywhere along the abstract/real-life dimension. It can be discussed in terms of the givens, the goal and the gap between them. The first step in problem solving is to clarify the givens and the goal.

4 Problem solving can involve specifying subgoals, working backwards from the goal as well as forwards from the givens.

5 Solving real-life problems involves taking into account the constraints of the actual situation in which the problem arose.

6 Mathematical enquiry (investigation) can be located anywhere along the abstract/real-life dimension, but is characterized by the child having the opportunity to specify the goal and direction of the enquiry and to think more creatively.

7 Creative thinking in mathematics is characterized by divergent, flexible thinking, showing originality and inventiveness and willingness to take risks. This is a significant component of being a good problem solver in mathematics.

8 Young children can be encouraged to think creatively by engaging in open-ended tasks with many possible responses, rather than simply answering questions with just one correct answer.

9 Formulating generalizations is a characteristic way of thinking mathematically. A generalization is a statement that is true about a number of specific cases and involves the use of language such as *each, every, all, any, always, whenever, if ... then*.

10 Some generalizations are statements about the way in which items in a sequence change each time, from one item to the next – for example, in a set of results that have been tabulated in order. This is focusing on transformation; that is, how specific cases are different.

11 Other generalizations are statements that describe what it is that stays the same for the items in a sequence, what is true about all of them. This focuses on equivalence.

12 A counterexample is a specific instance that shows that a generalization is false or that it needs to be modified or qualified in some way.

13 An important part of any mathematical investigation is communicating what has been discovered to others.

14 To be convinced of the truth of a generalization, a mathematician would demand a proof – that is, a valid logical argument. Mathematical proof is not something to be introduced in the primary years, but children can discuss whether they are sure about various assertions and, in some cases, begin to explain why certain results occur.

Suggestions for further reading

Chapters 4 and 5 of Haylock (2010) explain further some of the key processes in mathematical reasoning and problem solving.

We recommend a thought-provoking chapter by Lesley Jones entitled, 'The problem with problem-solving', in Thompson (2003).

Also have a look at the entries on Using and Applying Mathematics, Talk, Problem Solving, Investigation, and Generalization, and the suggestions for further reading for each of these, in Haylock with Thangata (2007).

Clarke and Atkinson (1996) provide an original approach that includes examples of investigational mathematics with young children that produce significant progress in mathematical learning.

Mike Ollerton, in a chapter entitled 'Using problem-solving approaches to learn mathematics' in Thompson (2010), describes how problem solving can be integrated into children's learning in primary schools and not just tacked on after children have learnt various skills and knowledge.

Schwartz (1995) describes strategies that teachers have developed to provide authentic use of mathematics through everyday activities in school, such as recording attendance and organizing school lunches.

Sellars and Lowndes (2002) give advice on how young children can be taught strategies to develop their ability to use and apply mathematics.

A key chapter for those who work in the Early Years Foundation Stage is 'A curriculum to promote mathematical thinking' in Pound (2006). This emphasizes the importance of fostering mathematical thinking in line with recognized principles of good practice in early childhood education.

The chapter by Griffiths on 'Mathematics and play' in Moyles (2010) is also well worth reading.

Finally, for those working with 3–5s we recommend Chapter 11 on problem solving in Gifford (2005).

Note: Solutions to Pause to Reflect problems.

The arrow in Figure 11.7 points to box number 33. This is the only number up to 50 that is 3 more than a multiple of 5, 1 more than a multiple of 4 and 2, and also a multiple of 3. Using similar reasoning, the alien in the photograph must have 52 beads underneath it.

REFERENCES

Aldrich, F. and Sheppard, L. (2000) 'Graphicacy: the fourth R?', *Primary Science Review*, 64: 8–11.

Ames, L. (1946) 'The development of the sense of time in the young child', *Journal of Genetic Psychology*, 68: 97–125.

Anghileri, J. (1995) *Children's Mathematical Thinking in the Primary Years*. London: Cassell.

Anghileri, J. (ed.) (2001) *Principles and Practices in Arithmetic Teaching: Innovative Approaches for the Primary Classroom*. Buckingham: Open University Press.

Anghileri, J. (2006) *Teaching Number Sense*, 2nd edn. London: Continuum.

Ball, D., Thames, M. and Phelps, G. (2008) 'Content knowledge for teaching: what makes it special?', *Journal of Teacher Education*, 59: 389–407.

Baroody, A. and Dowker, A. (eds) (2003) *The Development of Arithmetic Concepts and Skills: Constructing Adaptive Expertise*. Mahwah, NJ: Lawrence Erlbaum Associates.

Behr, M., Erlwanger, S. and Nichols, E. (1980) 'How children view the equals sign', *Mathematics Teaching*, 92: 13–15.

Bellos, A. (2010) *Alex's Adventures in Numberland*. London: Bloomsbury.

Blinko, J. (2000) *Shape, Space and Measure*. London: A. and C. Black.

Bobis, J. (2007) 'The empty number line: a useful tool or just another procedure?', *Teaching Children Mathematics*, 13: 410–13.

Brown, M. (1981) Levels of Understanding of Number Operations, Place Value and Decimals in Secondary School Children. Unpublished doctoral thesis, University of London.

Bryant, P., Christie, C. and Rendu, A. (1999) 'Children's understanding of the relation between addition and subtraction: inversion, identity and decomposition', *Journal of Experimental Child Psychology*, 74: 194–212.

Carpenter, T., Moser, J. and Romberg, T. (eds) (1982) *Addition and Subtraction: A Cognitive Perspective*. Hillsdale, NJ: Lawrence Erlbaum Associates.

Carruthers, E. and Worthington, M. (2006) *Children's Mathematics: Making Marks, Making Meaning*, 2nd edn. London: Paul Chapman Publishing.

Clarke, S. and Atkinson, S. (1996) *Tracking Significant Achievement in Primary Mathematics*. London: Hodder & Stoughton.

Clements, D. (1999) 'Subitizing: What is it? Why teach it?', *Teaching Children Mathematics*, 5(7): 400–5.

Clements, D. and Sarama, J. (2009) *Learning and Teaching Early Math: The Learning Trajectories Approach*. New York and London: Routledge.

Cockburn, A. (1999) *Teaching Mathematics with Insight: The Identification, Diagnosis and Remediation of Young Children's Mathematical Errors*. London: Falmer Press.

Cockburn, A. (ed.) (2007) *Mathematical Understanding 5–11*. London: Paul Chapman Publishing.

Cockburn, A. (2012) 'To generalise, or not to generalise, that is the question (with apologies to Hamlet and William Shakespeare)', in B. Maj-Tatsis and K. Tatsis (eds) *Generalisation in Mathematics at All Educational Levels*. Rzeszów, Poland: Wydawnictwo Uniwersytetu Rzeszowskiego, pp. 11–21. (This will become available on the web in due course. Please search for it under 'CME 12, Poland'.)

Cockburn, A. and Littler, G. (eds) (2008) *Mathematical Misconceptions: A Guide for Primary Teachers*. London: Sage Publications.

Cockburn, A. and Parslow-Williams, P. (2008) 'Zero: understanding an apparently paradoxical number', in A. Cockburn and G. Littler (eds) *Mathematical Misconceptions*. London: Sage Publications, pp. 7–22.

Desforges, A. and Desforges, C. (1980) 'Number-based strategies of sharing in young children', *Educational Studies*, 6: 97–109.

Dickson, L., Brown, M. and Gibson, O. (1984) *Children Learning Mathematics*. London: Cassell.

Donaldson, M. (1978) *Children's Minds*. London: Fontana.

English, L. and Watters, J. (2005) 'Mathematical modelling in the early school years', *Mathematics Education Research Journal*, 16(3): 58–79.

Falkner, K.P., Levi, L. and Carpenter, T.P. (1999) 'Children's understanding of equality: a foundation for algebra', *Teaching Children Mathematics*, 6: 232–6.

Fenna, D. (2002) *A Dictionary of Weights, Measures and Units*. Oxford: Oxford University Press.

Freiman, V. and Lee, L. (2004) 'Tracking primary students' understanding of the equality sign', in M. Hoines and A. Fuglestad (eds) *Proceedings of the 28th Conference of the International Group for the Psychology of Mathematics Education*, 2. Bergen: Bergen University College, pp. 415–22.

Gardner, M. (1991) *Mathematical Puzzles and Diversions*, new edn. London: Penguin Books.

Gelman, R. and Gallistel, C.R. (1986) *The Child's Understanding of Number*, 2nd edn. Cambridge, MA: Harvard University Press.

Gifford, S. (2005) *Teaching Mathematics 3–5: Developing Learning in the Foundation Stage*. Maidenhead: Open University Press/McGraw-Hill.

Gilmore, C. and Papadatou-Pastou, M. (2009) 'Patterns of individual differences in conceptual understanding and arithmetical skill: a meta-analysis', *Mathematical Thinking and Learning*, 11: 25–40.

Ginsburg, H. (2009) 'The challenge of formative assessment in mathematics education: children's minds, teachers' minds', *Human Development*, 52: 109–28.

Ginsburg, H. and Seo, K. (1999) 'The mathematics in children's thinking', *Mathematical Thinking and Learning*, 1: 113–29.

Gravemeijer, K. (1994) 'Educational development and developmental research in mathematics education', *Journal for Research in Mathematics Education*, 25: 443–71.

Hansen, A. (2012) *Games, Ideas and Activities for Early Years Mathematics*. Harlow: Pearson Education.

Hansen, A. (ed.) (2011) *Children's Errors in Mathematics*, 2nd edn. Exeter: Learning Matters.

Haylock, D. (1997) 'Recognising mathematical creativity in schoolchildren', *International Reviews on Mathematical Education*, 3: 68–74.

Haylock, D. (2001) *Numeracy for Teaching*. London: Sage Publications.

Haylock, D. (2010) *Mathematics Explained for Primary Teachers*, 4th edn. London: Sage Publications.

Haylock, D. and Warburton, P. (2013) *Mathematics Explained for Healthcare Practitioners*. London: Sage Publications.

Haylock, D. with Thangata, F. (2007) *Key Concepts in Teaching Primary Mathematics*. London: Sage Publications.

Hejný, M. (2008) 'Scheme-oriented educational strategy in mathematic(s)', in B. Maj, M. Pytlak and E. Swoboda (eds) *Supporting Independent Thinking Through Mathematical Education*. Rzeszów, Poland: Wydawnictwo Uniwersytetu Rzeszowskiego, pp. 40–8.

Hopkins, C., Pope, S. and Pepperell, S. (2004) *Understanding Primary Mathematics*. London: David Fulton.

Hughes, M. (1986) *Children and Number: Difficulties in Learning Mathematics*. Oxford: Blackwell.

Hunscheidt, D. and Peter-Koop, A. (2007) 'Constructing and connecting 2-D and 3-D shapes', in A.Cockburn (ed.) *Mathematical Understanding 5–11*. London: Sage Publications, pp. 57–71.

Inhelder, B. and Piaget, J. (1958) *The Growth of Logical Thinking from Childhood to Adolescence*. New York: Basic Books.

Jaslow, V.R. and Jacobs, J.B. (2009) 'Helping kindergartens make sense of numbers to 100', available at http://www.math.vcu.edu/g1/journal/Journal_11/11_Jaslow Jacobs.pdf (accessed 25/07/12).

Kamii, C. (1985) *Young Children Reinvent Arithmetic*. New York: Teachers College Press.

Kerslake, D. (1975) 'Taking time out', *Mathematics Teaching*, 73: 8–10.

Kieran, C. (1981) 'Concepts associated with the equality symbol', *Educational Studies in Mathematics*, 12: 317–26.

Klein, F. (1872) *Vergleichende Betrachtungen über Neuere Geometrische Forschungen*. Erlangen: Verlag von Andreas Deichert.

Leather, R. (2000) *Developing Shape, Space and Measures with 5–7-Year-Olds*. Leamington Spa: Scholastic.

Lewis, A. (1996) *Discovering Mathematics with 4- to 7-Year-Olds*. London: Hodder & Stoughton.

Linfield, R. and Coltman, P. (2008) *Planning for Learning through Shapes*, revised edn. Leamington Spa: Step Forward Publishing.

Long, K. and Kamii, C. (2001) 'The measurement of time: children's construction of transitivity, unit iteration and conservation of speed', *School Science and Mathematics*, 101: 1–8.

Lovell, K. (1966) *The Growth of Basic Mathematical and Scientific Concepts in Children*, 5th edn. Sevenoaks: Hodder & Stoughton Educational.

Luchins, A.S. (1942) 'Mechanization in problem solving', *Psychological Monographs*, 54, No. 248.

Marchini, C. and Papadopoulos, I. (2011) 'Are useless brackets useful tools for teaching?', in B. Ubuz (ed.) *Proceedings of the 35th Conference of the International Group for the Psychology of Mathematics Education*, 3. Ankara: PME, pp. 185–92.

Marchini, C., Cockburn, A., Parslow-Williams, P. and Vighi, P. (2009) 'Equality relation and structural properties – a vertical study', *Proceedings of the Sixth Conference of European Research in Mathematics Education*. Paris: Institut National de Recherche Pédagogique, pp. 569–78, available at http://www.inrp.fr/editions/cerme6

McGarrigle, J. and Donaldson, M. (1974) 'Conservation accidents', *Cognition*, 3(4): 341–50.

McGrath, C. (2010) *Supporting Early Mathematical Development: Practical Approaches to Play-Based Learning*. Abingdon: Routledge.

Montague-Smith, A. and Price, A. (2012) *Mathematics in Early Years Education*, 3rd edn. London: David Fulton.

Mosley, F. (2004) *Using Number Lines with 5–8 Year Olds: BEAM Number Line Bundle 4*. London: BEAM Education.

Moyles, J. (ed.) (2010) *The Excellence of Play,* 3rd edn. Maidenhead: Open University Press/McGraw-Hill.

Murphy, C. (2011) 'Comparing the use of the empty number line in England and the Netherlands', *British Educational Research Journal*, 37: 147–61.

Nguyen, D., Kemp, N. and Want, S. (2011) 'The effects of funny and serious task content and expectations of fun versus importance on children's cognitive performance', *Australian Journal of Psychology*, 63: 154–62.

Nunes, T. and Bryant, P. (1996) *Children Doing Mathematics*. Oxford: Blackwell.

Nunes, T., Bryant, P. and Watson, A. (2009) *Key Understandings in Mathematics Learning: A Review Commissioned by the Nuffield Foundation*. London: Nuffield Foundation.

Nunes, T., Schliemann, A. and Carraher, D. (1993) *Street Mathematics and School Mathematics*. Cambridge: Cambridge University Press.

Pepperell, S., Hopkins, C., Gifford, S. and Tallant, P. (2009) *Mathematics in the Primary School: A Sense of Progression*, 3rd edn. London: David Fulton.

Piaget, J. (1969) *The Child's Conception of Time*. London: Routledge and Kegan Paul.

Piaget, J. and Moreau, A. (1977) 'The inversion of arithmetic operations', in J. Piaget (ed.), trans. R.L. Campbell (2001) *Studies in Reflecting Abstraction*. Hove: Psychology Press, pp. 69–86.

Piaget, J. and Szeminska, A. (1952) *The Child's Conception of Number*. London: Routledge and Kegan Paul.

Pound, L. (2006) *Supporting Mathematical Development in the Early Years*, 2nd edn. Buckingham: Open University Press.

Rowland, T., Turner, F., Thwaites, A. and Huckstep, P. (2009) *Developing Primary Mathematics Teaching*. London: Sage Publications.

Ryan, J. and Williams, J. (2007) *Children's Mathematics 4–15*. Maidenhead: Open University Press/McGraw-Hill.

Sarnecka, B.W. and Gelman, S.A. (2004) '*Six* does not just mean *a lot*: preschoolers see number words as specific', *Cognition*, 92(3): 329–52.

Schwartz, S.L. (1995) 'Authentic mathematics in the classroom', *Teaching Children Mathematics*, 1(9): 580–4.

Sellars, E. and Lowndes, S. (2002) *Using and Applying Mathematics at Key Stage 1*. London: David Fulton, in association with NACE.

Shatz, M.,Tare, M., Nguyen, S. and Young, T. (2010) 'Acquiring non-object terms: the case for time words', *Journal of Cognition and Development*, 11(1): 16–36, available at http://www.ncbi.nlm.nih.gov/pmc/articles/PMC3258973/ (accessed 02/08/12).

Siegler, R.S. and Stern, E. (1998) 'Conscious and unconscious strategy discoveries: a microgenetic analysis', *Journal of Experimental Psychology General*, 127: 377–97.

Skemp, R. (1971) *The Psychology of Learning Mathematics*. Harmondsworth: Penguin.

Skinner, C., Ebbutt, S. and Mosley, F. (2004) *Teaching Mental Strategies, Years 1 & 2*. London: BEAM Education.

Spindeler, B. and Wollring, B. (2007) 'Communicating ideas about space and shape', in A. Cockburn (ed.) *Mathematical Understanding 5–11*. London: Sage Publications, pp. 28–50.

Tammet, D. (2012) *Thinking in Numbers: How Maths Illuminates Our Lives*. London: Hodder & Stoughton.

Thompson, I. (ed.) (2003) *Enhancing Primary Mathematics Teaching*. Maidenhead: Open University Press/McGraw-Hill.

Thompson, I. (ed.) (2008) *Teaching and Learning Early Number*, 2nd edn. Maidenhead: Open University Press.

Thompson, I. (ed.) (2010) *Issues in Teaching Numeracy in Primary Schools*, 2nd edn. Buckingham: Open University Press.

Tirosh, D., Tsamir, P. and Hershkovitz, S. (2008) 'Addition, subtraction, multiplication and division', in A.D. Cockburn and G. Littler (eds) *Mathematical Misconceptions*. London: Sage Publications, pp. 54–70.

Tucker, K. (2005) *Mathematics Through Play in the Early Years*. London: Paul Chapman Publishing.

Turner, S. and McCullough, J. (2004) *Making Connections in Primary Mathematics*. London: David Fulton.

Van den Heuvel-Panhuizen, M. (ed.) (2008) *Children Learn Mathematics: A Learning–Teaching Trajectory with Intermediate Attainment Targets for Calculation with Whole Numbers in Primary School*. Rotterdam: Sense Publishers.

Van den Heuvel-Panhuizen, M. and van den Boogaard, S. (2008) 'Picture books as an impetus for kindergartners', *Mathematical Thinking and Learning*, 10: 341–73.

Van Oers, B. (2010) 'Emergent mathematical thinking in the context of play', *Educational Studies in Mathematics*, 74: 23–37.

Wright, R., Martland, J. and Stafford, A. (2006) *Early Numeracy*, 2nd edn. London: Paul Chapman Publishing.

INDEX

Activities

Pauses to Reflect

Research Focuses

978-1-4462-0766-6

978-1-4462-0924-0

978-1-4462-1109-0

978-1-4462-0708-6

978-0-85702-535-7

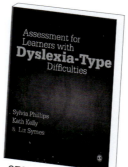

978-1-4462-6719-6

978-1-4462-6023-4

Find out more about these titles and our wide range of books for education
practitioners at **www.sagepub.co.uk/education**

EXCITING SPECIAL EDUCATION NEEDS BOOKS FROM SAGE

978-1-4462-5539-1

978-0-85702-924-9

978-0-85702-146-5

978-0-85702-093-2

978-0-85702-963-8

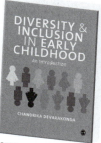

978-0-85702-851-8

978-0-85725-745-1

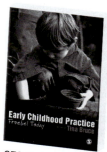

978-1-4462-1125-0

978-1-4462-0056-8

978-0-85725-741-3

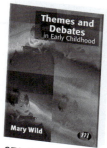

978-1-4462-5636-7

Find out more about these books and our wide range
of Early Years resources at **www.sagepub.co.uk/education**

**RECENT AND BEST-SELLING EDUCATION TEXTBOOKS
FROM SAGE AND LEARNING MATTERS!**